DIVINE DECADENCE

DIVINE DECADENCE

FASCISM, FEMALE SPECTACLE, AND
THE MAKINGS OF SALLY BOWLES

LINDA MIZEJEWSKI

PRINCETON UNIVERSITY PRESS

PRINCETON, NEW JERSEY

Published by Princeton University Press, 41 William Street,
Princeton, New Jersey 08540
In the United Kingdom: Princeton University Press, Oxford
All Rights Reserved

Library of Congress Cataloging-in-Publication Data

Mizejewski, Linda, 1952–
Divine decadence : fascism, female spectacle, and the makings
of Sally Bowles / Linda Mizejewski.
p.   cm.
Includes bibliographical references and index.
ISBN 0-691-07896-3   ISBN 0-691-02346-8 (pbk.)
1. Isherwood, Christopher, 1904–   Characters—Sally Bowles.
2. Isherwood, Christopher, 1904–   Goodbye to Berlin.
3. Isherwood, Christopher, 1904–   Adaptations.
4. Bowles, Sally (Fictitious character).
5. Berlin (Germany) in literature. 6. Decadence in literature.
7. Fascism and literature. 8. Women in literature.
I. Title.

PR6017.S5Z78   1992   823′.912—dc20   92-11858

This book has been composed in Linotron Baskerville

Princeton University Press books are printed
on acid-free paper, and meet the guidelines for
permanence and durability of the Committee on
Production Guidelines for Book Longevity
of the Council on Library Resources

Printed in the United States of America

10 9 8 7 6 5 4 3 2 1

10 9 8 7 6 5 4 3 2 1
(Pbk.)

For my parents, Ann and Edward Mizejewski

CONTENTS

LIST OF ILLUSTRATIONS AND CREDITS

TEXT AND MUSIC

ACKNOWLEDGMENTS

B ECAUSE THIS BOOK is about historical processes and how
they shape a story, these acknowledgments preface my argument by recognizing that a project like this is possible only by
virtue of a network of supportive people and circumstances. This
study begun in the English Department at the University of Pittsburgh just at the time when the department had organized its pro-
gram for Cultural and Critical Studies, enabling and encouraging me
to interweave literary, cinematic, and historical debates into a full-
length study. My mentors for this project were Lucy Fischer, Marcia
Landy, Dana Polan, and Sabine Hake, all of whom provided a challenging exchange of ideas, careful readings, and also the friendship
and sense of humor that humanized the entire process and made it
enjoyable. I feel fortunate to have worked with people who are so
strongly committed to the political implications of critical theory and
to the continuum between research and teaching. In particular, I owe
a great deal to Lucy Fischer, whose exciting teaching and scholarship
changed the direction of my studies and most directly engendered
this project.

A Mellon Predoctoral Fellowship from the University of Pittsburgh
made it possible for me to devote all my time to this manuscript for a
productive eight months in 1988 and 1989. Phil Smith, chair of the
English Department, further supported the project by offering me a
visiting assistant professorship that allowed me to devote my energies
to the revision process rather than to a new teaching position else-
where. During this time, I also traveled to Los Angeles to do research
at the Herrick Library. This trip was made possible through the gen-
erosity of my brother, Edward Vargas, whose love for cinema generated my own and started me in this direction long before we knew it
could be a field of study.

During the revision stage, I received invaluable help and many perceptive suggestions from Patrice Petro and Judith Mayne, to whom I
owe a great deal. Special thanks also go to Sarah Caudwell, whose
cooperation through correspondence and interviews allowed me access to the background of Jean Ross. I am also grateful for many
hours of conversation with Rose Gatens, Walter Renn, Angele Ellis,
and Claudia Johnson, all of whose insights into German fascism and
film are inscribed in many of my key arguments. Kay Schaffer de-
serves much gratitude for undertaking some formidable research
tasks on my behalf at the British Film Institute. The early stages of

my writing were abetted considerably by the cheerful computer wizardry of my good friend and neighbor, Dave Goldberg; in the last stages of rewriting, my research assistant, Joan Navarre, worked enthusiastically and meticulously to help me prepare this manuscript for publication. At Princeton University Press, Joanna Hitchcock offered unwavering support and clear-minded advice as we made the final decisions in regard to the manuscript. A publication subvention grant from the College of Humanities and the Office of Research and Graduate Studies at the Ohio State University provided funding for the illustrations and permissions for this book.

Throughout the period that I was writing and revising this book, as throughout my academic career, my parents, Ann and Edward Mizejewski, were a solid source of encouragement, homemade lentil soup, and faith. My first and most important good fortune was being born into this family—my father who drove a truck, my mother who loves books, diverse brothers and sisters who do scientific research, study Egyptology, teach kindergarten—all of whom value reading and writing and made it possible for me to imagine that it could be a way of life.

The person who most tirelessly lived with this project day in, day out, providing endless support of all kinds, is my husband, George Bauman, who experienced firsthand the alternating craziness, exasperation, and excitement that characterized the process of writing this book. My gratitude to him extends far beyond this particular manuscript, because his shared passion for writing and his confidence in me continue to energize and enable me in my work.

DIVINE DECADENCE

1. *Cabaret* (1972). As Sally Bowles, Liza Minnelli established this character's definitive iconography of wild Weimar decadence.

Chapter One

FANTASIES, FASCISM, FEMALE SPECTACLE

AN INTRODUCTION

Divine Decadence

THOUGH THE FICTIONAL character Sally Bowles has appeared in a variety of texts over the past half century, this figure acquired a definitive iconography with Bob Fosse's 1972 film *Cabaret*. In the widely publicized image, Liza Minnelli wears the unmistakable costume of Berlin-cabaret-decadence—black boots, gartered stockings, black hat—and is perched on a chair, one leg lifted in homage to the pose of her cabaret predecessor, Marlene Dietrich, in the similarly well-known image from *The Blue Angel* (*Der blaue Engel*) (1930). As a cultural sign, this representation is complicated because its significations extend from the campy to the pornographic, from homosexuality to sadomasochism. The image is certainly a quotation from other films, but it also reveals cultural transformations and uses of those films. These range from countless pop and camp representations of Dietrich in top hat and garter belt to the staged photos of blond, whip-snapping women and Nazi insignia on the covers of magazines in adult bookstores.

The closing scene of the Fosse film enacts the extended paradigm of this iconography. Wearing a different costume but nonetheless coded as Weimar siren, Liza Minnelli delivers the theme song, "Cabaret," in a performance that is filmed as mainstream musical act, privileging Minnelli's considerable stage presence and talent. She performs directly for the camera, directly to the film audience, and her performance is edited virtually to extinguish the historical references, the details of the diegetic Kit Kat Klub. But history is graphically and didactically reinvoked in what follows. Minnelli disappears backstage, and the emcee introduces a brief, startling montage of female and transvestite spectacle, shots from previous cabaret scenes; then the mirror wall reflecting the cabaret audience gradually begins to fill with uniforms displaying swastika arm bands. Considering how the cabaret has been characterized throughout the film, a historical cause-and-effect argument is suggested: the moral looseness of Weimar Berlin, in particular the sexual and bisexual play in Berlin nightlife, has made possible the tolerance of Nazism. The reflecting mirror wall further suggests that what the Nazis see onstage—the transvestites and sexually ambiguous emcee—are versions of themselves: grotesque, amoral, distorted—and homoerotic. That the inscriptive gaze also takes in the spectacle of female eroticism—Sally Bowles—only reinforces the stereotypes of Weimar decadence, the richness of its temptations, the multiplicities of its sexualities—a disruption of the "natural order" which leaves the society vulnerable to Nazism.

As a reductive reading of history, this may be no more serious than the cinematic fantasies that Nazism is as containable as the embalmed brains or genetic strands that haunt a certain kind of Nazi science fiction film—*They Saved Hitler's Brain* (David Bradley, 1963) or *The Boys from Brazil* (Franklin J. Schaffner, 1978), for example. Yet this psychosexual explanation of Nazism operates in other ways throughout our culture, and its investigation entails not only cultural disavowals of fascism, but also cultural versions of the fascinating, dangerous, ultimately horrendous sexuality that can be conflated into signification with Nazism. These cultural representations of Nazism, including the image of the secretly homosexual, beautifully costumed SS on parade, illustrate the complicated relationship between Nazi ideology itself—the Nazi cult of the visual, as Russell Berman describes it, or the aesthetization of politics, in Walter Benjamin's terms—and the subsequent cultural practices (in films such as *Cabaret*), which are themselves based on spectacle and obsessive delineations of sexual difference.

"Divine decadence, darling," gushes Minnelli as she flashes her green fingernail polish in the film. The Sally character herself is this century's darling of divine decadence, an odd measure of how dear to us is this fiction of the "shocking" British/American vamp in Weimar Berlin. Sally Bowles, the character created by Christopher Isherwood in his short story of the same name (published in the collection *Goodbye to Berlin*, 1939), has been re-created in four major stage and film adaptations, enjoying great popularity each time: in John Van Druten's stage play *I Am a Camera* (1951), in Henry Cornelius's film of the same name (1955), in Joe Masteroff's stage musical *Cabaret* (1966), and in Bob Fosse's film version of that musical (1972). A revival of the stage musical ran on Broadway and then on a road tour from 1987 to 1989; thus, Sally Bowles's story has been told and retold to diverse audiences in five different decades.

More accurately, the character of Sally Bowles has been rewritten to represent each decade's version of a historical dilemma, a haunting of conscience in the years since World War Two. The accumulations of Nazi horror stories—and the increasing willingness of Holocaust survivors to reveal their stories—raise uneasy questions. In dozens of popular films portraying mad Nazi scientists and monstrous Nazi prison guards, we can see some easily dispensed solutions. Who could possibly have been a Nazi? The madman, the monster, the psychopath, the sadist. Yet, as Alvin H. Rosenfeld points out, Western fascination with (and anxiety about) German fascism stems partially from our "resemblance" to Germans as Westerners sharing many of the same traditions and arts; in documentary footage of the crowds cheering Hitler, we find "familiar faces in the crowd, the look of neighborly, even family, resemblance."[1]

How can we posit and signify *our* difference, then, our horror at and moral superiority to what we would like to think of as a historical aberration and nightmare? The Sally Bowles story, I would argue, constitutes one such positing of "difference." In each adaptation, a male writer-protagonist who witnesses the rise of Nazism is temporarily fascinated with both Sally and the "wildness" of Berlin in the early 1930s; and in each version of the story, Sally's sexuality converges with "wild Weimar Berlin" to represent the threat and—more explicitly in the later adaptations—the historical horror that the writer must denounce. The political disavowal is enacted as sexual repudiation, and a particular heroism is made available for the protagonist. As a writer, he will serve as both witness and prophet, through whose authority we will come to understand Sally's "divine decadence"—as Sally herself cannot—as the moral corruption of a culture that is about to embrace the Third Reich.

"She's kind of eternal," Liza Minnelli said about the Sally character in a 1974 *Radio Times* interview.[2] But Sally's eternal returns are more historically specific. Isherwood's 1939 *Goodbye to Berlin*, with its foreboding accounts of growing anti-Semitism in the early part of that decade, became in retrospect even more chilling following the war. Although Isherwood's Sally makes thoughtless, casual anti-Semitic remarks, it would be impossible for any postwar Sally Bowles to do so in the wake of revelations about Auschwitz. The protagonist, after all, must be wholly fascinated by this character; thus her threat is manifest as sexual rather than political. Yet Sally becomes progressively more guilty in each decade's adaptation. "If you're not against all this, you're for it," Sally is told by the protagonist of the 1966 stage musical, who distinctly echoes the political rhetoric of that decade's confrontations with racism and the Vietnam War. In Fosse's film version

[1] Alvin H. Rosenfeld, *Imagining Hitler* (Bloomington: Indiana University Press, 1985), 16.

[2] Iain Johnstone and Jenny Rees, "Bowles Players," *Radio Times* (18 April 1974): 55.

six years later, no single line of accusatory dialogue is necessary; instead, the violence and brutality of the coming regime is graphically represented as the flip side of Sally's performances at the cabaret. That is, at the very time when political contention in the United States was being expressed increasingly in street spectacles and mass demonstrations, the "spectacle" of the rise of Nazism was itself represented as the cabaret, exhibiting issues of participation and guilt, performance and spectatorship. Likewise, the sexual disavowal of each adaptation is encoded differently with the shifting of each era's sexual anxieties, from specifically maternal discourses in the 1950s to the sexual revolutions of the late 1960s. Minnelli's garish makeup in the Fosse film is duplicated not only by the transvestite chorus girls among whom she performs, but also by the ambiguously gendered emcee, brilliantly played, with a sinister, heavily lipsticked smile, by Joel Grey. The cinematic cliché of the Nazi-as-monster takes on a particular sexual spin.

Central to these rereadings of both the Isherwood story and German fascism, the Sally Bowles character is inscribed in several cultural histories: the history of Weimar and the rise of the Third Reich, but also the popular, stereotyped version of that era; a fifty-year history of sexual politics; a history of the relationship between female sexuality and camera eye; and the evolution of a camp vision that has implanted Sally at the curious intersection of Nazism and eroticism—what Susan Sontag has termed "fascinating fascism." Thus, the Sally Bowles character provides a unique opportunity to examine the adaptation process as a function of the cultural production of social and political values. Rather than exploring these texts in a purely comparative way to determine how each medium constructs character and story, I want to investigate instead how the Sally Bowles character functions in each era as a paradigm of "shocking" female sexuality in the context of German fascism.

Although each adaptation demonstrates the textual pressures and codes of particular mediums and genres (for example, the harassed-bachelor comic narrative, or the formulas of the musical), these strategies are nevertheless employed as representations of a concept of history, roughly coded as "Weimar decadence." This history, in turn, is coded in each text not solely through textual or generic pressures, but through extratextual pressures that articulate "fascism" and "female sexuality" in specific ways. My questions, then, are directed not at how the adaptation process registers changes in character and narrative,[3] but rather at how particular strategies rework changing sex-

[3] For a summary of these character and plot changes, see Joe Blades, "The Evolution

ual and political anxieties in order to reproduce a story of disavowal, the tale of the male writer who is the authoritative witness to the "spectacles" of Sally Bowles and the rise of the Third Reich.

In addition, by focusing on the shifting gender dynamics in each text in relation to shifting historical conditions, I am suggesting that adaptations may provide for feminist theorists the opportunity to negotiate between materialist and psychoanalytic methodologies. As the analysis above suggests, the Sally Bowles texts demand work on both levels of theory. In a study of adaptation, a history is already present; the issues are already those of change. Yet what remains as a constant in these texts is a trajectory in which sexual anxieties and identities are paramount—and the female sexual image is devalued and disavowed by a male narrative authority and gaze. The key elements constructing the Sally Bowles character are precisely those that have most engaged feminist film theory of the past fifteen years: the dynamics of spectatorship and the impact of female spectacle, elements that operate in all five of the Sally Bowles texts and invite the use of feminist film theory across other media. But the psychoanalytic-semiotic model that has dominated that theory for the past several years is in itself inadequate in terms of explaining the uniquely historical hooks of this story about 1930s Berlin, as well as the persistence of this character and story in popular culture. Tracing these adaptations, then, demands the pursuit of divergent authorities or trajectories. On the one hand, the haunting, oedipal authority aims to reproduce the same story again and again, and it can only be thoroughly explicated with the tools of psychoanalysis. On the other hand, the authority of cultural experience—in particular, the experience that contemporary feminist scholarship seeks to expose as the underside of mainstream history—demands that the Sally Bowles paradigm be accountable to specific cultural shifts involving the construction and articulation of female sexuality.

The danger of Sally's story's being displaced by the oedipal one is immediately evident in a recent analysis of Fosse's *Cabaret* by psychoanalyst Stephen Bauer. Describing the repetition of Isherwood's *Goodbye to Berlin* over the past four decades as a cultural "preoccupation," Bauer is similarly interested in linking the adaptations to moments of historical crises—the McCarthy era, the Vietnam War. Bauer's interest in these texts concurs with mine in its basic premise that the very repetition of this story in culture points to an important

---

of *Cabaret*," *Literature/Film Quarterly* 1 (1973): 226–38. See also John Rove, "*The Berlin Stories, I Am a Camera, Cabaret*: An Analysis and Comparison" (M.A. diss., Memphis State University, 1976).

preoccupation or fantasy. However, Bauer's reading of the adaptations in relation to Isherwood's original text is perhaps most useful in its revelation of what happens to the issue of female sexuality—the character Sally Bowles—under the application of traditional psychoanalysis. Bauer reads the story as one of the oedipal hero's dealing with the death of the father(s), invoking parricidal fantasy and the concealed wish to submit to paternal authority. In terms of Isherwood's personal background—the death of his father in World War One—and the historical contexts of the later texts, Bauer makes a strong case for the repeated plot line of the missing father, rebellious son, and the impotent paternal figure in the background—Presidents Hindenburg, Eisenhower, Johnson. It is no surprise, then, that in this configuration, the character of Sally recedes into minor functions; in Bauer's reading, she is an embodiment of Weimar Germany, or she is a young boy in disguise, a same-sex fantasy that would be comforting to the hero abandoned by his father.[4] In short, the lady vanishes.

These interpretations of Sally, especially the possibility that she operates as a same-sex fantasy, touch on central issues in her construction by gay writers Isherwood and Van Druten. The displacement of Sally's story by the oedipal one is worth noting here, if for no other reason than that Bauer's interpretation illustrates the problem that has led many psychoanalytic feminist film theorists, who seek to establish grounds of female spectatorship, toward speculations of how the oedipal trajectory is resisted or even parodied in mainstream cinema.[5] Granted, as a psychoanalyst, Bauer would not be likely to interpret a film in terms of its uses of cinematic codes, and his description of Fosse's *Cabaret* as male trajectory is perfectly accurate; the camera's gaze is mostly the gaze of Brian Roberts (Fosse's version of the Isherwood narrator), and his voyage becomes our entrance into the cabaret world and our retreat from it at the end. What Bauer does not acknowledge is what recent feminist film theory has brought to the forefront: the impact of the female figure onscreen, especially in its powerful or threatening capacity which must be diminished or disavowed by narrative, camera work, or both. From this perspective, it is possible to focus not only on the representation and permutations of female sexuality in these texts, but also on the subversive moments in which the oedipal trajectory is often interrupted or seriously undermined.

[4] Stephen F. Bauer, "Cultural History and the Film *Cabaret*," *The Psychoanalytic Study of Society* 12 (1988): 175–66, 181.

[5] For example, see Tania Modleski's reading of Alfred Hitchcock's *Rebecca* (1940) in *The Women Who Knew Too Much: Hitchcock and Feminist Theory* (New York: Methuen, 1988), 43–55.

Yet to read these texts even within this framework of psychoanalytic feminist film theory is insufficient in terms of accounting for the adaptation process, in which the element of threatening female sexuality takes on specific historical coordinates. I am wary, that is, of submitting the Sally Bowles texts to an analysis in which "Sally" becomes a term of difference in a dynamic that seems to operate universally. In my discussion of the original Isherwood story, for example, I emphasize the development of a fictional female sexuality from within the specifically homosexual milieu of Isherwood and his colleagues; the "divine decadence" of Sally Bowles emerged therein as a joke about heterosexuality aimed at a culture (and a literature) that was compulsorily heterosexual, and the resulting satire of Sally's "shocking" behavior takes on a hostile edge. In turn, each adaptation has generated claims of a "subversive" or "shocking" treatment of sexuality or of female eroticism within the constraints of representation at a particular cultural moment. The 1950s adaptations clearly tested the limits of how female sexuality could be articulated on stage and on the screen, with the film version precipitating a widely publicized censorship debate. The two *Cabaret* texts, constructed during an era of noisy contentions concerning sexual freedom and expression, self-consciously read the German pre-Nazi era as a contemporary political warning, positioning "dangerous" sexuality as part of the spectacular Nazi "big show." The "dangerous" female eroticism in these latter texts closely resembles male homoeroticism at the very cultural moment in which a discourse of both women's liberation and gay liberation had emerged. Ironically, then, the very "liberations" of the Fosse film—the freedom to represent a gay or bisexual character and an openly promiscuous woman—abet a conservative or even reactionary trajectory, positing a phallic norm against which Nazism can be defined.

Thus if my insistence on Sally Bowles as focus of these texts is a reading against the grain, as feminist film theory uses the term, it is also a reading against the feminist film theory that has insisted on the primacy of the psychoanalytic framework of individual, male spectatorship. The anxieties of the oedipal story undeniably provide the paramaters of these texts; however, I am equally interested in the particular, changing historical conditions that provide the groundwork of each project. The very complexity of the productions featuring Sally Bowles, the inscriptions of her character in multiple codes and practices (for example, both legitimate theater and drag-queen parody), suggest that a single methodology will not account for the multiple conditions of these texts and their contexts, which include elements as diverse as camp, film censorship, and 1960s political activism. Although it is true that the psychoanalytic method offers powerful tools for understanding the relationships of spectatorship, I hope to show the intersections of the dynamics of individual spectatorship and wider historical forces, and consequently point to alternative methodologies for feminist film theory.

The Sally Bowles character provides other intriguing openings for a feminist analysis concerned with positionings of the powerful female figure in relation to traditional male heroism. The male protagonist of these texts is particularly problematic, an inheritance of Isherwood's repression of the Christopher character in the original story. Generally, critics of *Goodbye to Berlin* have been intrigued, if not obsessed, with the narrator precisely because his strained invisibility contradicts the demands for a "hero," or even a recognizable narrator.[6] This tension has been exacerbated by Isherwood's obsessive rewriting of his Berlin experience in which he increasingly stepped to center stage, to reveal that the story, after all, is "chiefly about Christopher."[7] But my own claim that the story is "chiefly about Sally Bowles" is amply supported by the history of the adaptations. In three of the four stage and film versions, the character of Sally has dominated the production, the reviews, and the publicity. Isherwood admits that he and John Van Druten "decided the play should be about Sally" when *I Am a Camera* was written,[8] and Van Druten's copyrighted title is *Sally Bowles*. The actresses playing Sally have received far more attention than the actors playing the putative heroes; in the 1974 *Radio Times* article cited above, Iain Johnstone and Jenny Rees interview "Bowles players" as the centers of each adaptation, and no mention at all is made of their leading men. Julie Harris was widely identified with the stage and screen Sally of the 1950s, in the same way that Liza Minnelli has come to be associated with *Cabaret*.

---

[6] "The trouble is that most readers do not enjoy identifying with self-proclaimed weaklings," Colin Wilson has said of the early "Chris" heroes. See Wilson's essay, "An Integrity Born of Hope: Notes on Christopher Isherwood," *Twentieth Century Literature* 22 (1976): 312–31. The Isherwood studies that focus on the "problem" of the detached-but-autobiographical narrator are too numerous to list, but see, for example, Alan Wilde's more historical positioning of the issue in *Christopher Isherwood* (New York: Twayne, 1971) and Paul Piazza's attempt to put into order the various theories of the narrator and the complications in Isherwood's heroes in *Christopher Isherwood: Myth and Anti-Myth* (New York: Columbia University Press, 1978).

[7] At the end of *Kathleen and Frank* (New York: Simon and Schuster, 1971), Isherwood's story of his parents told alternately through his mother's letters and his own commentary, he concludes ironically that perhaps this text, too, like all his writing since *The Adventures of Mummy and Daddy*, "that lost childhood work," is "chiefly about Christopher" (510).

[8] Henry Hewes, "Christopher Isherwood's Snapshots," *Saturday Review* (12 April 1952): 38.

FANTASIES, FASCISM, SPECTACLE 11

The Chris/Cliff/Brian character, on the other hand, has received far less attention. As the difference in names indicates, the leading man is a less durable or recognizable character, and the performers (William Prince, Laurence Harvey, Bert Convy, Michael York) were necessarily upstaged by the dynamic Sally Bowles. The only other character who has received the same attention is the emcee in the later adaptations, a role that has been overwhelmingly identified with Joel Grey, who got top billing in the 1987 revival of the stage musical. The importance of Grey's character certainly merits attention, as I will point out in the last two chapters, but there is no question that the emcee could be an oedipal hero, even if he is voyeur or, as Bauer suggests, an "embedded author" or "Greek chorus."[9]

Yet my project to read the figure Sally Bowles as a history (and cultural history through permutations of Sally Bowles) is haunted by another kind of oedipalization that occurs in popular readings of Weimar culture. A good example is Bauer's own historical source, Peter Gay's popular text, *Weimar Culture: The Outsider as Insider*, which inscribes the oedipal myth as the myth of Weimar. A chapter titled "The Revolt of the Son" describes Expressionism, and another, "Revenge of the Father," traces various forms of conservative backlash to the liberal trends in Berlin and the youth movements. Gay is so certain that the history of Weimar is a male history that he introduces his text with an assertion that he will confirm what "we" already know about the era as a story of "fathers and sons." Besides illustrating the gamut of cultural clichés and stereotypes about Weimar, his description is also significant for its positioning of female sexuality in this history:

> When we think of Weimar, we think of modernity in art, literature, and thought; we think of the rebellion of sons against fathers, Dadaists against art, Berliners against beefy philistinism, libertines against old-fashioned moralists; we think of *The Threepenny Opera*, *The Cabinet of Dr. Caligari*, *The Magic Mountain*, the *Bauhaus*, Marlene Dietrich. And we think, above all, of the exiles who exported Weimar culture all over the world.[10]

Gay's study eventually examines each of the phenomena he mentions here except for Dietrich, who appears again only in a photo and as a body part, a culturally recognizable fetish, in a sentence about a film in which she did not appear: ". . . Caligari continues to embody the Weimar spirit to posterity as palpably as Gropius' buildings, Kandin-

[9] Stephen F. Bauer, "Cultural History," 182.

[10] Peter Gay, *Weimar Culture: The Outsider as Insider* (New York: Harper and Row, 1968), xiii.

sky's abstractions, Grosz's cartoons, and Marlene Dietrich's legs."[11] But the buildings of Gropius are taken seriously, later analyzed by Gay as Weimar texts, whereas the reference to Dietrich is purely iconographic. Even her most noted film of that era, Von Sternberg's *The Blue Angel*, merits no more discussion than two sentences of the caption under the still, an illustration rather than a part of the "real" text. The contrast here is worth noting because it recurs in the retelling of the story of Sally Bowles on stage and in film, where female sexuality is opposed to "serious" text in a trajectory that opposes body and language; or it is posited in a tension between the blatant visibility of female spectacle and the nervous disavowal of what is unknowable about the female body.[12] By describing Weimar as a story of fathers and sons in which Marlene Dietrich appears as icon and fetish, Peter Gay's summary remarkably mimics the dynamics of mainstream Hollywood film as described in contemporary feminist film theory: the repetition of the oedipal trajectory, fetishization and disavowal of female sexuality, the visual representation of woman as term of difference, male trajectory/female spectacle, or—in Laura Mulvey's famous encapsulation, "Woman as Image, Man as Bearer of the Look."[13]

As can be seen in Bauer's historical source and his own understanding of history, the feminist analysis of adaptation necessitates a shift in focus to undermine the large cultural assumption that history is always the story of fathers and sons. Considering the Sally Bowles character in its later stages—*Cabaret* as a gay cult film, Sally's icono-

[11] Ibid., 102.

[12] See Peter Baxter's lovingly detailed explanation of the irresistible and terrifying hidden female space above Dietrich's legs in *The Blue Angel*, which he claims is a fascinating oedipal text about "the specific relationship of concealment and revelation" which "rivets the attention." "On the Naked Thighs of Miss Dietrich," *Wide Angle* 2 (1977): 23.

[13] Laura Mulvey, "Visual Pleasure and Narrative Cinema," *Screen* 16 (1975): 11. Gay's analysis is itself typical of a certain kind of historical discourse concerning Weimar history. Patrice Petro's recent work on gender and representation in Weimar Germany points out that the analysis of the era as "a breakdown of male identity" has had considerable impact, and that this "preoccupation with an allegedly ineffectual patriarchal authority" has produced a number of "blind spots" in Weimar history: specifically, the presence of women as spectators and co-producers of culture. See *Joyless Streets: Women and Melodramatic Representation in Weimar Germany* (Princeton: Princeton University Press, 1989), xviii–xix. Petro thus joins other recent feminist historians such as Renate Bridenthal and Claudia Koonz who have claimed that women's history in the Weimar years was no mere undercurrent but central to major movements and policies. See Koonz's *Mothers in the Fatherland: Women, the Family, and Nazi Politics* (New York: St. Martin's, 1987) and the anthology *When Biology Became Destiny: Women in Weimar and Nazi Germany*, ed. Renate Bridenthal et al. (New York: Monthly Review, 1984).

graphic status as the materialization of wild Weimar Berlin, the relationships of that iconography to pornography and sadomasochism—
we can discern a history of gender relationships that are closely connected not only to Weimar history but also to changing relationships
with that history. According to Bauer, the repetitions of the story indicate "there is something universal in such a work's being revised,
something close to the bone of author and audience, that also specifically meets the needs of and resonates with the historical moment."[14]
But in reading "the historical moment" as a singular, "universal"
one—the sons' anxieties concerning the Vietnam War—Bauer glosses
over the unsettling female presence in both film and history which is
precisely where my own study of Sally Bowles begins. Claiming this
set of adaptations as a series of cultural tests, articulations, and productions, my argument is that the Sally Bowles configuration operates across several intersecting histories that provide the grounds of
these texts. These include concerns with visibility and spectatorship
connecting German fascism and the motion-picture camera; the cinematic history of antifascist films; and the cultural readings of both
Weimar and Nazism as a peculiar sexual fascination—"divine decadence." These are the issues that need to be unpacked in order to
understand how the figure Sally Bowles operates as a sexual borderline, a handy delineation of fascism as sexual Other, which has pro-
pelled so much creative and cultural energy into the retelling of her
story over the past fifty years.

SALLY, LOLA, LILI MARLEEN

The relationship between the parallel development of fascism and
the motion-picture camera early in this century has often been addressed in film theory, most notably by Walter Benjamin, in his 1935/
1936 essay "The Work of Art in the Age of Mechanical Reproduction," with the warning that fascism works to repress freedom but
encourage mass expression. More recently, Thomas Elsaesser has
commented on fascism as being a particularly visual phenomenon, a
"specularization of consciousness" much like cinema; along the same
lines, Russell Berman reads Leni Riefenstahl's *The Triumph of the Will*
(1935) as the triumph of the visual over the written word, typical of
the fascist prioritizing of the sight or spectacle over language.[15] Fur-

[14] Stephen F. Bauer, "Cultural History," 174.
[15] Walter Benjamin, "The Work of Art in the Age of Mechanical Reproduction," in
Illuminations, ed. Hannah Arendt, trans. Harry Zohn (New York: Schocken, 1969),
241; Thomas Elsaesser, "Primary Identification and the Historical Subject," in *Narra-*

ther consideration of the sexual politics of these phenomena reveals an additional and startling alignment concerning the dynamics of visibility. Both in German fascism and in mainstream cinema, the heightening of sexual difference is crucial. In the biological order that the Third Reich worked to attain, the visible differences of gender and race served to confirm a "natural" hierarchy. The supporting "stars" of the Riefenstahl film, after all, the chorus lines of *Hitlerjungen* and the SS, suggest the "natural" hierarchy by which history is made and populated by strong, white males.

Likewise, mainstream cinema has inscribed the dynamics of spectatorship with a biologism (and racism) that is repeatedly posited as "natural": woman as body and image, man as narrative authority and voyeur. It is the cinema-loving Isherwood who constructs the original Sally Bowles as the object of literature's most famous metaphorical camera, as described by the narrator in the opening paragraphs of *Goodbye to Berlin*: "I am a camera with its shutter open, quite passive, recording, not thinking."[16] Ensconced from the start in the relationship between camera eye and woman, Sally's character is inherently positioned in a relationship that, as extensive studies by John Berger, Linda Williams, and others have shown, has been heavily coded and ideologically burdened in its representations of women since its beginnings.[17] In each of the five Sally Bowles texts, the male writer/authority confronts the woman who operates as body and spectacle, without a reliable or meaningful language of her own. As often described in feminist film theory, the mechanics of disavowal—fetishization and excess—produce the excessive props, costuming, and makeup that can be seen in the history of this adaptation from Julie Harris's green fingernail polish and long black cigarette holder to Liza Minnelli's garishly thick circles of eyeliner.

However, the popular image of Sally Bowles, especially since the Fosse film, is part of an even more specialized relationship between woman and camera eye, as my opening remarks on Dietrich and *The Blue Angel* suggest. In the postwar film history of this image, Sally Bowles has the dubious distinction of appearing both in its early

tive, Apparatus, Ideology, ed. Philip Rosen (New York: Columbia University Press, 1986), 535–49; Russell Berman, "Written Right Across Their Faces: Leni Riefenstahl, Ernst Jünger, and Fascist Modernism," in *Modern Culture and Critical Theory* (Madison, Wisconsin, and London: University of Wisconsin Press, 1989), 99–117.

[16] Christopher Isherwood, *Goodbye to Berlin* (1939) in *Berlin Stories: The Last of Mr. Norris and Goodbye to Berlin* (New York: New Directions, 1954), 1.

[17] In particular, see Linda Williams's description of excess and fetishization in representations of the female figure in turn-of-the-century film in "Film Body: An Implantation of Perversions," *Ciné-Tracts* 12 (1981): 19–35.

stages, in 1950s representations of Weimar stereotypes, and in its slickly stylized production twenty years later. The 1955 *I Am a Camera* added a cabaret scene to the plot of Van Druten's stage version so that Sally is firmly located in a *mise-en-scène* already familiar to viewers from Von Sternberg's *The Blue Angel*: the smoky cabaret, a rowdy audience, ominous sounds of broken glass and women screaming as the New Year, 1930, is welcomed in. Julie Harris's performance in this scene is both pathetically poor and oddly telling. With a minimal display of talent, she sings a strange tribute to the power of the visual, a song about love that is based only on sight, and then pops a monocle into one eye socket, suggesting both a caricature of the German upper class and an arrogant return of the audience gaze. Establishing herself as the nightclub singer associated with a world of spectacle and dubious relationships, a world in which the "spectacle" of Nazism is developing, Sally Bowles in her first film appearance demonstrates that a cinematic practice connecting female eroticism—in particular, the Dietrichesque cabaret singer—with Weimar "decadence" and the Third Reich was already established ten years after the war.

Regarding this iconographical connection, Patrice Petro has pointed out that the popular use of Dietrich as a figure of Weimar female sexuality is a "convenient" way "to project a reading of male subjectivity in crisis," especially considering Dietrich's siren roles as nemesis of men.[18] Lola Lola's song "Falling in Love Again" from *The Blue Angel* emphasizes her lethal irresistibility: "Men cluster around me like moths around a flame, / And if they burn, I'm not to blame." As the film has traditionally been read, Lola operates as pure body and materiality, a kind of natural, devastating life force, in the destruction of the intellect, willpower, and self-respect of the hapless Professor Rath, whose moral condemnation of the singer changes to fascination and then adulation. The turning point is Lola's performance of this song at the cabaret, when Rath as the wholly enamored spectator falls under her spell and ends up spending the night with her. Ironically, Rath's decision to take the "moral" route by marrying her leads to his own degradation, as the professor turns cuckold, clown, and fool, while Lola Lola's power and seductiveness continue undiminished.

The earliest and perhaps best-known political interpretation of this film is that of Siegfried Kracauer, who reads this and other Weimar films as reflections of the rise of fascism. In this reading, Professor Rath stands for the German middle classes, who submit to "powers far worse than those from which he escaped"; the students and the

---

[18] Patrice Petro, *Joyless Streets*, 159.

2. *The Blue Angel* (*Der blaue Engel*) (1930). This widely circulated image established Lola Lola (Marlene Dietrich) as the original Weimar cabaret siren fascinating the audience with a "dangerous" sexuality.

cabaret performers both manifest "sadistic cruelty" which "forces their victim into submission."[19] Kracauer's approach is rather narrowly allegorical, but instead of dismissing this interpretation altogether, I would prefer to position it as an important part of what Petro sees as the "gendered" readings of Weimar. This is true because certainly this reading of *The Blue Angel* is congruent with the psychosexual assumptions about German fascism evident in postwar popular culture, according to which the "fascination" of fascism is linked to sadism, submission, and seduction—the theatrical possibilities of which would be richly exploited by gay culture and camp. The powerful and hypnotic figure in this scenario is the dominating woman, who reveals an arch self-consciousness in the excessiveness of her costume, poses, and *mise-en-scène*, making Lola Lola's "Falling in Love Again" a popular subject for female impersonators. The curious route from Kracauer's moralism to transvestism and camp suggests the contradictions that will in fact be central to the two *Cabaret* adaptations, which similarly focus on fascism in relation to a sexuality that is posited as threatening and morally reprehensible, on the one hand, but also fascinating in its sexual play, on the other. Indeed, Dietrich herself as the key figure in this nexus complicates the ways in which Lola can be read. The self-consciousness of her performance invites not only camp impersonation but also feminist speculation that her defiant "return of the gaze" operates as a resistant force to the relationships of female spectacle and male voyeurism, and that her power and autonomy have considerable lesbian appeal as well.[20] The problem is that, for other readings, the association of the Lola Lola figure with gay and lesbian desires works to reinforce the "decadent Weimar" interpretation of German fascism, as is evident in the transvestite scene in *The Damned* discussed below. In general, the history of the Sally Bowles adaptations illustrates the persistence and cultural popularity of Kracauer's reading of fascism as the sexually dangerous spectacle that fascinates and seduces the middle classes.

This relationship of female spectacle (the cabaret singer teasing the

[19] Siegfried Kracauer, *From Caligari to Hitler: A Psychological History of the German Film* (Princeton: Princeton University Press, 1947), 218.

[20] E. Ann Kaplan discusses the subversive aspect of Dietrich in *Women and Film: Both Sides of the Camera* (New York: Methuen, 1983), 49–59. Also, for a reading of Dietrich's performance in relationship to the other women onstage in *The Blue Angel*, see Judith Mayne, "Marlene Dietrich, *The Blue Angel*, and Female Performance" in *Seduction and Theory*, ed. Dianne Hunter (Urbana and Chicago: University of Illinois Press, 1989), 28–46. Mayne also points out the male bias in traditional readings of Professor Rath as Lola's "victim" and demonstrates how a reading from a female point of view can break down the male gaze/female spectacle dichotomy by focusing on how the film "is structured by a tension between different modes of performance" (32).

audience with what is not visible: female sexuality) and an "invisible" politics (fascism lurking in the background) reveals a dynamic that has received attention in psychoanalytic terms in feminist film theory as the crisis of the "unknowability" of female sexuality.[21] The Sally Bowles case gives this dynamic specific historical hooks. Female sexual spectacle in the two Sally Bowles films plays on tensions of what is "knowable" about the Sally character, so that there is slippage between what the leading man in each text experiences as rise-of-the-Nazis and life-with-Sally. In the latter film in particular, visibility is situated as a crisis that is both sexual and political, in that the hidden nature of female sexuality is conflated with the hidden sexual secret of Nazi Germany. The Fosse film, in addition, hints at another kind of invisibility with disturbing historical resonance. The complication and frustration of the Reich's aim for visible, natural difference recurs in its aim for ethnic purity. Jewishness, unlike sex and race, is "invisible," and thus tests German fascism's privileging of visibility, the reliability of the image. In aiming to make Jewishness a physical trait, Nazi propaganda insistently portrayed a "typical" Jewish physical type, but records show that another kind of physical typing was actually used to identify Jewish males: the Jewish and non-German custom of circumcision. As I will point out in my final chapter, the Fosse film conflates female sexuality and Jewish identity as similar terms of genital anxiety, reworking a historical anxiety seamlessly into one of the strategies of mainstream film.

My argument is that the crisis of spectatorship inscribed within these films duplicates a wider cultural anxiety about the spectacle of Nazism. The on-screen Weimar audience that is fascinated with the cabaret singer will soon participate in this larger historical spectacle; in Fosse's *Cabaret*, in particular, the film audience finds itself in an uncomfortably similar position in regard to these diegetic spectators, necessitating a disavowal of pleasure on some level—a narrative punishment of the show girl, a qualification of pleasurable spectacle as "decadence." After all, how are we, as fascinated spectators, different from the European spectators fascinated by Nazism? The key here is

[21] See Mary Ann Doane's analysis of King Vidor's *Gilda* (1946) and *film noir*, "*Gilda*: Epistemology as Striptease," *Camera Obscura* 11 (1983): 6–27. She contends that female sexuality in this genre, like the lighting style, "confounds the relation between the visible and the knowable" because the "instability of the female sex is linked to the untrustworthiness of the image, to a conflict between 'looking' and 'being' " (11). Female sexuality is "unknowable," and thus an epistemological crisis, Doane claims, because it is "diffuse" rather than, like male sexuality, centered in the visible organ; whereas mainstream film is based on the reliability of the image, the unknowable nature of female sexuality can work against this reliability in a genre such as *film noir*.

the crisis of the reliability of the visual (surely they can't really look or be like us) that is projected onto the show girl as another kind of problem concerning what is or is not visible. This paradigm is reinforced by the reductive historical stereotype of Nazism itself as a sudden failure of vision, a vulnerability to spectacle, a fluke or aberration, rather than a phenomenon situated in mainstream European traditions. As referent for the image of the Weimar cabaret siren, Marlene Dietrich is herself part of the knowability crisis here—a "good" German who comes to the United States but suspiciously retains her European accent, style, "unknowability."

Already it is evident that "history" operates in the Sally Bowles texts as a motivated reading, a postwar disavowal of 1930s Germany. The understanding of that era ends up being iconographic rather than analytical. Thus Sally's appearance in the cabaret scene in Cornelius's *I Am a Camera* is a reference to a familiar code concerning Weimar Berlin, which in turn historically locates what is otherwise a conventional bachelor-versus-the-show-girl narrative. Like the stage play, the Cornelius film reveals its setting by scattering a series of such references throughout the text—the Brownshirts as thugs, the bread lines, the nightlife.[22] The character Sally Bowles, coded as dangerous female sexuality, operates as an oblique alignment of female (or transvestite) eroticism with fascism, not as part of the narrative per se but as part of a didactic trajectory contending with the question our culture faced after Auschwitz: How could any "normal" person become a Nazi? This question is central to the postwar constructions of Sally Bowles, in which political difference is inscribed as sexual difference, and the grounds of the question become male intellect versus female materiality, a positioning of the "innocent" British/American intellectual against the decadence of Weimar Berlin.

Fosse's 1972 *Cabaret* is part of a much slicker and well-established antifascist genre dealing with this question in films by Bernardo Bertolucci, Luchino Visconti, Constantine Costa-Gavras, and others. This genre most often suggests a psychosexual—often homosexual—explanation of the protofascist, even while positing a "historical" or socialist account.[23] Such a move is congruent with a popular explana-

[22] A similar use of history is evident in *Gilda*, according to Doane: "Fascism haunts the text," Doane says of *Gilda*; it "situates itself temporally by invoking history only obliquely, as an afterthought." Doane's further observations on the relationship between fascism and sexuality prove generally true in other postwar antifascist films: "the condemnation of homosexuality and a heterosexuality not properly constrained within the bounds of the 'normal' marriage gains force by its sleight-of-hand merger with an anti-fascist critique," ibid., 22.

[23] Joan Mellen, in her description of these films in "Fascism in the Contemporary

tion of fascism exemplified in T.W. Adorno's study of "the authoritarian personality," which accepts fascism as a historical given most likely to appeal to certain psychic constructions. However, the defensiveness of this argument, the positioning of fascism as Other in total opposition to "normal" culture and personality, has specific ramifications for mainstream cinema, in which the homosexual theory works in congruence with Hollywood homophobia, as happens in *Cabaret*. My claim here is that the representation of homosexuality in these films is in the long run related to the use of female spectacle as historical and psychological disavowal. Luchino Visconti's *The Damned* (*La Caduta Degli Dei*) (1969), which is an immediate predecessor of *Cabaret* in several ways, enacts this relationship with its protofascist character Martin von Essenbeck (Helmut Berger)—who, as homosexual, pedophile, cross dresser, and mother rapist is rather overdetermined as sexual Other. In a key scene, he performs in drag as Marlene Dietrich while the Reichstag burns. This scene, with its reference to Dietrich, its paralleling of spectacles (Reichstag fire, cabaret-drag-show), and its conflation of female eroticism and homosexuality is so heavily coded with postwar significations that it works at odds with the narrative's attempt at historical positioning.

The Dietrichesque cabaret singer is a key element in this postwar cluster of representations. In Liliana Cavani's *The Night Porter* (*Portiere di Notte*) (1973), which in other ways differs greatly from the antifascist genre, the cabaret performance of Lucia (Charlotte Rampling) is almost totally dissociated from the logic of plot and character development. In a highly stylized scene, Lucia appears bare chested in long black gloves and Nazi regalia, draping herself around a column and singing a sullenly Dietrichesque love song to a smoky roomful of soldiers. The scene is introduced ambiguously as a flashback that is never wholly explained as either memory, fantasy, or allegory. Max (Dirk Bogarde) says that it is "a story from the Bible," the Salome story, with Lucia's dance ending in the presentation of the severed head of a Nazi guard. But the impact of the scene resides in the culturally familiar elements that are far removed from either the Bible

---

Film," *Film Quarterly* 24 (1971): 2–19, analyzes the contradiction that occurs in the tension between an attempt at historical distancing and historical accuracy when the terms are sexualized. The protofascist in these films, she claims, is often the secret homosexual attempting to hide his "difference." Mellen claims that this representation accurately reflects Wilhelm Reich's theory of the protofascist as victim of patriarchal sexual repression. However, Mellen does not question this credible psychosexual trajectory in relation to what she sees as the failure of the historical trajectory in these films. In spite of their neo-Marxist theses, she admits, the films in the end take fascism as a "given," separate from historical causes, and instead focus on the latently homosexual personality attracted to it.

3. *The Damned* (*La Caduta Degli Dei*) (1969). Martin von Essenbeck (Helmut Berger) performs in drag as Marlene Dietrich while the Reichstag burns.

4. *The Night Porter* (*Portiere di Notte*) (1973). The "cabaret" performance of Lucia (Charlotte Rampling) stylizes the iconography of "Nazi eroticism" into the surreal.

or the concentration camp where the scene supposedly takes place;
Lucia's costume, song, and *mise-en-scène* are the shorthand for 1970s
popular understandings of "Nazi eroticism," here stylized to the point
of the surreal. Focus on sexual performances and spectatorship in
relation to Nazism are likewise encoded in films such as Ingmar Bergman's *The Serpent's Egg* (1977), István Szabó's *Mephisto* (1981), and
Rainer Werner Fassbinder's self-conscious tour de force, *Lili Marleen*
(1981).[24]

Lucia's performance in *The Night Porter* illustrates the power of the
cultural sign dissociated from its original conditions (Dietrich as Lola
in *The Blue Angel*) that circulates in so many other texts that it acquires
significations with multiple meanings (homosexuality, sadomaso-

[24] See Thomas Elsaesser, "*Lili Marleen*: Fascism and the Film Industry," *October* 21
(1982): 115–40.

chism, German fascism) not necessarily connected with its original text. The Dietrichesque cabaret performer has become the kind of popular cultural figure described by Tony Bennett and Janet Woollacott in their analysis of the James Bond character. Fictional characters such as Bond or Robinson Crusoe, they argue, can "achieve a semi-independent existence," recognizable even by those who do not know their original texts: "Functioning as focal points of cultural reference, they condense and connect, serve as shorthand expressions for, a number of deeply implanted cultural and ideological concerns."[25] Dietrich's cabaret singer, though widely recognizable as cultural reference, is not as fixed a character as Bond, nor has she saturated popular culture as completely as Fleming's famous spy. But as prototype and visual icon, she circulates as referent in a variety of texts, from the pornographic to camp, as a similar kind of "shorthand."

The Sally Bowles character operates as a specific function of this cultural perception and phenomenon, which continues to be supported and produced as the figure of Lili Marleen or Lola Lola, coded within what is perhaps the Third Reich's oddest legacy: the specifically erotic component of "fascinating fascism." Susan Sontag's well-known essay on this topic is an important point of departure not only because she gave the subject an enduring name but also because the trajectory of her essay itself reveals a significant cultural positioning. The essay begins with a resistant reading of Leni Riefenstahl's new biographical packaging connected to her "nonfascist" work as a photographer of the Nuba tribe in Africa. The issue is fascist/nonfascist, and Sontag quickly breaks down this distinction not only by correcting Riefenstahl's euphemistic official biography but also by revealing the continuum of fascist aesthetics, whether the subject be SS costumes on parade or African tribesmen. Sontag goes on to explain the popularity of fascist aesthetics in our culture by pointing out their common ground with various mainstream institutions and movements, from Art Deco to Busby Berkeley, reading the fascination of fascism as a recognition of cultural similarities.

But Sontag has a much more difficult time dealing with the specific phenomenon of Nazism as sexual fantasy. Noting how SS regalia and scenarios have been eroticized, transformed into the materials of pornography, she becomes increasingly didactic in her questions and tone: "Why has Nazi Germany, which was a sexually repressive society, become erotic? How could a regime which persecuted homosex-

25 Tony Bennett and Janet Woollacott, *Bond and Beyond: The Political Career of a Popular Hero* (Hampshire, England: Macmillan Educ., 1987), 14.

uals become a gay turn-on?" Sontag claims that the link between sadomasochism and fascism is theater, but she is not as interested in
fascism's theatricality as in its role in "an oppressive freedom of
choice in sex." Nazism, says Sontag, is now available as the "master
scenario" for a sexuality that enacts—or rather, wishes for and "re-
hearses"—domination and submission—and, she concludes, "the fantasy is death."[26]

What is notable about Sontag's analysis is the deliberate bifurcation
of her essay. The first part, her meditation on Riefenstahl's *The Last
of the Nuba*, is a long, thoughtful critique that makes uncomfortable
connections, a reading of fascism that breaks its historical boundaries
to illustrate its more pervasive presence in Western culture. But the
second part, her much shorter commentary on a paperback copy of
SS Regalia, takes a strident oppositional stance. Although yielding
borderlines generously in terms of fascist and mainstream culture on
the topic of aesthetics, Sontag draws the borderline firmly when the
topic is sexual fantasy. Her attitude is progressively moralistic and
finally fatalistic. Once the sexual imagination seeks out the theatricality of fascism, she insists, it is wishing for its own demise.

This split reading by Sontag is worth noting for several reasons. In
conceding that at least some aspects of German fascism have common
ground with "respectable" Western traditions and arts, Sontag is
much more perceptive, and less defensive, than the makers of antifascist films who portray fascism as a monstrous aberration. When the
subject is sexuality, however, Sontag draws the line and evokes the
monstrous, even though the horror of Nazism is as much implicit in
a sympathetic viewing of *Triumph of the Will* as in a sexualized reading
of *SS Regalia*. What, then, is *not* acknowledged as common ground
here, in the connections among fascism, theatricality, and sexual fantasy? Is sadomasochism the only kind of sexual practice with political
implications? Surely not, as Andrea Dworkin has forcefully pointed
out, although the subject of sadomasochism has often split feminists
on the subject of "politically correct" sex, with those such as Pat Califia defending leather sex and Nazi scenarios as potentially liberating:
"If you don't like being a top or a bottom, you switch your keys. Try
doing that with your biological sex or your race or your socioeco-
nomic status. . . . Not everyone who wears a swastika is a Nazi."[27] The

---

[26] Susan Sontag, "Fascinating Fascism," in *The Susan Sontag Reader* (New York: Farrar, Strauss & Giroux, 1982), 323, 325.

[27] Pat Califia, "Feminism and Sadomasochism," *Heresies* 3 (1981): 32. Califia is the
spokesperson for the organization Samois, which advocates lesbian sadomasochistic
practice as feminist. For the feminist debate about this issue, see the essays in *Against*

latter comment in fact discloses the possibility of the empty sign, the image that circulates in popular fashion in virtual isolation from its "meaning," such as the use of swastikas in punk fads. But perhaps the larger question is to what extent all sexual "taste" (including the sexual codes of punk or other fads) in patriarchal culture adheres to a dominance-submission paradigm, for which Nazism provides both a theatrically rich model and a grim reminder of what happens when the power paradigm of this sexuality is literalized into state politics. Thus the signs of Nazism are never wholly emptied so much as easily absorbed into less visible sexual ideological apparatuses.

The character Sally Bowles is situated centrally in the map of fascinating fascism as drawn by Sontag, if only to illustrate that the lines need to be adjusted. On the one hand, Sally is related to many mainstream traditions that make her recognizable and sympathetic. She is inscribed in the codes of comedy, the musical, and camp culture; with Liza Minnelli her citizenship has been expanded to include the United States, and her theme song, "Cabaret," turned into a popular tune. On the other hand, her connections to the darker side of Sontag's landscape are clear, too. Though she has never explicitly appeared in pornography or the scenarios of sadomasochism, her cabaret costume is that of the Sadeian woman, and the two films (especially the latter) contain scenes and narrative lines that are at least implicitly sadomasochistic. Because of the sexual subtext in the Isherwood and Van Druten texts, and the more openly gay references in the Fosse film, Sally is also firmly entrenched in gay culture—where, says Sontag, "the eroticism of Nazism is most visible."[28] As these issues suggest, the history of Sally Bowles's "divine decadence" is a history of contentions concerning boundary—heterosexual/homosexual, male/female, Nazi/anti-Nazi—contentions that in turn are embedded in the "ambivalent" relationship between Nazism and homosexuality, in Nazi sexual politics, in the sexual politics of mainstream cinema, and in postwar theories of German fascism.

FANTASIES AND BOUNDARIES OF GERMAN FASCISM

The most serious premise in my analyses of this adaptation series is that generally, as "antifascist" productions, the Sally Bowles adaptations end up duplicating the fascist politics they strain to condemn,

---

Sadomasochism: A Radical Feminist Analysis, ed. Robin Ruth et al (E. Palo Alto: Frog in the Well, 1982).

[28] Susan Sontag, "Fascinating Fascism," 324.

reproducing the homophobia, misogyny, fascination for spectacle, and emphasis of sexual difference that characterize German fascism. The issue here is a cultural misreading of Weimar culture and "decadence" that is central to the Sally Bowles paradigm, in that each text positions Nazism as an Other that emerges in a cause-and-effect way from the Otherness of "wild Weimar." Without attempting a comprehensive history of this era, I would argue that popular misreadings of Weimar culture conveniently situate fascism as a result of liberal errors rather than conservative ones. Berlin in the 1920s and early 1930s was in fact the locus of an avant-garde culture that included a proliferation of gay and lesbian bars, talk of an emancipated New Woman (of whom Sally Bowles is a caricature), and the toleration of a liberal attitude toward sexuality, as seen in Magnus Hirschfeld's famous Institute for Sexual Research. But the liberal sexuality, the liberated roles of women, and the profligate behavior in the cabarets comprised only one strand of experience in the Germany of that time; moreover, these emergent social shifts were exactly the elements targeted by Nazi propaganda in order to posit a cleaner, more traditional Third Reich—one in which everyone knew his and her place.

For example, though the National Socialists later exploited popular conceptions of the New Woman as threat to male power, a considerable gap existed between the image and the reality, as documented by more recent feminist histories.[29] Weimar attitudes toward homosexuality were likewise contradictory and edgy, revealing again that the later Nazi backlash had mainstream appeal. While the liberal inquiries of the Hirschfeld center and the boy bars beloved by Isherwood were tolerated in Berlin, hostile theories of homoeroticism were far more popular, as evidenced in Hirschfeld's repeatedly unsuccessful attempts to repeal Germany's Paragraph 175, the nineteenth-century national law that made homosexual activity a crime. As for the sexual liberation of women in Weimar, contemporary research again reveals complications and gaps in the stereotype and histories. Atina Grossman's study of the Weimar Sex Reform movement, for instance, concludes that the long-range goals of the Sex Reformers coincided neatly with the Third Reich's later goals of eugenics and control of "deviance." Taking the standards of male heterosexu-

---

[29] See Claudia Koonz, *Mothers in the Fatherland*, on Weimar women in the work force, 45–47. See also Patrice Petro, *Joyless Streets*, on the representational function of the New Woman in various Weimar discourses, 90–110. Significantly, in analyzing the impact of the media on the construction of gender in Weimar, Petro claims that she needs to point to some of the institutions and presses that Peter Gay's analysis failed to include because they did not conform to his oedipal model of political affiliation (86).

ality as the norm, these medical and sociological experts fused the ideology of motherhood with "liberated" goals of sexual intimacy so that the celebrated New Woman could be domesticated. Obsessed with categorization and "types" of women and sexual response, the Sex Reformers ultimately posited a "normal" sexuality so that "the boundaries defining deviant groups and behavior sharpened."[30] We find here, as in many cases, that certain Nazi obsessions, such as absolute sexual categorizations, were not suddenly imposed by a new ideology but grew out of existing institutions, traditions, and ideas.

Generally, National Socialism was able to draw on deep middle-class anxieties about the exact elements in Weimar Berlin that often attracted foreign visitors: for example, the sexual liberalism and the loss of traditional German values concerning women. It was the "disorder" of Weimar Berlin that Hitler's party promised to eradicate; in Nazi jargon, the Weimar Republic was "the period of the system"—a point in the cycle during which decadent liberal messes could be "excreted."[31] But there is a distinction to be made between the actual political and economic disorders—the problems with the multiparty parliament, the inflation, the war debts, the "crises in hegemony" described by Nicos Poulantzos and others—and the appeals to a middle-class "order" by which National Socialism represented itself. It attacked what had always been an emergent, never a dominant, cultural liberalism in German life. The backlash against the emancipated woman, for example, did not originate with National Socialism, though the latter was easily able to draw on the reactionary flood of "scientific" evidence that appeared from 1925 through 1933 condemning feminism as "unnatural."[32] Mainstream, nonfascist middle-class and religious leaders were quick to support the series of morality ordinances passed by the Reich during the spring of 1933 outlawing "obscene" writing and performances, closing down homosexual gathering places, and cracking down on prostitution and public contraception-vending machines. Berlin cabaret life encapsulated all these issues and was similarly targeted. The imagination and sexual energy of the cabarets, far from being precursors of Nazism or entertainment for the SA, as Fosse's *Cabaret* insinuates, were actually points of resistance. Cabaret humor often took on the Nazis as their targets of satire, so that after 1933, the famous emcees who had most

[30] Atina Grossman, "The New Woman and the Rationalization of Sexuality in Weimar Germany," in *The Powers of Desire: The Politics of Sexuality*, ed. A. Snitow et al. (New York: Virago, 1983), 158–59, 166.

[31] Annemarie Troger, "The Creation of a Female Assembly-Line Proletariat," in Bridenthal, 239.

[32] Claudia Koonz, *Mothers in the Fatherland*, 99.

openly performed such satires were persecuted, and by 1935 most of the cabarets were forced out to London, Prague, and Vienna.[33]

The "order" that the National Socialists promised to restore was a deeply hierarchical and biological one. Surely the appeal of Nazism to both mainstream cinema and to camp parody is its obsession with sexual difference, an obsession that is directly connected to its obsession with racial difference. The connection is the biological need for Aryan mothers of the new master race (thus the banishing of women from professional life back to the home) and the fanatic idealization of motherhood in the Reich, as seen in the political uses of a national Mother's Day (but only for women who were "genetically fit"). My concern here is with the apparently paradoxical elements of adulation and contempt in the motherhood/traditional-woman campaign, because it is not an exclusively Nazi methodology but is a paradigm that has parallels in older cultural traditions (for example, the simultaneous adoration/repression present in the courtly-love tradition), and in more recent discourses concerning motherhood (for example, the "Momism" and "bad mother" syndrome of the 1950s, as will be discussed in chapter 3). Moreover, it reproduces itself in other (eroticized) ways in forms such as classic cinema. The paradox in the Nazi schemata is this: The "pure" woman is the racial defense against pollution by the Jew, but what is contemptible in the Jew is in fact "womanliness." As racial propaganda, this worked two ways, in that the Jew represented the threat of liberalism and education that was posited as a parallel to the threat of women in traditionally male spheres: "Everything urbane and intellectual in a female was seen as a sign of 'Jewish decadence.' "[34] The economic failures of Weimar liberalism could be explained against a "natural" order that put progressive women and Jews in their places.

Yet whereas this line of reasoning implicitly condones the "traditional" woman for her submission and passivity in a masculine ordering of the world, another line of anti-Semitic propaganda ruthlessly undermines any respect for femininity. George Mosse's *Nationalism and Sexuality* documents in detail the connection between the masculinism of German fascism and its anti-Semitism, pointing out how the Third Reich was able to draw on the German cultural and "scientific" movements of the early part of the century that condemned Judaism specifically for its effeminacy—even while other strands of anti-Semitism worked on the contradictory assumption that Jews were danger-

[33] See Lisa Appignanesi, *The Cabaret* (New York: Universe, 1976), 101–3, 156, 161.

[34] Annemarie Troger, "The Creation of a Female Assembly-Line Proletariat," in Bridenthal, 239.

ous because of their aggressive lechery, especially as it was directed toward Christian women.[35] The contradiction stems from the representation of Jewish "lechery" as itself secretly female—that is, insatiable and uncontrollable.

Mosse points out the enormous influence of the Austrian writer Otto Weininger's 1903 racist/sexist treatise *Sex and Character* (*Geschlecht und Charakter*) which is worth examination in that it blatantly foregrounds the issue of boundary (the human being is the autonomous male) and the danger of pollution (by less human creatures, the Jew and the woman). Weininger condemns women and Jews specifically for "lack of a free intelligible ego"—that is, to hearken back to the visibility problem—they are less "knowable." Their characteristics and impulses are less differentiated: "In the Jew and the woman, good and evil are not distinct from one another," Weininger tells us. His conclusion to his chapter on Judaism ends with an apocalyptic description of his times. The modern age, he says, has seen the end of all art, "genius," philosophy, greatness; it is an age of "superficial anarchy," communism, capitalism, Marxism, materialism. "Our age," he says in summary, "is not only the most Jewish but the most feminine."[36] What is notable about these passages is that a postwar reading of them is bound to focus on the anti-Semitism and its direct links to the ideology of the Third Reich; less conspicuous perhaps is Weininger's solid grounding in the Western tradition of the autonomous self, which links him as much to mainstream ideas of "healthy ego" as to Nazism. His warnings about the "less-defined" female/Jewish character, for example, take on new resonance in light of Carol Gilligan's recent descriptions of cultural models of autonomy. Gilligan contends that the autonomous-healthy-ego model idealized in our culture is actually a male model of self-perception, as opposed to female self-perception which tends to be more "fluid" in terms of ego boundary.[37] The other notable element of Weininger's discourse is that its paranoia is sharpened by a self-hatred that was also self-destructive; Jewish and homosexual, he committed suicide in 1903.

Weininger's characterization of modernity as both female and Jewish neatly dovetailed with other conservative theories linking all three to the dangers of urbanity: the theory that modernity itself has boundary lines and can be located specifically—in the city—and therefore contained. Contemporary historians find repeatedly that

[35] George Mosse, *Nationalism and Sexuality: Respectability and Abnormal Sexuality in Modern Europe* (New York: Fertig, 1985), 144.

[36] Otto Weininger, *Sex and Character* (1906; New York: AMS, 1975), 307–9, 329.

[37] Carol Gilligan, *In a Different Voice: Psychological Theory and Women's Development* (Cambridge, Mass., and London: Harvard University Press, 1982).

Weimar anxieties about the modern age were expressed as gender anxieties. Patrice Petro has documented how often artists and writers of the time "responded to modernity by imaginatively reconstructing Berlin as demonic, as alienating, and as female"; Peter Gay gives examples of the descriptions of Berlin as "a highly desirable woman, whose coldness and coquettishness are widely known."[38] At the same time, Berlin was being characterized by nationalists as the cause and site of all aberrant sexuality, with the result that there was a public discourse aimed toward sharper definition of normal versus aberrant sexual behavior, and subsequent hostility toward homosexuality—in particular, male homosexuality, which had made itself more "visible" through the activities of Hirschfeld and others, and which could be posited as a more urgent threat to the masculinist ethos of the Reich.[39] Mosse documents how a variety of theorists early in the century contributed to the stereotype of urban life as intrinsically unnatural, a "home to outsiders—Jews, criminals, the insane, homosexuals—while the countryside was the home of the native on his soil."[40] In the continuum linking femininity, Judaism, urbanity, and illicit sexuality in opposition to a rural male norm, homosexuality was inevitably linked to the "confusing of genders" that occurred in liberal big cities where women attempted to take on the jobs of men. The homosexual could be bracketed with the Jew as dangers to a "natural" biological order.[41]

Paradoxically, in popular postwar representations, the Third Reich has been consistently linked to male homosexuality in spite of its own explicitly homophobic platform. A reason often cited is the historical incident that is now known as the Night of the Long Knives, an event portrayed as grand spectacle in *The Damned*, when the SA and its leader, Ernst Röhm, were overthrown and murdered by Heinrich

[38] Patrice Petro, *Joyless Streets*, 43; Peter Gay, *Weimar Culture*, 132.

[39] Richard Plant, in *The Pink Triangle: The Nazi War Against Homosexuals* (New York: Henry Holt, 1986) contends that though lesbianism was persecuted by the Reich when it was made obvious, lesbians escaped the all-out "war against homosexuality" enforced against gay men, 114–17.

[40] Mosse, *Nationalism and Sexuality*, 32.

[41] Plant attributes the extensive and systematic persecution of gay men by the Third Reich both to the cultural backlash against some of the liberalism of the Weimar period and to the personal homophobia of Reichsführer SS Heinrich Himmler, who eventually made the decision that "the Final Solution was as inevitable for gays as for Jews" (90). The number of gay men who died in concentration camps has been estimated at between a quarter and a half a million. Plant claims that this documentation has been readily available but consistently overlooked since the end of the war; postwar culture, he claims, has been much more interested in the stereotype of the secretly homosexual Nazi than in Nazi homosexual persecution.

Himmler and his SS. Later historical accounts suggest that Röhm's well-known homosexuality was not the cause, but the later justification of the massacre. Apparently Röhm's sexual tastes were tolerated by Hitler so long as he was of use, but they could conveniently be used as an example for Nazi moralism once Röhm and his SA were no longer needed.[42] As a sign of the secret homosexuality of Nazism, the popular references to this event constitute a historical misreading, since only a small percentage of the SA was involved in Röhm's affairs, and the more "typical" Nazi male was perhaps the "straight" misogynist heterosexual. Yet in spite of this popular reading of the Night of the Long Knives, it is not the SA, but the SS that has been simultaneously eroticized and "camped-up" with homosexual overtones. As Susan Sontag points out, the SA shared the same rhetoric and reputation for brutality but "have gone down in history as beefy, squat, beerhall types; mere brownshirts," whereas the SS has become the material for fantasy—precisely because the latter "was designed as an elite military community that would be not only supremely violent but also supremely beautiful."[43]

Heinrich Himmler was himself deeply aware of the homoerotic danger in the SS's style and aesthetics. After the Röhm scandal, his homophobic rhetoric heightened and he engaged in a paranoid series of measures to guard against male homosexuality within the Reich and in particular within his elite SS, a threat that he saw as inevitable in a commune of men where virility and the perfect, male, athletic body were idealized in isolation from female eroticism or influence. The popular Third Reich propaganda film *Hitlerjunge Quex* (Hans Steinhoff, 1933) illustrates the problem Himmler was addressing. Here the male commune of the Hitler Youth Corps replaces the availability of female sexuality (in the film, represented by a floozy Communist street girl) with the steady company of handsome, fit, blond boys led by an especially handsome troop leader. Heini, the working-class adolescent protagonist, is able to shed his confining, unenlightened family so that he can join the "higher" family of beautiful boys in gleaming uniforms. The overweight, older, ineffective father is replaced by the trim, energetic young *Bannführer* who is an adolescent fantasy of a father not much out of adolescence himself. The mother, meanwhile, is both venerated and evaporated (she conveniently kills herself) to facilitate Heini's transition to the *Hitlerjungen* family. Once Heini is part of this attractive new group, he gains

---

[42] See Hans Peter Bluel, *Sex and Society in Nazi Germany*, trans. J. Maxwell Brownjohn (Philadelphia: Lippincott, 1973), 218 and Plant, 101.

[43] Susan Sontag, "Fascinating Fascism," 322, 321.

the strength to engage in the exhausting us-versus-them mentality necessary for a National Socialist victory over the decadent forces that would otherwise lead Germany to chaos—represented as the drinking, sex, and rowdiness of the rival Communist youth group. In all, *Hitlerjunge Quex* reads like a literal enactment of Mosse's theory of the cult of the masculine at the heart of radical nationalism. The "homosexuality" here operates as a fantasy that is oddly puritanical, a wish for a world without female sexuality but also without any physical desire that cannot be transcended into an ideal male bonding that works for a higher cause.

The relevance of all this is that Nazi sexual politics, the obsession with both difference and sameness, is not an imaginative creation of postwar cinema (and camp parody) but, along with economic and sociological differences, was a powerful dynamic in situating individuals within ideology. The development and history of the Third Reich has been of special interest to feminist historians precisely because this era powerfully illustrates how gender relations intersect with racist politics. The connection of racism and sexism is not new to feminist theory, but the further connection to German fascism is recent— and threatening to certain concepts of history. The habits of thinking that posit absolute boundaries between sexes and races also posit boundaries between fascism and nonfascism. It has taken forty years for some historians to break past this habit and to begin to ask questions not about how different the Nazi is, but how similar, and to seek out the repressed histories (of women Nazis or persecuted homosexuals) that oppose the cultural stereotypes.[44]

Perhaps the most profound recent challenge to traditional histories of Nazism comes from the German historian Klaus Theweleit in his two-volume study, *Männerphantasien* (*Male Fantasies*), which takes a controversial stand against defensive theories that insist that fascism is really "about something else"—homosexuality, irrationality, class struggle, authoritarianism. Theweleit examines fascist language as a way to "see" the workings of Nazism, and he insists that readers first "experience" the language rather than instantly assume that it is symbolic, or fantasy. The bottom line, he argues, is that German fascism produced men capable not just of murder but of methodical massacre as well, so he examines the diaries, letters, novels, and battle de-

---

[44] See, for example, Alice Yaeger Kaplan's review of postwar theories of fascism in *The Reproduction of Banality: Fascism, Literature, and French Intellectual Life* (Minneapolis: University of Minnesota Press, 1986), 3–35, as well as Russell Berman's introduction, xi–xxiii. See also Sidra deKoven Ezrahi, *By Words Alone: The Holocaust in Literature* (Chicago: University of Chicago Press, 1980) on how the very language and concept of "the Holocaust" can work as containment and evasion, 2.

scriptions of what he calls "soldier-males," beginning with the German Freikorps, the troubleshooting World War One veterans who remained professional killers and became the vanguard of National Socialism. He begins with a study of language used by this group, asking the startling question, "Is there a true *boundary* separating 'fascists' from 'nonfascist' men?"[45] His point of departure is a basic and otherwise overlooked element of the everyday reality of these men—the language they use to describe their relationships with women, or what Theweleit calls the "relations of production" that result in certain male-female relationships.

The value of Theweleit's approach—his refusal to categorize these men by drawing borderlines—can best be seen in a comparison to Mosse's treatment of the Freikorps in *Nationalism and Sexuality*. Mosse, too, acknowledges the importance of this group as a clue to the masculinism of National Socialism, noting that for this group of men, "all those excluded from their masculine band were mere objects; this included women, Jews, and the Slavic peoples."[46] This is part of Mosse's explanation for why Jews were later bracketed with homosexuals as threats to the Reich. Yet Mosse never acknowledges that the "fascist" attitudes toward women that he documents as part of racism—the assumption that women lack "moral sense" or inevitably cause disorder and degeneracy—are not just "sexual attitudes" but *sexist* attitudes not unique to Germany, nationalism, or fascism, and that he is talking specifically about a relation between misogyny and anti-Semitism.

Theweleit, on the other hand, in tracking down female stereotypes (and absences) in the Freikorps texts, relentlessly pursues their coordinates throughout Western culture—in contemporary political advertisements, Renaissance art, ads in the *New York Times*, and Hollywood film posters. Theweleit's point is not that every misogynist is a fascist, but rather that the representations of women that are directly connected to violence and death in the fascist texts are not a special category of images but part of a spectrum that is considered mainstream and acceptable.

The Freikorps' female stereotypes are so obviously connected to a defensive/aggressive killer-soldier's point of view that they may seem at first too obvious as "Nazi" caricatures. But from the perspective of film studies, they are remarkably parallel to the representations of women that Michael Renov finds in wartime cinema in Hollywood—

[45] Klaus Theweleit, *Male Fantasies*, vol. 1, *Women, Floods, Bodies, Histories*, trans. Stephen Conway (Minneapolis: University of Minnesota Press, 1987), 27.
[46] George Mosse, *Nationalism and Sexuality*, 125.

the "neutralizations" of female eroticism or desire through marriage, death, or the congealing of individual women into groups. Renov's point is that wartime sociological shifts resulted in male sexual anxieties that were experienced more acutely than class conflict or other kinds of differences during the war years; the disavowals of female eroticism that Mulvey finds in mainstream film took on specific, historical applications.[47] Theweleit, on the other hand, claims that fascist prose of the 1920s and 1930s reveals the same priority of concern, that "one of the primary traits of fascists is assigning greater importance to the battle of the sexes than to the class struggle, even in their *conscious* thinking. They view the class struggle as an irrelevant issue, one that can easily be taken care of by the establishment of the folk-community."[48] For Theweleit, the sexual anxiety concerning women is not an accidental trait but a central fascist issue concerning boundary and self-versus-other.

Although Theweleit's suggestions and theoretical foundations are often problematic,[49] his extensive documentation of the soldier-males' texts is invaluable. These texts repeatedly illustrate blatant aversions to female sexuality, or extinctions of sexual women, or fears of being lost or "dissolved" in sexual union. The male response is to "freeze up, become icicles in the fact of erotic femininity" so that "the man holds himself together as an entity, a body with fixed boundaries." Theweleit insists that the obsessive fear and response is not even unconscious, not analyzable as castration anxiety because it is not even symbolic. Erotic woman is "that unfamiliar, nameless flesh, that living territory of *becoming*."[50] In further readings, Theweleit shows that the aversion is not only to female sexuality but also to any "waves" or "surges" of fluidity, passion, or loss of control that contradict the idea of the bounded, autonomous self. Thus Theweleit explains the aesthetics of Nazism, the channeling of fluidity into choreography, the freezing of fluidity into a "monumental world" of "massive exteriors and solid forms," submission to designs that put everyone into constrained positions: "The monumentalism of fascism would seem to be a safety mechanism against the bewildering multiplicity of the living. The more lifeless, regimented, and monumental

[47] Michael Renov, "From Fetish to Subject: The Containment of Sexual Difference in Hollywood's Wartime Cinema," *Wide Angle* 5 (1982): 16–27.

[48] Klaus Theweleit, *Male Fantasies*, vol. 1, 169.

[49] See, for example, Chris Turner and Erica Carter, "Political Somatics: Notes on Klaus Theweleit's *Male Fantasies*," in *Formations of Fantasy*, ed. Victor Burgin et al (New York: Methuen, 1986), 201–13. See also Tania Modleski, "A Father is Being Beaten: Male Feminism and Feminist Theory," *Discourse* 10.2 (1988): 62–73.

[50] Klaus Theweleit, *Male Fantasies*, vol. 1, 244, 125.

reality appears to be, the more secure the men feel. The danger is being-alive itself."[51] (Surely this gives us an insight into the Nazi slang about the Weimar Republic as the "period" of the system with its revolting "excrescences.")

In examining the sexual and racial politics of the Third Reich, postwar histories and theories of Nazism, and the Sally Bowles texts, this is the intersection I find, or the recurring operation and "production of reality," as Theweleit would say: a concern for boundary and delineation, an aversion to fluidity and to the "blur of categories" celebrated by camp. It is the nervous positing of a unified, male subjectivity that "holds himself together as an entity, a body with fixed boundaries," to use Theweleit's description, in various disavowals of likeness. In locating the Sally Bowles character as a cultural construction—that is, as a locus of historical, literary, theatrical, and cinematic codes—I am particularly interested in the drawing of these borderlines, the construction of fascism as an absolute Other through language and structures that distance us from it. The distancing devices in these texts, however, work to confirm the very lineages they seek to deny; in constructing the borderline as a sexual one, the border of female eroticism or effeminacy (or conversely, the reified, super-masculine-but-secretly-female SS),[52] they reproduce the sexual polarizations of Nazism and illustrate that Nazi sexual politics—far from being an aberration or a contained, historical fluke—is an extension of sexual politics so familiar to us in the twentieth century that they appear seamlessly in forms such as classic Hollywood cinema. Susan Sontag readily admits the shared ground of fascist aesthetics and such nonfascist productions as the 1930s musical. But in connecting the sexual politics of theater and film with the sexual politics of the Third Reich, my own argument here pushes to connect the two sides of Sontag's essay, interrogating the possibility that sexual theatrics that use the Nazi scenario are likewise more similar to rather than absolutely distinct from mainstream sexual power relations.

By analyzing the constructions of the Sally Bowles figure in relation to changing cultural perceptions of German fascism, I aim to read

[51] Ibid., 218.

[52] In *Male Fantasies*, vol. 2, trans. Erica Carter and Chris Turner (Minneapolis: University of Minnesota Press, 1989), Theweleit points to a male bonding of his "soldier-males" which may or may not extend to physical acts of intercourse, but which he claims remains oddly asexual, precisely because it seeks to maintain the absolute boundaries of the self, including a reluctance to succumb to pleasure. As opposed to popular stereotyping of Nazism and homosexuality, Theweleit distinguishes between homosexuality as a pleasurable sexuality and, conversely, as a certain kind of institution within some military (and academic) settings (323–25).

these texts and contexts symptomatically, examining the cultural codes and anxieties, as well as the specific textual codes and conventions, that seek to make that understanding in each era. Though the nationality, lovers, and adventures of the Sally Bowles character may vary in the texts, the common denominator in each version is Sally as body, as icon, as physical presence, set in contention against language and intellect. This "habit of thinking," which I have suggested here closely parallels that of German fascism, lends itself to a particular kind of narrative as well—one that flirts with and denies homoeroticism, one that valorizes female reproductive power while simultaneously repressing female eroticism. This is the trajectory of *Hitlerjunge Quex*, but also of all the Sally Bowles texts. "Doesn't my body drive you wild with desire?" Sally asks in the Fosse film. An examination of Sally's various constructions reveals that she is in fact the locus of multiple and contradictory desires positioned in both historical and psychological anxieties.

Chapter Two

"GOOD HETER STUFF"

ISHERWOOD, SALLY BOWLES, AND THE VISION OF CAMP

THE OBLIGATORY STARTING point of any critical discussion of Christopher Isherwood, for many readers, is his most famous sentence: "I am a camera . . ." which is the opening of the second paragraph of *Goodbye to Berlin*. In an examination of Isherwood's most famous—and most iconographic—character, Sally Bowles, it seems likewise obligatory to begin with a photograph, an image that has become ubiquitous in biographies of Isherwood and in other texts concerning young English writers in Weimar. This is Stephen Spender's 1931 full-length photo of Jean Ross, Isherwood's acquaintance in Berlin and the model for his character Sally Bowles. In beret and bell-bottom trousers, obviously posed for the camera, Ross stands with legs straddled, hands in pockets, and offers a wry smile. Even though Spender's 1985 *Journals 1939–1983* do not otherwise discuss Ross, the photo is included with the illustrations for this text; and though the photo is identified in other biographies and memoirs as "Jean Ross ('Sally Bowles')," here the identification reads "Sally Bowles (Jean Ross)," both an allusion to the popular status of Sally as cultural artifact by 1985 and an odd validation of the fictional character as historically "real"—more real than the parenthetical Jean Ross.[1]

On the other side of the page is a photo of an early Nazi street meeting, in which men and women in civilian clothing extend their arms in salute. Considering our cultural coding of the documentary camera as "proof" or validation for verbal or written text, the fictional character Sally Bowles operates in the same status as the civilian Nazis here, "proof" of a certain era and Spender's witnessing of that era. To some extent, this photo in Spender's published journal encapsulizes the problematics surrounding this Isherwood character as she appears in all her subsequent texts: the female subject of the

---

[1] In addition to its inclusion in Spender's *Journals 1939–1983* (New York: Random House, 1985), the photo appears in the two major authorized Isherwood biographies, Jonathan Fryer's *Isherwood:A Biography of Christopher Isherwood* (New York: Doubleday, 1978) and Brian Finney's *Christopher Isherwood: A Critical Biography* (New York: Oxford University Press, 1979). It also appears in Spender's article "On Being a Ghost in Isherwood's Berlin," *Mademoiselle* (Sept. 1974): 138–39ff.

5. Jean Ross (circa 1931), photographed by Stephen Spender.

"objective" camera, the juxtaposition of female spectacle and Nazi street spectacle, the female body as historical text. To use John Berger's thesis, Jean Ross seems positioned for the camera as if conscious of her status as being-looked-at, the object of the gaze. However, the photo also suggests a dynamic between subject and photographer that is more complicated, or at least not without resistance. Unlike the Nazis in the opposite picture, Jean Ross is posed deliberately and even theatrically; her body position and costuming (the trousers, the straddle, the hands in pockets) imply a self-conscious bohemianism and opposition to conventional codes of femininity. It would not be difficult to read the image as a self-conscious posing as "a character."

As this reading of the photo implies, the camera is no innocent or objective recorder, and a narrator who sets himself up as a "camera" is not necessarily passive, trustworthy, or detached—the very qualities Isherwood's critics have traditionally attributed to the narrator of *Goodbye to Berlin*, based on the famous self-description: "I am a camera with its shutter open, quite passive, recording, not thinking. . . . Some day, all this will have to be developed, carefully printed, fixed."[2] In terms of the major narrative developments, the Christopher narrator is in fact mostly outside the action; yet the self-positioning as "camera" is itself a mediation, a particular kind of intervention in the telling of the stories. Moreover, the positioning as outsider to the action defers to a specific historical constraint: the pressures on Isherwood, at the time of publication, to conceal publicly his own homosexuality. Biographer Brian Finney, summarizing many critical speculations in regard to the narrator, concludes that the narrative device is simply Isherwood's aesthetic mistake, necessitated by this need to conceal his homosexuality, resulting in continual misreadings. "The more Isherwood represses him," he claims, "the more out of his control the narrator becomes."[3]

[2] Christopher Isherwood, *Goodbye to Berlin*, in *Berlin Stories: The Last of Mr. Norris and Goodbye to Berlin* (New York: New Directions, 1954), 1. For Colin Wilson, this opening is a marker of Isherwood's cameralike "honesty." See "An Integrity Born of Hope: Notes on Christopher Isherwood," *Twentieth Century Literature* 22 (1976): 316. G. S. Fraser, in *The Modern Writer and His World* (New York: Penguin, 1964) goes so far as to identify Isherwood's technique as related to British documentary film of the period—that is, the objective eyewitness account (133, 137–39). David P. Thomas, on the other hand, points out that the analysis of technique as actually cameralike is misleading on several counts since the most celebrated "cameralike" passages of description actually make narrative moves and generalizations impossible for any kind of camera; he suggests instead that the camera reference reveals "a defensive mask . . . attempting to protect a vulnerable personality against the terrors of isolation." See "*Goodbye to Berlin*: Refocusing Isherwood's Camera," *Contemporary Literature* 13 (1972): 43–52.

[3] Brian Finney, *Christopher Isherwood*, 145.

The problem with such a model of reading is that it posits some center of intentionality in the text that is absolute and that guides the reading in a single direction (and that can make a mistake upsetting the intended effect, so that the strategy goes "out of control"). Likewise the assumption that the narrator is literally cameralike tends to attribute absolute qualities to cameras (objectivity, passivity, honesty) without accounting for the various ideological codings and uses that mediated film and photography in the 1930s.[4] Jean Ross's hairstyle, clothing, and bodily pose are clearly aligned to the masculinized images of the New Woman that appeared in a variety of Weimar media. Although Ross seems to take on this pose self-consciously for the photographer, Isherwood's inscription of Sally Bowles as part of a wider modern political danger, urban and unmaternal, works as part of the continuum that operated in a number of Weimar discourses and representations locating Berlin in relation to dangerous, nontraditional female sexuality.

Reading both Isherwood's metaphor and Spender's photograph in tandem, I am suggesting that Isherwood and the most famous object of his "camera," Sally Bowles, need to be located within this network of material conditions and representations. This is true because the "I am a camera" line points to a specific kind of perception made possible in the first decades of the twentieth century. Walter Benjamin points out the "shock" effect of inventions that enable a complex process to take place through one abrupt hand movement. Of all these inventions, he says, "the 'snapping' of the photographer has had the greatest consequences. A touch of the finger now sufficed to fix an event for an unlimited period of time. The camera gave the moment a posthumous shock, as it were."[5] Isherwood's paragraph, with its powerful suggestion of the shot—the instant recording and the process of development leading to something "fixed"—has probably had such great impact because it directly addresses this twentieth-century sensibility described by Benjamin as more alert, more able to "cushion" the trauma of the continuous, multiple shocks of modernity—but also as more fragmented or reductive, the sensibility of the crowd or the workers who "could express themselves only au-

[4] Patrice Petro's detailed account of photojournalism in the Weimar Republic in *Joyless Streets*, for example, calls attention to the relationship between photography in popular print media and images in the film industry during that era, and further describes the ideological codings within these images that directly address crises of gender identity, in particular with the use of the androgynous New Woman and her relationship to modernity (84–139).

[5] Walter Benjamin, "On Some Motifs in Baudelaire," in *Illuminations*, 174–75.

tomatically."[6] Considering the political context of Isherwood's Berlin tales, the camera metaphor appeals to the detached or helpless spectatorship of international events made possible by the news camera. In the 1930s, the newsreel had already been established as an important public medium that had recorded, for example, the 1934 double assassination of King Alexander of Yugoslavia and French Foreign Minister Jean Louis Barthou in Marseilles. For postwar readers of Isherwood who had no doubt seen newsreel footage of marching Nazis in the 1930s or later television news coverage of other wars, the famous camera self-description is particularly resonant in regard to the multiple "shocks" of modern history for the subject who feels positioned like the helpless, passive spectator—or, as I will argue later, who can find a safe defensiveness in this position: I saw it happening, but could do nothing.

If the camera metaphor is a clue to Isherwood's awareness of the impact of the camera on modes of perception, rather than a literal clue about style or character, then it is fruitless to track down Isherwood's "shots" as either photos or footage. However, in tracking down the construction of the Sally Bowles character as a product of this particular twentieth-century sensibility, there are multiple biographical clues that Isherwood as a writer was under the specific influence of the cinema. Throughout his lifetime he was involved as self-described "film fan" and later as writer of screenplays for mainstream films. By the time he completed the short story "Sally Bowles" in 1936, he had already worked on his first motion picture, a melodrama with Berthold Viertel, and was about to write an autobiography of his Cambridge years that discusses his love of cinema and its impact on his writing. Although Isherwood's literary crowd is often identified historically as the generation between the wars, or the generation whose fathers died in the trenches in France, critics have only recently begun to identify this group of writers as the one that witnessed the development of the century's most popular cultural medium—the motion picture and, in particular, the Hollywood movie.[7]

Looking specifically at the construction of the Sally Bowles character in this context, I aim to read from the outside in, so to speak, in order to track down the emergence of this character in the vortex of

[6] Ibid., 176.

[7] Bernard Bergonzi's *Reading the Thirties: Texts and Contexts* (Pittsburgh: University of Pittsburgh Press, 1978), for example, points out the impact of Greta Garbo as commodity and icon for this generation of writers who were the first to grow up with cinema, and whose poetry and prose commented extensively on such cultural phenomena as the palatial cinema house and revolutionary perceptions as the close-up, the ability to see the icon/star as the giant face on the screen (124–33).

several contending conditions. First, of great importance is Isherwood's intention to produce a popular, mainstream text about a heterosexual character, complicated by his simultaneous self-identification as not just gay, but as ideologically opposed to heterosexuality as well. Directly at issue here is the position of the historical Jean Ross amidst a closely knit group of gay intellectuals who would invent their own legend about their days in wild, Weimar Berlin. This contention is parallel to Isherwood's similar position in relation to film, the medium that he claimed had the most impact on his writing—that is, his position as marginal/gay in relation to an apparatus that is—at least institutionally—overwhelmingly mainstream/heterosexual. The relationship between these contentions, I will argue, is the special vision or codings of camp, a particular means of access to popular culture from a gay point of view, a stylization that both satirizes the construction of female sexuality in the character of Sally Bowles, and at the same time problematizes the status of this character by retaining the ideological dynamics of female spectacle in popular cultural representations.

In the long run, the problem that emerges is the contradictory position of female sexuality within camp discourse and iconography, an ambivalence between sympathy and hostility that haunts camp humor and that is vividly illustrated in the construction of the figure of Sally Bowles. For a feminist analysis of Isherwood, the complications are immediately evident. As a critic of traditional gender role-playing, Isherwood hardly represents the villainous male mainstream literature that certain kinds of feminist critique could attack. As I will point out later, the campiness of the Sally Bowles story is very much a coded response to a homophobic culture and publishing industry that repressed gay identification. Within this context of compulsory heterosexuality, the story "Sally Bowles" brilliantly satirizes the sexual economics in which female "sexiness" operates as a strategy with specific market value, and which further suggests, as an artificial construction, the artifice of other culturally defined sexual roles. The comedy of camp itself disarms feminist critique with its playful breaking down of gender boundaries and exposure of cultural rules and constructions concerning sexual behavior. But whereas masculinity is also parodied in camp humor in other ways, the comic satirizing of gender in camp is frequently the representation of specifically *female* sexuality as grotesque or monstrous—the overwhelming mother, the garish whore, the carnivalesque hag: female stereotypes that circulate within other cultural texts with specifically misogynist overtones. The Sally Bowles story as a joke may target mainstream cultural constructions of gender, but if the comedy resides in the "joke" of female sexuality, the question for feminist query is to what extent this repositions woman as object, not subject, of the humor—especially in a discourse that has historically appealed to gay men more than to lesbians.

The beginning of these contentions is certainly the presence and "story" of Jean Ross in the context of Isherwood and his friends in what would become their legendary Berlin days. It was a legend they would build deliberately for themselves, though its most popular version is enacted in Isherwood's two Berlin novels, *The Last of Mr. Norris* (1935) and *Goodbye to Berlin* (1939), frequently referred to together as *The Berlin Stories* since their joint publication under that title by New Directions in 1954. In *Goodbye to Berlin*, the story "Sally Bowles" is positioned among much more serious texts: the grim framing sketches, "A Berlin Diary (Autumn 1930)" and "A Berlin Diary (Winter 1932–3)"; the unhappy homosexual affair described in "On Reugen Island"; the working-class sketch "The Nowaks," which ends with the overwhelmingly gloomy sanitorium scene; and "The Landauers," which recounts the narrator's friendship with the charming Jewish department-store owner who refuses to acknowledge the imminent danger of the Nazis. Within this dark context, the comedy and theatricality of Sally and her adventures take on an uneasy edge. Likewise, the serious abortion sequence of "Sally Bowles" is oddly positioned between the two major jokes that make up the narrative: the jilting of Sally and Chris by the wealthy, drunken American Clive and the tricking of Sally by the fake movie agent/con man.

As is true of most of the other narratives in this book, these events are freely based on Isherwood's experience in Berlin, in this case his interactions with Jean Ross. Both Isherwood and Spender have since come forth with supporting details. Spender has clarified that it was he, not Isherwood, who set up Ross with the con man, and he notes how "impressed" he was with the fact that Ross had had an abortion.[8] Isherwood recalls of Ross that "like Sally, she boasted continually about her lovers" to the point that he thought she was exaggerating. "Now I am not so certain," he adds.[9] But Ross herself in later years contradicted these accounts except to confirm that, like Isherwood and his friends, she was in Berlin as a young rebel: " 'Chris's story was quite, quite different from what really happened. But we were all utterly against the bourgeois standards of our parents' generation.

[8] "On Being a Ghost in Isherwood's Berlin," 138–39.
[9] *Christopher and His Kind, 1929–1939* (New York: Farrar, Straus & Giroux, 1976), 61.

That's what took us to Berlin. The climate was freer there, I suppose nowadays you'd call us hippies.' "[10]

Nevertheless, Spender's use and identification of Jean Ross's photo in his *Journals* reveal that the prevalent account of Ross in Berlin would not acknowledge that her story was "quite, quite different" from Isherwood's fiction. Ross's objection to the fictionalized version is made clear in a 1986 essay by her daughter, Sarah Caudwell. Protesting that her mother's actual accomplishments have been overshadowed by "progressively cruder" portrayals of Sally Bowles, Caudwell tells a story with disturbing resonances. First, she emphasizes that although her mother later became a journalist, journalists themselves did not want to listen to Ross's story of her earlier Berlin years. Ross would complain that " 'they want to know about Berlin in the Thirties. But they don't want to know about the unemployment or the poverty or the Nazis marching through the streets—all they want to know is how many men I went to bed with.' "[11] That is, sexual politics displaces national politics; the sensational personal story overshadows the sensational public story. The "spectacle" of the Nazis marching in the streets is not as interesting as the legend of Sally Bowles, sexual spectacle of stage and screen.

Already a familiar story takes shape: a woman's silence and the acquisition of her story in a series of male texts. But the entanglements of history, stereotype, and popular culture are even more complicated than this summary implies. As Caudwell points out, Jean Ross was hardly a silenced woman. The daughter of a staunchly liberal, anti-Tory family, she was engaged in political activities for nearly all of her adult life, ranging from her antifascist writings in the 1930s to activism against nuclear weapons and the war in Vietnam. Ross may have spent eighteen months or so as a "hippie" in Berlin between 1932 and 1933, but during this time she became fluent enough in German so that, upon her return to England, she was able to work as a bilingual scenarist in the British film industry with German directors who had fled the Third Reich. She married Claud Cockburn in 1934, and together they worked as journalists and political activists against British and Spanish fascism. When the Spanish Civil War broke out, she was writing in Madrid for *The Daily Express*. After Cockburn left Madrid to fight on the Republican side, Ross filed stories under his name for *The Daily Worker* and continued her own reports for the *Express* as well. She later also wrote for *The Daily Worker*

---

[10] Iain Johnstone, "The Real Sally Bowles," *Folio* (Autumn 1975): 33–34.
[11] Sarah Caudwell, "Reply to Berlin," *The New Statesman* (3 Oct. 1986): 28.

as a film critic.[12] Yet the identity of Jean Ross has been nearly wholly occluded by the fictional characterizations. Sally Bowles, on the other hand, is deeply embedded in this century's imagination as vamp, camp, femme fatale, and iconographical statement about 1930s Berlin.

A major issue here is Isherwood's frankly autobiographical methodology, the conflation of truth/fiction and its subsequent romanticizations, especially by his own crowd—Spender, W. H. Auden, Edward Upward, John Lehmann—who, as Colin Wilson points out, did "what looks like deliberate legend-building to self-consciously set themselves up as the Next Generation (after Joyce, Huxley and Eliot)."[13] Thus Spender writes a chatty article for *Mademoiselle* in the wake of the popularity of Fosse's *Cabaret*, again using his 1930s photo of Jean Ross and claiming (with an odd use of verbs) that he "lived this girl becoming Sally Bowles upon Christopher's watchful smile." Though the story and character are "invented," he says, "it yet seems . . . that everything Sally says in the story is what I remember her actually saying (whether I was present or not)." All the people in Isherwood's Berlin boardinghouse, he proclaims, are now "the truth that is the fiction."[14]

Jean Ross is not the only person to be appropriated in this truth/fiction conflation by Isherwood and Isherwood's closest readers. That group of readers comprises a considerable cast of his characters, mostly his Cambridge school chums thinly disguised in his account of those days, *Lions and Shadows* (1938), who then recur in his other novels: Spender is Stephen Savage, Upward is Chalmers, Auden is Weston, Lehmann is simply John, just as Forster is E.M. They appear in his fiction from the 1930s (*All the Conspirators*) to the 1960s (*Down There on a Visit*), and for anyone unable to break the code, Isherwood supplies a who's-who throughout his 1972 autobiography, *Christopher and His Kind*. These writers were also one anothers' first readers and advisors when it came to their own poetry and prose; Spender reports how Isherwood was "the Critic in whom Auden had absolute trust. If Isherwood disliked a poem, Auden destroyed it without demur."[15] For Isherwood, it was Edward Upward who remained a lifelong trusted critic, the "final judge" of his prose; in turn, as Brian Finney points out, Auden's early poetry is indebted to myths and im-

[12] These biographical details come from Sarah Caudwell, letter to the author, 2 Jan. 1989.

[13] Colin Wilson, "An Integrity Born of Hope: Notes on Christopher Isherwood," 312–13.

[14] Stephen Spender, "On Being a Ghost in Isherwood's Berlin," 138.

[15] Stephen Spender, *World Within World* (New York: Harcourt Brace, 1951), 92.

ages of Upward "transmitted through Isherwood."[16] Spender wrote
to Lehmann that "whatever one of us does in writing or travelling or
taking jobs, it is a kind of exploration which may be taken up by the
other two or three."[17] Spender's autobiographical novel of the Berlin
years, *The Temple* (1988), reveals Auden and Isherwood as merciless
teacher-critics who considered all their work as collaborative, and
they are of course the main characters in this text.

The result of all this is a remarkably incestuous circle of writers-
readers-characters who shared not just common cultural codes (for
example, their class and university background) but private ones as
well. In *Lions and Shadows* Isherwood describes the elaborate private
fantasy world he and Upward had constructed at Cambridge in order
to make university life bearable—the imagining of a "metaphysical
University City" infused with "enemy agents" and the gradual discovery of an alternative "Other Town." Every street sign could be reread
as part of the fantasy, so that they "often conversed in surrealist
phrases."[18] This kind of private language was not limited to their university years. The American writer Paul Bowles remarks that when
he met Isherwood and Spender in Berlin, they were like "two members of a secret society constantly making references to esoteric data
not available to outsiders."[19] Isherwood reports that in those days, the
world was dualistically divided between their own allies versus "The
Others"—who could be, for example, the "mere merchants" who
might decline to publish one's books.[20] Through these elaborate, divisive codes, outsiders were either rejected or transformed into the
multiple fictions and allusions that this set of colleagues kept in circulation.

A good example, especially in relation to the Jean Ross/Sally
Bowles construction, is the enterprising Gerald Hamilton, Isherwood's model for the main character in his first Berlin novel, *The Last
of Mr. Norris.* Whereas the vices of the Sally Bowles character are
more subtly connected to Berlin politics, Mr. Norris's sexual decadence (his penchant for women with whips and boots) is clearly related to underhanded dealings and dishonest politics. Introducing
the young narrator, William Bradshaw, into a world that at first seems
merely eccentric and excessive, Mr. Norris is eventually revealed to
be trading government secrets and secrets of the local antifascist

[16] Brian Finney, *Christopher Isherwood*, 40.
[17] John Lehmann, *Christopher Isherwood: A Personal Memoir* (New York: Henry Holt, 1987), 8–9.
[18] *Lions and Shadows* (1947; New York: Pegasus, 1969), 67, 69.
[19] *Without Stopping* (New York: Peter Owen, 1972), 110.
[20] *Christopher and His Kind*, 80.

Communist party. Yet in spite of his villainy, Mr. Norris is also a comic character whose wig, pornography, and debauchery are a source of constant fascination for the relatively innocent narrator. Apparantly, Norris's adventures are closely tied to the business affairs of the real-life Gerald Hamilton, though Norris's sexual naughtiness is put into heterosexual terms for the 1934 fiction. Hamilton himself, though somewhat older than Isherwood's crowd and an outsider to the literary business except for a venture in pornography, became involved with them despite their suspicions about his more "sinister" dealings in politics.[21] Hamilton's reply to Isherwood's fictionalization is his own 1956 autobiography, good-naturedly entitled *Mr. Norris and I*, a breezy, gossipy retelling of his "true" story which slips seamlessly into Isherwood's. Ironically self-mocking and melodramatic, the discourse Hamilton uses to describe his Berlin days is strikingly "in character" with Mr. Norris. Further effacing the distinction between himself and the fiction, he even appropriates "the original of 'Sally Bowles' " in a brief anecdote illustrating the shocking behavior that characterized "Bohemian" Berlin: "She asked me to come in the next morning for a talk, but arriving punctually at the time I was invited, I was told she was not yet up. However, hearing I was there, she called out gaily, 'It's all right, come and talk to me while I have my bath, darling.' I knew I was in Berlin's Bohemia at last."[22] Hamilton's willingness to "play" his character no doubt encouraged the collaborative imagining/remembering of Berlin. Colin Wilson reports a 1956 meeting with Isherwood and Spender in which the three of them "immediately plunged into a discussion about Gerald Hamilton" with an anecdote confirming that "Mr. Norris had not changed in twenty-five years."[23]

Considering Isherwood's own autobiographical commentaries on his writing, in his 1970s texts and in multiple interviews, it is not surprising that one result is the peculiar kind of discourse noted above in Spender and Wilson, in which fictional character and real-life reference are conflated rather romantically. Another result is that critical work on Isherwood has tended to be biographical, investigating the elusive first-person Christophers in his texts and his appropriations of history and people into his various mythologies. The effect dovetails neatly with traditional literary criticism's assumption that characters are in fact whole persons rather than rhetorical strategies or effects of discourse and culture. Thus the Sally Bowles figure has

[21] See Brian Finney, *Christopher Isherwood*, 85–86.
[22] Gerald Hamilton, *Mr. Norris and I* (London: Allan Wingate, 1956), 128–29.
[23] Colin Wilson, "An Integrity Born of Hope: Notes on Christopher Isherwood," 313.

been noted as Isherwood's most "normal" or "identifiable" female character, in light of Isherwood's more obvious interest in male characters.[24] However, my own point of departure in this analysis is both a resistance to the conflation of the historical Jean Ross with the character—resistance to the analysis of "Sally Bowles" as "person"—and, at the same time, an insistence on the impact of Ross as one of the conditions in the construction of what has become a powerful and long-sustained cultural artifact.

Given the circumstances in which Isherwood and his friends had banded together to become the Next Generation in literature, the positioning of Sally Bowles involves political and psychological issues far more complicated than identifiability—although the terms of the "normal" are very much at stake. On the one hand, the British writers of the 1930s emerged from powerful social and cultural norms. These include their childhood experience of World War One and the losses of their fathers in that war; their experience in the public-school system—almost invariably Cambridge or Oxford; and their strong upper-class bonds.[25] On the other hand, the subgroup of Isherwood and his friends emerged in a particular contention with that culture. Isherwood explains in *Christopher and His Kind* that he and Auden were in Germany from 1929 to 1933 not in idealistic self-exile from their stuffy upper-class British world but because, in certain sections of Berlin, they could practice more openly the homosexuality that was illegal in their own country: "Berlin meant Boys."[26] Yet as sexual outsiders in England, they were, paradoxically, very much in a mainstream tradition; the recent cultural history of the "construction" of homosexuality in Great Britain repeatedly points out how public definitions and condemnations of homosexuality were formulated in the latter part of the nineteenth century at exactly the same time as single-sex public schools were rapidly expanding. At some of the leading schools, homosexuality was virtually institutionalized.[27] Thus generations of the most privileged British boys were quickly positioned in contradictory terms of cultural identity, as both mainstream and marginal, privileged and deviant. This is an important factor in understanding how Isherwood and his friends identified themselves as rebels against but also very much a part of mainstream

[24] Jonathan Fryer makes this argument in "Sexuality in Isherwood," *Twentieth-Century Literature* 22 (1976): 347.

[25] See Bernard Bergonzi, *Reading the Thirties: Texts and Contexts*, 10–37.

[26] *Christopher and His Kind*, 2.

[27] See Jeffrey Weeks, *Coming Out: Homosexual Politics in Britain from the Nineteenth Century to the Present* (New York: Quartet, 1977), 13–17, 34–35.

British literary and cultural life in spite of their self-exiles to Germany.

Late in his life, Isherwood read his early sexual orientation as a deliberate social, ideological defiance. As a young man, he says, he realized that heterosexuality would make life easy: "You wouldn't be out of step with nearly everybody else." But this realization made him both angry toward and conscious of a sexual politics of resistance. His early formulation of resistance (at least as he remembers it) is notable in that he pinpoints a definition of ideology that is remarkably Althusserian; but he then proposes that it can be subverted through his "nature," and he suggests that his "nature" may itself be a deliberate subversion of ideology:

> Girls are what the state and the church and the law and the press and the medical profession endorse, and command me to desire. My mother endorses them, too. She is silently brutishly willing me to get married and breed grandchildren for her. Her will is the will of Nearly Everybody, and in their will is my death. *My* will is to live according to my nature, and to find a place where I can be what I am . . . But I'll admit this—even if my nature were like theirs, I should still have to fight them, in one way or another. If boys didn't exist, I should have to invent them.[28]

This passage is also worth noting in that the positioning of self against "Nearly Everybody" was an important factor in the private codes of Isherwood's friends in the 1930s. In *Christopher and His Kind* Isherwood makes clear the primacy of his self-identity as gay—especially in a society not just homophobic but in which all private homosexual acts were officially criminal. While homosexuality was technically illegal in Germany, too, it was well known that the Berlin police seldom bothered to harass the famous boy bars. So the years in Berlin, Isherwood explains, literally gave him a language in which to speak the forbidden desires—because it was a foreign language. While he had "hinted and stammered in English" with sexual partners in London, he could "ask straight out in German for what he wanted. . . . he wasn't embarrassed to utter the foreign sex words, since they had no associations with his life in England."[29]

The subculture that Isherwood and his friends constructed for themselves was specifically homosexual. Isherwood points out the awkward moments that occurred at times with the only heterosexual member of his group, Edward Upward. Speaking of sexual matters, "Christopher was conscious that Edward trod carefully. When he

[28] *Christopher and His Kind*, 12.
[29] Ibid., 31.

spoke of 'buggers' and 'buggery' . . . he did so in exactly the right tone of voice."[30] On the other hand, it was specifically through his homosexuality that the older, nonuniversity-educated Gerald Hamilton could fit comfortably into this group. It was "the most enduring bond between Gerald and Christopher," Isherwood tells us. His description of the friendship is again marked by the positioning of self versus Nearly Everybody: "When it came to breaking the laws which had been made against the existence of their tribe, Christopher was happy to be Gerald's fellow criminal."[31] Hamilton's autobiography is laced with private references and insider jokes about his sexual orientation, especially about the fact that Isherwood transformed him into a heterosexual masochist in *The Last of Mr. Norris*, a perversion he could coyly deny. Referring to the fictional Norris's penchant for women with boots and whips, Hamilton admits that there are many similarities between himself and Norris, but "not, I hasten to say, in the sex life of that worthy."[32] The joke here is especially ironic; although Hamilton's real sexual activities were still illegal in England, there was no law against the heterosexual masochism at which he pretends to be shocked.

In contrast to Hamilton's good-natured cooperation with his fictionalization, Jean Ross's response was much more ambivalent and, according to her daughter, never a happy one: "She never liked *Goodbye to Berlin*, nor felt any sense of identity with the character of Sally Bowles."[33] Isherwood himself noted her possible disapproval: "After I wrote the Berlin stories in the thirties, I sent everyone who appeared in them a draft for their approval before they were published. Only Sally stalled. It was two months before she finally agreed, but she stuck to her word."[34] But John Lehmann, the editor at Hogarth working with the story, reports that much more than courtesy was involved in getting Ross's approval. Because of the abortion sequence, Ross's permission was sought in order to avoid a libel suit. Though he himself was "fascinated" by the abortion story, Lehmann was "nervous whether our printers—in the climate of those days—would pass it." When he warned Isherwood about this and encouraged him to drop the sequence, Isherwood's reply in a 1937 letter is telling: "It seems to me that Sally, without the abortion sequence, would just be a silly little capricious bitch. Besides, what would the whole thing lead up to? And down from? The whole idea of the study

[30] Ibid., 47–48.
[31] Ibid., 78.
[32] Gerald Hamilton, *Mr. Norris and I*, 133.
[33] Sarah Caudwell, "Reply to Berlin," 28.
[34] Iain Johnstone, "The Real Sally Bowles," 33.

is to show that even the greatest disasters leave a person like Sally essentially unchanged."[35]

The "climate of those days" to which Lehmann refers was one in which the abortion issue in Great Britain had become particularly sensitive. Though abortion had been illegal and punishable by life imprisonment (in theory, for both the mother and the doctor) since 1861, few cases had been brought to trial. But beginning in 1934, roughly a hundred inquests a year were carried out in cases in which women had died in illegal abortion procedures. At the time Isherwood was writing "Sally Bowles," the topic of abortion had become both public and controversial; a variety of pressures on the British Medical Association led it to produce a lengthy public report in 1936 considering legalization. This in turn led to the formation of a national coalition, the Abortion Law Reform Association, which intended to sort out legal problems, definitions, and justifications, although this work was contested and eventually defeated by increasingly antifeminist sentiment in the years before the war.[36]

Thus the stakes for Ross were quite different than for Gerald Hamilton in being identified with illegal activity concerning sexuality. While Hamilton's gay identity is repressed or rewritten in Isherwood, Ross's abortion becomes public text and justified as the "whole point" of her story. As Isherwood's biographer Jonathan Fryer points out, "Anyone who knew Jean Ross during the 1930s would have had very little trouble in recognising her as the basis for Sally Bowles." Though Ross eventually gave her permission, she had changed quite a bit in the meantime, unlike "Sally," having returned to London and gotten involved with serious left-wing politics, partially in response to growing fascist sentiment in Great Britain. "Several of Jean's friends were shocked by the book," reports Fryer, "and, unlike Gerald Hamilton, she avoided all possible publicity connected with it. She was a brave and kind woman, by now deeply committed to left-wing causes, and the book did not help her image much among those comrades who realized she was the model."[37]

These accounts of Hamilton/Norris and Ross/Bowles reveal a series of ironies and contradictions. While the Norris character is a political villain far more corrupt than the Bowles character, his real-life counterpart is capable of participating in the literary discourse that pro-

[35] This story and the quotation from Isherwood's letter are in John Lehmann, *Christopher Isherwood*, 28–29.

[36] See Barbara L. Brookes, *Abortion in England, 1919–1939: Legal Theory and Social Practice* (Ph.D. diss., Bryn Mawr, 1982); also Anthony Horden, *Legal Abortion: The English Experience* (Oxford: Pergamon, 1971).

[37] Jonathan Fryer, *Isherwood*, 164.

duced him and that built the Berlin legend, reproducing the same ironies and inside jokes. The result is another text, *Mr. Norris and I*, certainly not as privileged in the canon as *Goodbye to Berlin* but a fairly standard reference in criticisms and histories of Isherwood, especially in that Isherwood himself privileges the book with an introduction. On the other hand, the real-life counterpart of the Sally Bowles character (whose politics in *Goodbye to Berlin* range dubiously from apathy to anti-Semitism) becomes a real-life political activist against fascism, making the fictionalization an embarrassment to her cause. Aligned with a leftist group for whom Weimar Berlin signifies neither sexual liberation nor decadence, but rather political crisis, she declines from the legend building altogether. Caudwell, complaining of the lifelong identity of her mother with Sally, is especially upset by the casual anti-Semitism attributed to the Sally character—Sally's line about "an awful old Jew" who wants to sleep with her—pinpointing it as part of a literary convention of the empty-headed, attractive young woman whose thoughtlessness in this case inadvertently links her to Nazism. Insisting that her mother was always as antiracist as antifascist, Caudwell says of Ross, "She may well, at 19, have been less informed about politics than Isherwood, five or six years older; but, when the Spanish war came and the fascists were bombing Madrid, it was she, not Isherwood, who was there to report it."[38]

In the long run, the homosexual nature of Isherwood's group became part of the legend, explicitly detailed in their later published letters, diaries, and autobiographies. The Sally Bowles character, on the other hand, would become an altogether different, iconographic presence in the production of these texts carrying on the legend, and Jean Ross's continued silence—her daughter claims she simply "never cared enough" to make "any public rebuttal"[39]—reinforces her status as outsider to this group. But she is a particular kind of outsider; the language used to describe her veers between hostility and awe. This is the sexually active woman whose abortion "impresses" and "fascinates" these writers; yet when Isherwood describes the character he is creating or transcribing, the abortion is the plot device that saves what is otherwise "a silly little capricious bitch."

The hostile edge to this latter description must certainly be put into the perspective of Isherwood's many later remarks about both Jean Ross and the character Sally Bowles, indicating his great affection for both. In *Christopher and His Kind* he describes the genuine friendship he enjoyed with Ross in their Berlin days, and in his 1954 introduc-

[38] "Reply to Berlin," 29.
[39] Ibid., 28.

tion to *The Berlin Stories*, he expresses his delight with the character Sally as played by Julie Harris and rewritten by John Van Druten: ". . . being a creature of art, she had been created out of pure love."[40] It seems to me that the contradiction between these warm recollections and the sharper tone of the remark to Lehmann is part of the wider problem of female sexuality in relation to gay male psychology, politics, and culture. The character Sally Bowles is a useful case illustrating what is at stake. This is true because one of literature's most raucously heterosexual characters was produced in the immediate milieu of a closely knit, homogeneous group of gay intellectuals who were bonded not just through the literature they were producing, but also through private loyalties to one another as the secret enemies of Nearly Everybody—the identification of themselves as both criminal and consciously opposed to the ideology of heterosexuality. The group's aims and commitments are somewhat parallel to what Eve Kosofsky Sedgwick has termed homosocial desire, a "social force" or "glue" that bonds a group of men for the sake of their own interests and to the exclusion of women. Although Sedgwick is more concerned with homosexual desire that is displaced in male bonding and not necessarily limited to gay men, her study makes clear that lack of interest in women—by heterosexual or homosexual men—often leads to conservative attitudes toward them in spite of other more progressive thinking among these groups.[41] In the case of Isherwood, this contradiction is most evident in the inscription of Sally Bowles within *Goodbye to Berlin*, as I will point out later, in which a radical critique of the status of women in heterosexual politics is coupled with deep suspicion of the sexually free New Woman who takes on male prerogatives.

The presence and status of Jean Ross within this group is unfortunately romanticized and obscured in their own memoirs, mainly because she has been so overwhelmingly identified as Isherwood's Sally and the Sally of the adaptations. Isherwood himself admits in his later memoirs that he can no longer clearly remember Ross because she has been recreated by so many later actresses, but he maintains that he and Ross were "truly intimate" as "brother and sister." There was no question of concealing his homosexuality from her; he recalls "a rainy, depressing afternoon when she remarked, 'What a pity we can't make love, there's nothing else to do,' and he agreed that it was and there wasn't."[42] In his 1951 recounting of the Berlin days, Ste-

[40] See *Christopher and His Kind*, 63, and "About This Book," in *The Berlin Stories*, vii.

[41] Eve Kosofsky Sedgwick, *Between Men: English Literature and Male Homosocial Desire* (New York: Columbia University Press, 1985).

[42] *Christopher and His Kind*, 63.

phen Spender barely mentions Ross except to give her a few walk-on descriptions as one of the "characters" who would appear sometimes in Isherwood's flat. But in his 1974 memoir, he admits that Jean Ross's language "repelled" him, being explicitly "physiological" in a way that could not be reproduced by Isherwood for publication in the 1930s.[43] If Edward Upward felt that he had to use "exactly the right tone of voice" to make sexual references in this homosexual world, then the presence of Jean Ross with her casual conversations about lovers would have indeed created a dissonant note in Isherwood's milieu.

In fictionalizing Jean Ross, however, Isherwood was contending with much more than censorship codes having to do with her language. Jonathan Fryer perhaps pinpoints the key terms in describing her as more "normal" or "identifiable" than Isherwood's previous female characters. What we can read here as normal/identifiable is the privileging of certain characteristics in literature. Sally is young, British, upper class, attractive; her world revolves around men, love affairs, and money. Such characters not only populated mainstream fiction, but had recurred in popular culture as the sexually free New Woman since the end of World War One. The character Sally Bowles is in fact such a major departure for Isherwood partially because she is recognizable from a variety of other character codes that he had previously refrained from using precisely because those codes are dependent upon heterosexual desire.

In a 1936 letter to John Lehmann while he was working on the story "Sally Bowles," Isherwood specifically names the literary precedent he has in mind: "It's rather like Anthony Hope: 'The Dolly Dialogues.' It is an attempt to satirize the romance-of-prostitution racket. Good heter stuff."[44] Isherwood's reference here, even if a joke, is a telling one—or at least a clue to the sort of "heter stuff" he was joking about. Popular British writer Anthony Hope was himself the author of a text that would remain a favorite through several adaptations, *The Prisoner of Zenda* (1894). Hope's *Dolly Dialogues* also had a long-playing cultural life; originally serialized in *The Westminster Gazette* in 1892 and throughout that decade, then printed as a volume in 1899, they were further popularized as readings during Hope's later speaking tours and broadcast on British radio in the 1920s. So Isherwood was naming as precedent a character instantly recognizable in popular culture, and he was naming his own project to appeal

[43] "On Being a Ghost in Isherwood's Berlin," 138.
[44] John Lehmann, *Christopher Isherwood*, 27.

to a mainstream audience and a desire foreign to himself: "good heter stuff."

The character Miss Dolly Foster—Lady Mickleham in the later dialogues—provides a rich prehistory of Sally Bowles if she is read as the focal point of several heterosexual codes of popular fiction with and against which Isherwood was writing. The *Dialogues* are mostly just that; there is little or no description or action in the short scenes between Dolly and the first-person narrator, "Mr. Carter," a former boyfriend who—to use the discourse—alas, has lost her to another. With minimal physical description, little history or setting (except for suggestions of the upper class and a comfortable amount of money), Dolly consists of her conversational games and flirtations; through a certain kind of language, Hope is able to suggest a desirable, somewhat comic young woman who appealed to British audiences for over thirty years.

Dolly's world is populated by less interesting women (rivals or formidable dowagers) and men who are smitten by her. The problems that emerge in these sketches are never more serious than the question of whether to tell her husband about her former boyfriends, or the disapproval some society woman expresses about Dolly's flirtatiousness. Devoid of political or moral questions, dependent on entertaining, noncontroversial dialogue, *The Dolly Dialogues* read like an 1899 version of situation comedy. Hope's format, in fact, as a series of dialogues rather than more traditional narrative, is indicative of the coming shift in popular culture from literature to other media, the shift from pulp fiction to radio adventure shows. Dolly emerges as pop-culture heroine alongside other widely recognized popular fictional characters (Nick Carter, Sherlock Holmes, Tarzan) who were later adapted to radio or film.

Citing *The Dolly Dialogues*, Isherwood is pointing to the popular heroine who is not especially admirable, but is especially "charming"—that is, who is entirely constituted and justified by male desire. Though the conventions of Dolly's world, with its formalities, decorum, and rules of courtship, are often satirized, what is never satirized is Mr. Carter's wistful infatuation with Dolly that is the trajectory of every sketch. Dolly is good at sustaining interest in herself and getting men (particularly Mr. Carter) to admit they are fascinated by her:

"Why are you looking at me?" she asked.

"Because," said I, "there is nothing better to look at."

"Do you like doing it?" asked Dolly.

"It is a privilege," said I politely.

"Well, then!" said Dolly.

"But," I ventured to observe, "it's rather an expensive one."

"Then you mustn't have it very often."

"And it is shared by so many people."

"Then," said Dolly, smiling indulgently, "you must have it—a little oftener."[45]

This kind of coyness and flirtatiousness can be discerned in the Sally Bowles character in Isherwood's short story, but in Isherwood, the discourse is exaggerated and distanced by parody, and unlike Dolly, Sally rarely has the last line or laugh. In the opening sequence of "Sally Bowles," the narrator's friend Fritz hints that he is ready for a new romance because it has been two years since his last one. Sally responds according to the codes of flirtatiousness, pretending a polite interest in the last affair, but simultaneously drawing attention to herself in the hint that she could be the next one. Yet the response is so theatrical that the effect is more comic than flirtatious: " 'How marvellous!' Sally puckered up her nose and laughed a silvery little stage-laugh: '*Doo* tell me—what was the last one like?' "[46]

Similarly, in Dolly's breathless sentences given over to childlike enthusiasms, we can catch the nuances of a discourse (and a desire) Isherwood could find useful in constructing Sally Bowles—the assumption that the rather silly, self-preoccupied upper-class young woman is an attractive, desirable character. For example, Hope's sketch entitled "The Very Latest Thing" satirizes Dolly's new enthusiasm—the fashion of acquiring an autograph book in which friends write out opinions of the book's owner—but also justifies the attractiveness of Dolly's wish for such a self-serving item in that it provides an opportunity for intimacy and flirtation with Mr. Carter. The sketch begins:

"It's the very latest thing," said Lady Mickleham, standing by the table in the smoking-room, and holding an album in her hand.

"I wish it had been a little later still," said I, for I felt embarrassed.

"You promise, on your honour, to be absolutely sincere, you know, and then you write what you think of me. See what a lot of opinions I've got already," and she held up the thick album.

"It would be extremely interesting to read them, " I observed.

"Oh! but they're quite confidential," said Dolly. "That's part of the fun."

"I don't appreciate that part," said I.

"Perhaps you will when you've written yours," suggested Lady Mickleham.[47]

[45] Anthony Hope, *The Dolly Dialogues* (London: Victoria House, 1899), 56.

[46] *Goodbye to Berlin*, 23. All page numbers in the text refer to this earlier cited edition.

[47] Anthony Hope, *The Dolly Dialogues*, 73.

But as even this brief quotation indicates, Dolly's attractiveness is codified through a wariness, or paternalism, on the part of the narrator, his ability to react with archness or irony to her lines. The dynamic of these sketches is the interaction of Dolly's flirtatious baits—codified as childlike enthusiasm or naïveté—and Mr. Carter's wit, his ability to play with the language, to reveal and conceal his desire through the polite codes of the visitor-to-the-married-lady. In "The Very Latest Thing" this dynamic is enacted more literally, as the narrator agrees to play Dolly's album game and put her into words to her own self-satisfaction. The narrator's language is privileged as the creator of Dolly, the context in which Dolly's own language emerges as both comic and charming—or rather, amusing from the perspective of the more knowing narrator and capable of securing itself into the text's network of desire.

In Isherwood's short story, the dynamic between Sally Bowles and the narrator is likewise one that involves the contextualizing of her own language—which he cannot take seriously—into his own, one that is inscribed as more serious, superior, validated as "real." The scene in which he confronts her with her own language begins with Sally's failed attempt to impress him with her frankness about her "marvellous new lover." Getting no response, she asks, " 'Do I shock you when I talk like that, Christopher darling?' " The narrator replies with a long analysis, explaining that he is not shocked because he recognizes her language as "just nervousness" with strangers, and the subsequent " 'trick of trying to bounce them into approving or disapproving of you, violently.' " He admits that he uses this trick himself at times. However, his professorial analysis itself begins to flatter Sally because it again establishes her as the center of his attention—an attention that is, precisely, his authority to name her, in contrast to her less "objective" rendering of reality—and herself:

> ". . . If you go to bed with every single man in Berlin and come and tell me about it each time, you still won't convince me that you're *La Dame aux Camélias*—because, really and truly, you know, you aren't."
>
> "No . . . I suppose I'm not—" Sally's voice was carefully impersonal. She was beginning to enjoy this conversation. I had succeeded in flattering her in some new way: "Then what *am* I, exactly, Christopher darling?"
>
> "You're the daughter of Mr. and Mrs. Jackson-Bowles" (33).

The impending joke of this particular sequence is that in reply to Chris's serious, "objective" naming of her as someone's daughter, Sally immediately launches into a posed, theatrical account of her love affairs in relation to her work as an actress, using exactly the discourse Chris had just attempted to deflate:

"Of course," said Sally gravely, after a pause, "I'd never let love interfere with my work. Work comes before everything. . . . But I don't believe that a woman can be a great actress who hasn't had any love-affairs—" she broke off suddenly: "What are you laughing at, Chris?" (33–34).

While the Dolly sketches satirize silly affectations such as the opinion album, Isherwood's object of satire in "Sally Bowles" is certainly racier—the "romance-of-prostitution racket," the examination of the gold digger, who is more ambitious in the use of her charms than Lady Mickleham. Dolly surrounds herself with admirers who play courtly-love games with the desirable but unattainable woman. Her "worth" in society is the extent to which she is still valuable as a lure for these men and this kind of socializing. Sally Bowles's attractiveness is valuable on a much more tangible basis. It is the currency for meals and—she hopes—her entrance into show business. Yet the line between Dolly Mickleham and Sally Bowles is fairly straightforward; these are characters whose location in the dynamic of the trajectory is sexual interaction with men, from flirtation to fucking. Dolly's coy turn-of-the-century fishing for compliments is the acceptable language for what Sally Bowles will ask more directly in the 1972 film adaptation: "Doesn't my body drive you wild with desire?"

And that very question—the question of the female body as object of desire—is the problematic basis of Isherwood's "heter" project, the project of producing the subject and story of heterosexual desire from the context of a marginal, gay subgroup that had deliberately exiled itself from mainstream culture, in particular the heterosexual desire of Nearly Everybody. Isherwood's reference to Hope's popular character reinforces the fact that he and his friends had no intention of creating a marginalized, underground art. Lehmann recalls Spender's description of their group as a "heroic band who were out to create an entirely new literature."[48] That this "new literature" would be mainstream is evident in Isherwood's history of publication. The publisher of his first novel, All the Conspirators, was no obscure operation but the venerable Jonathan Cape; the publisher of his second was the prestigious Hogarth Press. When Isherwood remarks, in his 1972 autobiography, that some of the poses or dramatic moments in his early work were purely "playing to the gallery,"[49] he is pointing not to his small group of reader-friends, but to the mass readership composed of exactly the homophobic state/church/law/press/medical profession that comprised Nearly Everybody. The young writer who went to Berlin because he was hesitant to speak his homosexual de-

[48] John Lehmann, Christopher Isherwood, 8.
[49] Christopher and His Kind, 53.

sires in English was nevertheless part of the "heroic band" whose ambition was to become part of mainstream English literature. And they succeeded. Beyond their presence in the literary anthologies, they are acknowledged as "the" writers of the thirties, honored in 1976 by an exhibit at the National Portrait Gallery in London—which Isherwood criticized because "nowhere was it mentioned that so many of the leading figures of that literary generation had been homosexual or bisexual."[50]

The result of this contention between mainstream and marginal location of desires is the curious representation of female eroticism and heterosexuality found in the story "Sally Bowles." Unlike the sketches in *The Dolly Dialogues*, in which the trajectory or tension is dependent upon the mutual sexual attraction of narrator and character (Will they confess their desire? Will they act on it?), Isherwood's story relates the interaction of the desirable, accessible woman and the narrator who is wholly without desire for her, in spite of strong fictional codes requiring their attraction. This has been an especially troubling problem for the stage and screen adaptations. Isherwood himself described the dilemma in a 1975 interview, pointing out that "this has left all the succeeding playwrights and script writers with this problem: what *is* it about Chris? Why doesn't he do something about this very available, attractive girl?" In the same interview, Isherwood explains the strategy of the fictionalized relationship in terms of the limitations imposed on the writer of the 1930s, the impossibility of using a homosexual narrator because it would have introduced a subject more controversial and distracting than anything else in the book: "Now, if I had made the 'I' a homosexual, especially in *those* days, I would have made him overly-remarkable, and he'd have gotten in the way of the other characters." Isherwood confesses that he had to sacrifice some of the comedy that resulted from his actual relationship with "Sally"—"how, at one time I had no money, we actually shared our room and slept in the same bed, and, of course, the relations between my boy friends and her! It would have created comedy, certainly, but at what a cost. It would have become tiresome, because it's not what the book is *about*."[51]

My argument is that the repression of one kind of comedy here— and the repression of homosexuality, in fact—causes the book to be "about" another kind of comedy and satire of the heterosexual. Beyond being "a satire of the romance-of-prostitution racket," "Sally

[50] Jonathan Fryer, *Isherwood*, 287.
[51] Norma McLain Stoop, "Christopher Isherwood: A Meeting by Another River," *After Dark* 7 (1975): 62.

Bowles" satirizes and reveals the entire construction of female sexiness as performance, theater, elaborate "sham," to use Isherwood's word. A distinctive relationship between narrator and character is deployed to maintain this effect. Although the Dolly character in her flirtations is at times just as theatrical and posturing as Sally Bowles, "Mr. Carter" is willing to take on the proper role and engage in this sexual theater, though with some archness and irony, because he has a stake in it: his own desire. But in "Sally Bowles," that stake or interest is missing; Sally's exaggerations and posturings, her bids for attention and sexual interest, are played out to a narrator for whom it is only theater. Her language trips on its own attempts at drama or tension: " 'I feel all marvellous and ethereal,' " Sally gushes about her newest lover, " 'as if I was a kind of most wonderful saint, or something' " (39). In the economy of desire (the expectations of the reader, based on codes of fiction) and the great sexual energy suggested by the narrative (Sally's promiscuity), something has been displaced or gone awry. What should be sexy is only "sexy." What poses as passion—for example, Sally's description of a lover—cannot possibly be taken seriously: " 'He was so marvellously primitive: just like a faun. He made me feel like a most marvellous nymph, or something, miles away from anywhere, in the middle of the forest' " (39). The awkward qualification of her descriptions—"or something"— points at once to the borrowing of this discourse from other sources, and also her own inability to generate a more original or sincere way to speak of desire; but it is also a comic way to deflate the grandiose pronouncements.

The combination of humor, ironic distance, and satire of gender role at work in this discourse has been described and developed as camp. Considering that the later Sally Bowles film and stage vehicles, the two *Cabaret* texts, are gay cult favorites as camp artifacts, it is not unreasonable to trace elements of camp sensibility in Isherwood's original story. It has been pointed out that the Sally Bowles figure provides the campy comedy that works in contention with the growing political discourses in *Goodbye to Berlin*; eventually, these stories are no longer funny because of the outrageous political scene, in which the camp sensibility of exaggeration has been out-parodied by the far-from-amusing Nazis.[52] However, the camp comedy in relation to Nazism is greatly complicated by the peculiar sexual politics of this text, in which the cultural construction of female sexuality is at stake—the identification of a certain kind of "sexiness" as artifice, the-

[52] Peter Thomas makes this argument in " 'Camp' and Politics in Isherwood's Berlin Fiction," *Journal of Modern Literature* 5 (1976): 117–30.

atricality, role-playing. Unable to step out of character, so to speak, Sally is always "on"; the narrator describes her attempts to be serious as "a kind of theatrically chaste effect, like a nun in grand opera" (27). Likewise, her language is constantly onstage, puffed with flamboyant hyperbole—a conscious acting-out of "sexiness": " 'That's the man I slept with last night,' she announced. 'He makes love marvellously. He's an absolute genius at business and he's terribly rich—' " (23). And this very quality of sex-in-quotation-marks reveals not just its parodic nature, but also its affinity to similar posturings in other texts that approach heterosexuality ironically. The real question here is how this ironic distancing from the cultural "sexual woman" permits a conflation with the other necessary distancing in this text—from Nazism. This question, in turn, raises the difficult issue of the relationship of woman to the comedy, carnival, and grotesqueries of camp.

Camp playfulness can be discerned throughout even the earliest of Isherwood's work, in the ironic uses of the recurring Chris/Christoph/Isherwood/Issyvoo persona and in his self-conscious references to texts-within-texts. The titles of *Prater Violet* (1945), *Lions and Shadows* (1947), and *The World in the Evening* (1954), for example, are all actually titles of other fictional texts described in the works, as if the titles were in special quotation marks. The embedded texts are often jokes themselves: "Lions and Shadows" is a bad novel that never gets written, and "Prater Violet" is the corny movie musical on which "Isherwood" is working. Moreover, though most dictionaries of slang pinpoint the use of "camp" as homosexual slang since the 1930s, one of the earliest attempts at a formal definition of camp comes, significantly, from Isherwood himself, filtered through a gay character in his 1954 novel, *The World in the Evening*.

In this novel, the character Bob Wood differentiates between camping in "queer circles," or "Low Camp"—drag versions of Marlene Dietrich—and to "High Camp," which "always has an underlying seriousness. . . . You're expressing what's basically serious to you in terms of fun and artifice and elegance. Baroque art is largely camp about religion."[53] Although this distinction apparently separates "High Camp" from a homosexual orientation, the context of the conversation in this novel does not. "High Camp" is a way of seeing or understanding that needs to be "taught" by Bob Wood to the heterosexual main character, Stephen (whose heterosexuality is literally in quotation marks in this novel, evident only in the embedded texts of letters and flashback). Their discussion of cultural high camp sug-

[53] *The World in the Evening* (London: Methuen, 1954), 125.

gests not so much inherent styles or traits of artists as a way of understanding or approaching their art. From this point of view, Mozart is camp, but Beethoven is not; Flaubert and Rembrandt are not, but El Greco and Dostoevsky are camp. As Bob Wood explains, " 'You have to meditate on it and feel it intuitively.' "[54] The interesting question is to what extent this intuition is related to a gay sensibility, and this is the question that has informed debates about camp ever since.

Susan Sontag, in what has become the most well-known definition of camp, uses the concept of a special reading or interpretation by suggesting that "Camp sees everything in quotation marks. It's not a lamp, but a 'lamp'; not a woman, but a 'woman.' To perceive Camp in objects and persons is to understand Being-as-Playing-a-Role."[55] Sontag's 1964 essay sketches out an affinity between camp and homosexuality based on aestheticism, a neutral point of entry into culture, but she argues that this relationship is not exclusive or intrinsic. Thus she lists a number of artifacts (Tiffany lamps, *Swan Lake*, and *The Enquirer*) and characteristics (artifice, self-conscious style) that are not necessarily aligned with gay identity but that point to camp as a more general cultural vision. A more recent study, Mark Booth's book *Camp*, which aims not to explain so much as to define by multiple example, takes issue with both Isherwood and Sontag in pointing out that the origins of camp excess and theatricality can be traced to the court of Louis XIV in Versailles. Booth insists that the notion of camp as a gay invention of the 1930s is erroneous, and that in fact "camp people tend to be asexual rather than homosexual." Conceding that marginality is the common ground for camp and gay identity, Booth argues that although "many homosexuals are camp, only a small proportion of people who exhibit symptoms of camp behaviour are homosexual."[56]

Nevertheless, the term has been greatly politicized and continues to be appropriated as a specific factor of gay sensibility and culture. Its use in this relationship is particularly relevant for an understanding of Isherwood's approach to a popular, mainstream representation of heterosexuality—the construction of "good heter stuff." Sontag emphasizes camp as a challenge to fixed notions of boundary. For the resisting reader of culture, the most glaring example of things-being-what-they-are-not is the artificial construction of gender. This awareness of the artificial-construction-of-gender boundary is a constant play in camp humor, often evident in celebrations of excessive-

[54] Ibid., 126.

[55] "Notes on Camp," in *The Susan Sontag Reader* (New York: Farrar, Strauss & Giroux, 1982), 109.

[56] Mark Booth, *Camp* (London: Quartet, 1983), 20.

ness or hyperbole: Busby Berkeley's female bodies turned into geometry; Joan Crawford's masculinity/femininity and incredible shoulders.[57] So for the homosexual, whose self-definition is out of sync with the prevailing network of gender definitions, camp works as a subversive celebration of marginality, a style and humor that is intrinsically political.[58]

I would argue, too, that this playful opposition to dominant culture and deliberate violation of boundary is closely related to Mikhail Bakhtin's theories of comedy and parody, particularly with regard to his well-known discussions of the carnivalesque as subversive body and discourse. Like camp, the carnivalesque operates through reversals of hierarchy, the use of mask and grotesquery, and the breakdown of delineations between art and life. Bakhtin attributes the carnivalesque to a disruption of dominant structures of knowledge, a moment of cultural crisis partly due to a contention between two languages (Church Latin as opposed to the vernacular.)[59] Likewise, what is involved in camp is similarly a crisis in knowledge and knowability, but at a much more basic level, testing an entire sign system's positioning of gender. In a performance of Holly Woodlawn or in Joel Grey's emcee in *Cabaret*, the sign system of gender topples as the gap between signifier and signified comes under a kind of open, public acknowledgment. If the emergence of camp style at the turn of the century (with Oscar Wilde and other fin-de-siecle stylists) is one response to the creation and definition of "the homosexual" as described by Foucault, then we can understand camp historically positioned as a part of a crisis in knowability, and a serious crisis at that: the challenging of heterosexual ideology, the defiance of binary sexuality and order through the deliberate imposition of ambivalence, reversals, and laughter.

My point is that Isherwood, in constructing Sally Bowles for a heterosexual audience from which he is essentially self-isolated, uses the

[57] Al LaValley mentions these as examples of camp's "too-muchness" in "The Great Escape," *American Film* 10 (1985): 28–34.

[58] For further discussion of gay politics in relation to camp, see Jack Babuscio, "Camp and the Gay Sensibility," in *Gays and Film*, ed. Richard Dyer (New York: Zoetrope, 1984), 40–57. See also Andrew Ross's extended discussion of this topic in his chapter "Uses of Camp" in *No Respect: Intellectuals and Popular Culture* (New York: Routledge, 1989), 135–70.

[59] Mikhail Bakhtin, *Rabelais and His World*, trans. Helen Iswolsky (Cambridge, Mass., and London: MIT Press, 1968). Strictly speaking, Bakhtinian carnival can be applied to camp only to describe camp's most inclusive or participatory activities, because Bakhtin claims that carnival "does not acknowledge any distinction between actors and spectators" and "is not a spectacle seen by the people; they live in it, and everyone participates because its very idea embraces all the people" (7).

strategies of camp—humor, incongruous contrast, theatricality—as a way to satirize the artifices of the "sexy" woman—the woman who has learned to construct herself for this cultural definition and who thus puts herself into a specific market, "the romance-of-prostitution racket," a labeling that itself critiques the status of women in regard to power in heterosexual relationships. The conception of the Bowles character may be literally based on a destabilization of sexual identity that is essential to camp; Caudwell claims that her mother always suspected that Sally Bowles was based on a male friend of Isherwood, and Isherwood himself admits that he named the character for the American writer Paul Bowles, whose "looks" he had liked.[60]

The excesses of Sally's sexual poses often create the self-conscious "too-muchness" of camp. Part of the excessiveness of the Sally Bowles character involves the incongruous contrasts within her own language, her willingness to slip from one outrageous discourse to another:

> ". . . He wants me to be his mistress, but I've told him I'm damned if I will till he's paid all my debts. Why are men always such beasts?" Opening her bag, she rapidly retouched her lips and eyebrows: "Oh, by the way, Fritz darling, could you be a perfect angel and lend me ten marks? I haven't got a bean for a taxi" (24).

The reversals here are telling: a deadpan acceptance of the economics of sexual exchange (with cool pragmatism: "I'm damned if I will . . .") is followed by the accusation that men are "beasts" for not following the rules of this exchange. But the sentence is clearly out of another, altogether different discourse and set of expectations, a prurient *tsk-tsk* platitude by women about the male sexual appetite: "Why are men always such beasts? " Yet the joke ends not here but in Sally's gesture to "retouch" her face—to check her costume for the part—and then to revert to exactly the discourse and code she has just complained about, with a flirtatious appeal to Fritz as the "perfect angel" who will lend her money for a taxi.

Describing Sally's behavior and voice, Isherwood continually plays up their theatricality and artifice: her "little stage-laugh" (23); her deliberate positioning of herself into a "pose" for effect (27); her ability spontaneously to come up with "some really startling lies" that she "half-believed" herself (35). Her flirtation on the telephone is a "performance" not only for the person she is calling, but for her observers: " 'Hilloo,' she cooed, pursing her brilliant cherry lips as though

---

[60] See Sarah Caudwell, "Reply to Berlin," 28 and Christopher Isherwood, *Christopher and His Kind*, 60–61.

she were going to kiss the mouthpiece: '*Ist dass Du, mein Liebling?*' Her mouth opened in a fatuously sweet smile. Fritz and I sat watching her, like a performance at the theatre" (22–23). When Sally attempts to be traditionally feminine in a later scene, wearing a modest dress and "daintily curled up" on the sofa, she is "absurdly conscious" of her own beauty (27). But in incongruous contrast to the dainty costume and pose, Sally reveals in this scene her admiration for her friend Diana, " 'the most marvellous gold-digger you can imagine' " (28), tells Chris the story of how she invented a pregnancy to escape from school, and sighs that her younger sister " 'would nearly die if she knew what an old whore I am' " (30). Likewise, her self-descriptions as a "whore" contrast with a mock-elegant language in which nearly everything is "most marvellous" and in which she "adores" or is "adored" by nearly everyone.

The narrative of "Sally Bowles" is based on the series of jokes revealing the contrast between Sally's supposedly worldly sexual economics and her failures at actually transacting any profit from them. Early in the story, the narrator observes that Sally is not a very effective gold digger when he sees her at work at the Lady Windermere: "For a would-be demi-mondaine, she seemed to have surprisingly little business sense or tact. She wasted a lot of time making advances to an elderly gentleman who would obviously have preferred a chat with the barman" (26). After her affair with Klaus, which she had described characteristically as full of "adoration," Sally gets a letter from him in which he jilts her by using the same overblown language: " 'My dear little girl, you have adored me too much. If we should continue to be together, you would soon have no will and no mind of your own' " (41). But the letter then hints of his new relationship with an Englishwoman who " 'is related to an English lord' " (41)—a hint that Klaus is doing some gold digging on his own. Later in the narrative, when Sally's grandiose expectations about life with the wealthy Clive are likewise shattered, the satire of Sally's sexual economics is more literal; Clive leaves her and Chris only three hundred marks. " 'I'm afraid we're not much use as gold-diggers, are we, darling?' " Sally remarks (50). Momentarily disillusioned, she declares, " 'I'm sick of being a whore. I'll never look at a man with money again' " (51).

Yet even these earnings as a "whore" become part of the dynamic by which Sally's sexual exploits backfire, for she has to use the money to get an abortion for her pregnancy by Klaus. The "joke" on her here is more problematic, and points to an uneasy tension in the comedy of this text, the oscillation between a camp send-up of heterosexual game playing and a more hostile positioning of Sally as female

sexuality that is demystified and put in its place. The closure of the
story and the major episode after the abortion is a final joke on Sally
that is set up by the narrator: her manipulation and theft by someone
claiming to be an American film agent who turns out to be a sixteen-
year-old, mentally disturbed Polish con man. Promising her a contract with MGM, he manages to go to bed with her and get away in
the morning, having extracted from her exactly three hundred
marks—robbing her of her "earnings" from Clive. Explaining herself
later, Sally admits that she not only fell for his act but even agreed to
marry him at some point: " 'You see, I thought, that, being in films,
he was probably quite used to quick engagements, like that: after all,
in Hollywood, it's quite the usual thing . . .' " (74).

It can surely be argued that the subtext and grounding for these
jokes is the absurdity of the position of woman in the sexual exchanges of a ruthless market, her exclusive value as virgin or whore.
When Sally receives the letter from Klaus about the new girlfriend,
she and Chris speculate that Klaus is probably not sleeping with
her—that is, he might indeed marry her because she is still in circulation as one kind of valuable commodity, the virgin. Sally, on the
other hand, who is much more practical in the business of sex in exchange for favors, survives by the commodification of her body at the
other end of the spectrum in that market. This automatically dis-
qualifies her for the other kind of exchange. Men, however, are able
to have access to both kinds of women, those who are "nice" and
those who are more like Sally. The notion of the "nice" girl is played
upon early in the story. " 'Is she nice?' " the narrator asks Fritz at the
beginning when the subject of Sally comes up. In reply, "Fritz rolled
his naughty black eyes" and describes Sally in her own language:
" '*Mar*-vellous!' he drawled" (21–22). Sally not only recognizes her
status but is also able to name the entire construction of male desire
in explaining to Chris why men always leave her: " 'I'm the sort of
woman who can take men away from their wives, but I could never
keep anybody for long. And that's because I'm the type which every
man imagines he wants, until he gets me; and then he finds he
doesn't really, after all' " (50).

This critique of heterosexual ideology, the campiness of Sally's posturings and satire of her gold digging, stands on its own as a progressive discourse that is easily identified with Isherwood's conscious
agenda of rebellion and hostility against "the state and the church
and the law and the press and the medical profession" which endorse
these traditional roles for women and men. But this trajectory in
"Sally Bowles," in which patriarchal exchanges of women are turned
into a series of jokes, is undermined by another, far more serious,

and even hostile positioning of Sally's sexuality. Part of this is evident in the nature of these jokes, and in the odd location of the abortion sequence amid the comic sequences of Clive and the Polish con man. As Freud reminds us in *Jokes and Their Relation to the Unconscious*, jokes have considerable power in the dynamics of aggression: "A joke will allow us to exploit something ridiculous in our enemy which we could not, on account of obstacles in the way, bring forward openly or consciously."[61] In addition, the plot line of this series of jokes that structures the narrative is qualified by problematic historical and metonymic strategies that embed within these jokes not just Sally's abortion, but also the crisis of Weimar politics precipitating the emergence of the Third Reich.

First, the comedy of Sally's vampiness is explicitly reversed and inscribed within a troubling historical framework through a series of anti-Semitic references. When Sally's exclamation about men as beasts is followed by her flirtatious request for money from Fritz, the effect is comic and campy. But there is another effect altogether when she repeats this in anti-Semitic terms in a later scene: " 'And then there's an awful old Jew who takes me out sometimes. He's always promising to get me a contract; but he only wants to sleep with me, the old swine' " (31). In the later story "The Landauers," Sally makes a cameo appearance when Chris arranges a meeting with the prudish, elegant Natalia, a member of the prominent Jewish family, as an "experiment" (160). Sally's social lapse upon her arrival is similarly too offensive to be amusing. " 'I've been making love to a dirty old Jew producer,' " she says. "I'm hoping he'll give me a contract— but no go, so far . . .' " (161). In all the postwar adaptations of this story, these episodes and dialogues are retained but the anti-Semitic slurs are cut; with full postwar knowledge of Hitler's agenda, it would have been impossible to impute this casual racism to Sally without wholly alienating the reader from her character. However, even at the time that Isherwood wrote this in 1936, he was fully aware of the anti-Semitism of the Third Reich's ideology, as is made clear by the other references to it in *Goodbye to Berlin*. Later, in the story "The Landauers," Natalia's brother is killed by the Nazis, and the story ends with the narrator learning this by eavesdropping on a casual conversation laced with hostile references to and jokes about Jews (184–85).

The abortion sequence, which Isherwood claimed is the "whole idea" of the Sally Bowles story, is likewise marked by the anti-Semitic

---

[61] Sigmund Freud, *Jokes and Their Relation to the Unconscious*, trans. James Strachey (New York: Norton, 1960), 103.

discourse that, in the sequence of stories, saturates Berlin slowly and completely, so that the conversation about the murder of Jews at the end of "The Landauers" is casual and unquestioned. In "Sally Bowles," one of the narrator's co-lodgers, a music-hall *Jodlerin* who had been specifically identified as a Nazi, comes forward with a warning when Sally is about to go off to the nursing home: " 'The doctor isn't a Jew, I hope?' Frl. Mayr asked me sternly. 'Don't you let one of those filthy Jews touch her. They always try to get a job of that kind, the beasts!' " (53). It is impossible not to hear in this language a continuation of Sally's own railings about men, and about her cynical sexual/monetary relationship with the "awful old Jew" she had mentioned previously. Thus the comedy of Sally's earlier exploitations of sexuality is metonymically extended into another, decidedly noncomic trajectory in which racial difference is conflated with sexual difference as the ground for anxiety about exploitation of power.

In the abortion sequence, Sally's previous camp language and poses are similarly strained by other agendas. When Sally tells the nurse a fake, melodramatic story about her pregnancy, she admits she does it because the real story (being jilted by Klaus) " 'isn't particularly flattering' " (53). Later, Sally claims she regrets having had the abortion and wildly imagines supporting the child through prostitution: " '. . . how it'd grow up and how I'd work for it, and how, after I'd put it to bed at nights, I'd go out and make love to filthy old men to pay for its food and clothes' " (55). Positioned as this is immediately after the abortion and after the political and racial qualifications of Sally's sexual economics, the comic hyperbole of this discourse is considerably dampened. Sally likewise uses her customary, overdramatic language to explain her sadness and moodiness about the operation: " 'Having babies makes you feel awfully primitive, like a sort of wild animal or something, defending its young' " (55). Rather than amusing the narrator, this conversation disturbs him so much that he suddenly decides to leave Berlin: "It was partly as the result of this conversation that I suddenly decided, that evening, to cancel all my lessons, leave Berlin as soon as possible, go to some place on the Baltic and try to start working" (56).

Significantly, then, the turning point in the narrator's relationship with Sally is paralleled by a turning point in his relationship to Berlin and to his writing. It is also the framework of a historical turning point; he returns in mid-July 1931 to witness the major financial debacle and closing of the banks. The headline he sees in the newspaper reads " 'Everything Collapses!' " (58). But the joke about Sally's promiscuity seems to have collapsed, too. When he next sees Sally, her gold digging has shifted to something more serious; she is set up in a

fashionable apartment and apparently is " 'moving in financial circles' " (60), as Chris puts it. Their interaction is bristly and unpleasant; the "racket" of her sexual life is no joke when it is successful.
The narrator "felt puzzled and vaguely embarrassed" (59), no longer
able to laugh about her ploys:

> "Got a new boyfriend?"
> But Sally ignored my grin. She lit a cigarette with a faint expression of
> distaste. "I've got to see a man on business," she said briefly.
> "And when shall we meet again?"
> "I'll have to see, darling. . . . I've got such a lot on, just at present. . . . I
> shall be out in the country all day tomorrow, and probably the day af-
> ter. . . . I'll let you know. . . . I may be going to Frankfurt quite soon."
> "Have you got a job there?"
> "No. Not exactly." Sally's voice was brief, dismissing this subject (59).

The comedy sequences of the "Sally Bowles" story are thus undercut
not only by the abortion, but also by a gradual repositioning of Sally's
"racket" as less amusing. At the same time, the text's references to
Nazism and the political situation escalate; the ensuing stories in
Goodbye to Berlin move away from comedy entirely. In the last section,
the Third Reich is in power, and the entire positioning of camp takes
on political seriousness.[62]
However, the encroaching Nazi reality in "Sally Bowles" operates
in relation to two other dynamics that problematize camp comedy
with considerable impact. What is both puzzling and telling about the
Sally story is that although sexual tension is displaced by comedy/par-
ody, the structuring "jokes" of the narrative reveal a distinctly sexual
anxiety about Sally as body and materiality. This tension is in turn
displaced as a challenge to the narrator's ability to tell the story at all.
The conflict shifts to the narrator's status as a writer as opposed to
Sally's status as a would-be actress, gold digger, and self-proclaimed
"whore." While the latter is camped-up parody of Sally's poses, lies,
and theatrics, the former is posited not only as "real" but also as the
means of understanding Sally as comic and camp.
In examining this problematic positioning of camp in "Sally
Bowles," Bakhtin's analysis of the carnivalesque—which is celebratory
and never nihilistic—is less useful than his analysis of parody in The
Dialogic Imagination. Here Bakhtin describes parody as language

[62] Noting this movement and subsequent transformation of camp in these stories,
Peter Thomas remarks in his essay, " 'Camp' and Politics in Isherwood's Berlin Fiction," that "The Nazi reality is Camp without comedy" (130). Indeed, as I have pointed
out in chapter 1, Nazi reality consists of exactly the kind of radical emphasis on difference and hierarchy that makes it prime material for camp.

"used 'with conditions attached,' every word enclosed in intonational quotation marks."[63] Looking at the novel as a "*system* of languages that mutually and ideologically interanimate each other,"[64] Bakhtin suggests that parody arises to show the limitations of a certain discourse. Parody can be understood, then, as a resistance to a single, monolithic understanding of reality. It resists by suggesting repressed or unarticulated alternatives; it points to contradictory languages and meanings. I find this an especially accurate way to describe the camping up of heterosexuality in a gay discourse, and also an insight into the power of camp as both liberating and threatening: its ability to highlight unsettling contradictions.

Bakhtin makes useful distinctions between the "two languages" involved in parody. First, he points out that what occurs in the text as parody is not the thing itself but its representation, its style. The Sally Bowles character is likewise not a parody of female sexuality but the stylizations of its representations—the vamp, the femme fatale, *La Dame aux Camélias*, Anthony Hope's Dolly. But if these are the representations being parodied, we are left with the question of what is doing the parodying. Bakhtin differentiates between "the language being parodied" and "the language that parodies," the positing or suggestion of a norm against which the parody is played. And this is the particular problem of the position of Sally Bowles in the Isherwood story and in the subsequent adaptations: the identification of what Bakhtin calls "an actualizing background for creating and perceiving."[65] While camp comedy often depends on the privileging of a gay authority and point of view—the deliberate subversion of the binary, heterosexual sign system—this is not the authority of the narrator in *Goodbye to Berlin*, whose gay identity is repressed and whose authority stems from the much more traditional status of "author."

By repressing the homosexuality of the narrator and minimalizing the narrator as a character with accumulated personal traits, Isherwood claims he intended merely to highlight the other stories involved—"he'd have gotten in the way of the other characters."[66] But unlike the other narrative positions in *Goodbye to Berlin*, the narrator in "Sally Bowles" is also the actualizing background, the normative perception against which the comedy of Sally is played out. A good deal of the comedy, in fact, involves Sally's dialogue, her exaggerated

---

[63] *The Dialogic Imagination: Four Essays*, ed. Michael Holquist (Austin: University of Texas Press, 1981), 76.

[64] Ibid., 47.

[65] See Bakhtin's discussion of the two languages of parody and this actualizing background, ibid., 75–76.

[66] Norma McLain Stoop, "Christopher Isherwood: A Meeting by Another River," 62.

and theatrical language against which the normative language of the narrator is played for effect. In the opening scene of the story, the narrator establishes himself as an authority on language, an English teacher, in his interaction with Fritz; he automatically corrects Fritz's English usage "from force of professional habit" (21). Fritz goes on lazily speaking bad English and is joined by Sally, who demonstrates that she not only speaks bad German but also speaks English with such hyperbole that there is a similar difficulty with meaning. She asks to use Fritz's telephone but dramatically begs the two men not to leave the room: " 'For heaven's sake, don't leave me alone with this man!' she exclaimed. 'Or he'll seduce me down the telephone. He's most terribly passionate' " (22). Critic Alan Wilde, reading Isherwood in the context of 1930s "realism," describes Sally's "vivid but imprecise language" as a frustration of "the relationship assumed to exist between word and thing in the essentially 'realistic' thirties."[67] But this gap between sign and referent is positioned in relation to another, supposedly trustworthy, sign system: the narrator's. Given Sally's breathless exaggerations and Fritz's claim that he is " 'speaking a lousy English just now' " (21), the narrator emerges as the "corrective" for both.

The narrator's position in the plot as a writer, an authority with regard to language, is brought to the fore as topic of discussion and contention throughout this story. Chris is the deconstructor of Sally's language who can tell her coolly that her "shocking" talk is a "trick" forcing strangers "violently" to approve or disapprove of her (33). Later, Sally specifically praises Chris's ability to " 'understand women most marvellously,' " because, she says, this will surely help him " 'write the most marvellous novel which'll sell simply millions of copies' " (43). Pleased with this act of faith in himself, Chris then admits that his own faith in Sally is more vague: " 'Well . . . I'm quite certain you'll make a terrific success at something—only I'm not sure what it'll be. . . . I mean, there's so many things you could do if you tried, aren't there?' " (43).

The narrator's position as writer is inscribed into the narrative as the "reality" against which Sally's fantasies and imaginings are played. This works in an odd reversal even when Sally's version of Chris as writer renders him as campy "Writer" through her dramatic imagination:

[67] Alan Wilde, "Language and Surface: Isherwood and the Thirties," *Contemporary Literature* 16 (1976): 483. Wilde similarly finds in *The Berlin Stories* a "moral" use of language that "is meant to establish a norm against which the reader gradually comes to measure the linguistic (and, by extension, the social, political, and psychological) situation in prewar Berlin" (481).

"I think," said Sally, "it must be marvellous to be a novelist. You're fright-fully dreamy and unpractical and unbusinesslike, and people imagine they can fairly swindle you as much as they want—and then you sit down and write a book about them which fairly shows them what swine they all are, and it's the most terrific success and you make pots of money" (44).

Yet the very publication of "Sally Bowles" and its later "terrific success" as the source of many adaptations adds another level to the irony here, and further validates the position of Chris as writer.

Most importantly, the issue of Chris's writing precipitates the final sequence of the narrative, the setup with the Polish con man that occurs after the abortion and considerably problematizes Isherwood's claim that the abortion sequence is the narrative fulcrum, the "whole point" of "Sally Bowles." If the "point" is to show that "even the great-est disasters leave a person like Sally essentially unchanged," then what is "unchanged" in Sally is revealed in the two remaining and troubling episodes, her argument with the narrator and his revenge. The terms of this argument—Chris's status as a writer—and its re-sult—the "joke" of Sally's sexual and financial manipulation by the con man—foreground a hostility or anxiety that is latent in the odd gap between Sally's postabortion regrets and the narrator's immedi-ate decision to leave the city so that he can "start working"—or get back to the valorized and even "moral" world of writing as opposed to whatever is happening in Berlin. The concluding joke that satirizes patriarchal exchange of women situates Sally squarely within a phal-locentric discourse in which she literally has no credible language.

The crisis and testing point of the relationship between Sally and Chris is their argument about an article that Sally asks him to com-pose for her, "The English Girl"—an ironic self-reference to the status of his own text "Sally Bowles." Like the narrator of *The Dolly Dialogues* who inscribes Dolly into her opinion album, the narrator Chris agrees to play the game, but Sally rejects his article because it is " 'not nearly snappy enough' " (62). In the ensuing quarrel, Sally crit-icizes Chris for not being " 'strong' " and " 'ambitious,' " and she spe-cifically taunts him with the success of another writer she knows who " 'earns pots of money' " working on cinema scenarios (62). As op-posed to truly successful writers, she tells him pointedly, there are conceited " 'young men who, because they've written one book, start talking about Art and imagining they're the most wonderful authors in the world' " (63). Sally's attack is vicious; his kind of artistic posing, she says, makes her " 'sick.' " She specifically explains her impatience as her female need to respect male strength. " 'If you ever care for a woman,' " she tells him, " 'I don't advise you to let her see that you've got no ambition. Otherwise she'll get to despise you' " (63).

The Sally that emerges in this scene is no campy show girl but classic castrating woman, aiming directly at the source of authority in this text, which is certainly phallic in the Lacanian sense that Chris emerges as writer, the authority on language, the keeper of the symbolic order, in which her own language has been consistently ineffective and inappropriate. " 'What an utter little bitch she is,' " the narrator concludes furiously (64). His response to this scene is classic Lacanian scenario. "It was the cheapest, most childish kind of wounded vanity," he realizes, but this realization cannot stem his anger. "The awful sexual flair women have for taking the stuffing out of a man!" he reflects. His rationalization that Sally's language and intelligence can be dismissed is not enough to placate him: "It was no use telling myself that Sally had the vocabulary and mentality of a twelve-year-old schoolgirl, that she was altogether comic and preposterous; it was no use—I only knew that I'd been somehow made to feel a sham" (65). But his revenge for this threat and humiliation provides the closure for the Sally narrative; approached by the Polish con man, Chris deliberately sends him to Sally, "perhaps, out of malice," he admits (67). As a result, Sally's castrating threat is diminished. She is wholly fooled, sexually exploited, and robbed, thus properly punished by a "comic" scenario that restores her to Chris's good graces by the end of the story:

> "You know, Sally," I said, "what I really like about you is that you're so awfully easy to take in. People who never get taken in are so dreary."
> "So you still like me, Chris darling?"
> "Yes, Sally. I still like you."
> "I was afraid you'd be angry with me—about the other day."
> "I was. Very."
> "But you're not, now?"
> "No . . . I don't think so" (75).

But to work backward from this resolution, one might ask what questions are answered by this happy ending. Sally, characterized by language that is consistently empty or inappropriate, is positioned throughout the text as body, materiality, theatricality, but also as specific sexual threat: "The awful sexual flair women have for taking the stuffing out of a man!" Positioned opposite her is the narrator whose introduction of himself as a "camera" also positions him as reliable narrator of a specific kind. Within the story, his authority as writer is validated not only within the text, but also in the fact of its eventual publication, while her status as would-be actress is continually undermined as part of her comic discourse. The authority of his own language reveals the emptiness of hers. More than that, it serves as the demystification of her sexuality; Chris can locate her sexiness as a "trick" (33) but also can know her—as she apparently cannot know herself—as someone who can be tricked with the flimsiest kind of appeal. Sally attacks this authority of Chris as writer—an authority that in fact denies her own subjectivity, her own ability to know—on the grounds of her own sexual power, a sexual power and threat that the pregnancy and abortion had made clear. But this sexual threat is diminished by an elaborate humiliation that is the final joke of a narrative aiming, after all, at comedy: the resolution of a reconciled Sally and Chris, made possible because Sally's "likability" is that she is "so awfully easy to take in." Thus the narrative can literally move across Sally's body—signified constantly as economic stake, as surface, as site of fecundity posited opposite Chris's "fertility" as a writer—but can ultimately disavow its sexual power—strictly speaking, in Lacanian terms, its threat of lack, castration—because Sally's sexuality has been recontained by the symbolic order in which it cannot speak itself but can be spoken of—here, quite literally as a joke.

Such an analysis, a fairly standard feminist semiotic treatment of this dynamic, seems to take this study far outside the realm of materialist analysis and into a radically ahistorical framework, far removed from 1930s Berlin and from Isherwood's group of gay exiles. Yet the argument for its use here is specifically historical, considering Isherwood's appeal to a modern sensibility that would understand a particular positioning of spectatorship and spectacle: "I am a camera . . ." The dynamics outlined above, both of body/image versus narrative authority, and female sexual threat disavowed by punishment or humiliation, are remarkably parallel to the dynamics of mainstream cinema as described in feminist film theory in one of its most basic tenets, the positioning of the woman as image across which the authoritative male narrative is constructed. Isherwood's "Sally Bowles" does not, of course, consist of the apparatus and visual conditions that are the framework of semiotic psychoanalytic theories of cinema. Nevertheless, the social habit of those visual conditions (Isherwood as film fan) is my interest here, and my point of intersection for articulating the parallel semiotic and historical positionings of Sally Bowles. I am positing that the habit of those visual operations representing female sexuality constitute conditions in Pierre Macherey's sense, or ideologically charged aesthetic modes, as Terry Eagleton uses the term. Isherwood had had considerable experience with cinema by the time he wrote "Sally Bowles" and would shortly thereafter comment on the impact of cinema on his writing. Without taking the "I am a camera" stance literally, it is possible to include mainstream film as an important condition of production here—a powerful apparatus, along with "the state and the church and the law and the press" in constructing woman as the object of sexual desire—and in the case of Hollywood mainstream film, constructing particularly artificial models of gender.

In *Lions and Shadows*, Isherwood describes himself not just as a "born film fan" but as a writer whose methodology has clearly been influenced by this medium. The cinema, he says, coincides with his fascination for "the outward appearance of people—their facial expressions, their gestures, their walk, their nervous tricks," and in imagining a fictional scene, "it is simplest to project it on to an imaginary screen. A practised cinema-goer will be able to do this quite easily."[68]

There is strong evidence that Isherwood's cinema experience, at least at the time he was writing *Goodbye to Berlin*, was even more directly influential. His experience with the film industry had actually begun much earlier, as he describes in *Lions and Shadows*, when he took a short-lived job as an extra for a film at Lasky Studios during his university days and for the first time experienced the frenetic, costumed studio world where, he says, "everybody was addressed 'dearie' or 'darling.' "[69] In spite of an exhausting and dizzying day's work, his own few seconds on camera never appeared in the final version. Far from being disillusioned by this experience, Isherwood took up the challenge to write the screenplay for Berthold Viertel's *The Little Friend* in 1933–34 (an opportunity arranged by Jean Ross). This involved the adaptation of a sentimental Austrian novel about a little girl who reconciles her alienated parents by attempting suicide. His short novel *Prater Violet* (1945), which fictionalizes his experience

[68] *Lions and Shadows*, 85–86. Critics often comment on the unusually visual or "cinematic" nature of Isherwood's prose. Paul Piazza claims that *Goodbye to Berlin* is especially cinematic in style. Calling attention to Isherwood's love of the gothic and the surreal evidenced in his Cambridge fantasies, Piazza argues that the "camera" in the Berlin stories should be connected to the distorting, shadow-producing camera work of German Expressionism, with "montage" effects, sudden "cuts" from scene to scene, and uses of shadows and black-and-white contrasts. See *Christopher Isherwood: Myth and Anti-Myth*, 117–25. The precedents for this kind of analysis are weighty: Sergei Eisenstein's description of the "cinematic" properties of Charles Dickens, for example, in "Dickens, Griffith, and the Film Today," *Film Form: Essays in Film Theory* (New York: Harcourt, 1949), 195–255 and more recently, John Fell's compelling argument that increasingly visual effects are noticeable in Victorian and turn-of-the-century fiction writers, including Anthony Hope, in *Film and the Narrative Tradition* (Berkeley, Los Angeles, and London: University of California Press, 1974), 54–86.
[69] *Lions and Shadows*, 87.

with Viertel's film, documents the chaos of film production, with its breakdowns of equipment, tedious reshootings, and last-minute changes of script. The scenarist "Isherwood" in this novel finds his first sound stage "uncanny . . . a half-world, a limbo of mirror-images, a town which has lost its third dimension." The inhabitants of this unnatural "half-world" are collaborators to produce illusion; the actors and actresses are treated and think of themselves as images: " 'Where's Timmy?' Anita demands, in a bored, melodious voice. The makeup man hurries forward. 'Timmy darling, is my face all right?' "[70]

Isherwood indicates in *Christopher and His Kind* his knowledge, as a young man in Berlin, of films such as Richard Oswald's *Different from the Others* (*Anders als die Andern*) (1919) that deal with homosexual themes. But there is no indication throughout his lifetime work with the film industry that Isherwood was interested in alternative or underground film with explicitly gay topics. His friendship with Viertel, a Hollywood director, led him to further screenplay work with MGM and eventually with Warner Brothers and Paramount on films such as *Rage in Heaven* (1941), *A Woman's Face* (1941), and *Crossroads* (1942). By choosing to remain in major studios rather than work with experimental or avant-garde filmmakers, Isherwood was restricted by the Production Code of the Motion Picture Producers and Distributors Association in those days, and thus committed to an institutionalized censorship of the topic of his own sexual identity. Yet even his much later screenplay projects, though imaginative and intelligent, were far from experimental or specifically aimed at a gay audience. With Don Bachardy he wrote *Frankenstein: The True Story* for British and American television, for example (1973), and with Terry Southern he wrote the screenplay for Evelyn Waugh's campy send-up *The Loved One* (1965), directed by Tony Richardson.[71] Far from positioning himself as subversive or antagonistic toward Hollywood, though certainly able to satirize it in the Richardson film, Isherwood moved easily there as a worker and colleague, befriending stars such as Jennifer Jones, Rita Hayworth, and Ingrid Bergman. When *Radio Times* arranged a meeting of Isherwood and Liza Minnelli two years

[70] *Prater Violet* (New York: Random House, 1945), 71, 77.

[71] The number of screenplays that Isherwood wrote actually exceeded those that were successfully produced. " 'It was great fun working on them,' " Isherwood commented in an interview with Gilbert Adair, "Isherwood in Hollywood," *Sight and Sound* 46 (1976). " 'But something would always go wrong. . . . I seem to have put my bad luck into film-writing and all my good luck into the rest of my life! It would be a bore to complain; but, really, the films I wrote have nearly all ended in disaster, mitigated or unmitigated' " (25).

after her award-winning performance in *Cabaret*, he reminisced about his connections with her Hollywood family: "I knew her father Vincente quite well when he was directing at MGM and I was a writer there. He loved crane shots and he would take me up on the camera—and I'd occasionally meet Judy Garland at parties and things."[72] Although Isherwood's interviews at this time expressed his disapproval of the treatment of homosexuality in *Cabaret*, he never disapproved of Hollywood.

Nor is his position here unique. As Richard Dyer and others have pointed out, the Hollywood business of illusion making and role-playing has special relevance for the gay who often must play straight as a survival tactic. On the other hand, a more subversive tactic is possible, too: "We could pilfer from straight society's images on the screen such that would help us build up a subculture."[73] Camp is of course a major discourse in this subculture and has important connections to cinema, not only in its openly subversive moments (John Waters's films) but also with the possibility of a campy reading-against-the-grain of classic film, a marginalist reading that can turn the trajectory on its head. An example of this kind of reading actually occurs in the cinema episode in "Sally Bowles," in which Sally and Chris go to see "a film about a girl who sacrificed her stage career for the sake of a Great Love, Home and Children. We laughed so much that we had to leave before the end" (42). Outsiders to the middle-class codes of family and romance, these characters recognize the terms of the trajectory as Pure Ideology and can reverse the melodrama into comedy.

Given this condition, the writer who both loved cinema and thoroughly understood it as artifice and illusion, Isherwood had available to him a powerful and ubiquitous model of "good heter stuff" that would appeal to a mainstream audience. Because, as his own description reveals, he was in the habit in the 1930s of projecting his fictional scenes onto an imaginary cinema screen, there is good reason to argue that mainstream Hollywood cinema is an important factor in the construction of the original Sally Bowles, and that we can see in this character the status of female sexuality in Hollywood film as it has been described repeatedly by feminist film theory of the past several years: Sally's empty, inappropriate language as opposed to the narrator's privileged one; Sally as surface, as body to-be-looked-at, set up into elaborate poses; and finally, female sexuality that is eventually demystified in order that its threat be contained. If Isherwood was

[72] Iain Johnstone and Jenny Rees, "Bowles Players," 54.
[73] Richard Dyer, "Introduction," *Gays and Film*, 1–2.

drawing on this popular aesthetic mode *and* a particular ironic positioning of spectatorship in constructing a popular Sally Bowles, his own ambivalence in regard to this character is more understandable.

What emerges here, too, is the ambivalence of mainstream cinema itself, which is certainly "good heter stuff" institutionally, but which also operates in more fluid ways in the processes of its readings. As Andrew Ross points out, "there is no guarantee that what is *encoded* in these film scenarios will be *decoded* in the same way by different social groups with different sexual orientations."[74] That is, the very elements of Hollywood cinema mentioned above that have been most criticized by feminist theorists—the heightening of sexual difference, the representation of woman as surface, pose, body—can be reread or deliberately misread as ironic commentary on the exclusion of other kinds of sexuality. Isherwood's own lifelong fascination with Hollywood is perhaps most usefully read in conjunction with his impassioned denouncement of "what the state and the church and the law and the press and the medical profession endorse, and command [him] to desire." Though mainstream film may also presume and direct desire, it is not at all as monolithic as these other institutions in its relationship to the subject—although in film theory we often critique it as though it were. The point is that Isherwood's self-description as both "born film fan" and as alienated from "Nearly Everybody" suggests how easily mainstream film's appeal to Nearly Everybody can be appropriated by those it seems to exclude.

Yet the case of Sally Bowles presents additional complications. Unlike the persona of Marlene Dietrich, or Bette Davis, or Mae West—favorite figures for such gay and lesbian appropriation—the character Sally Bowles operates as parodic and excessive in relationship to *another* authority—the author/narrator of this text. While the "too-muchness" of Dietrich and West may point ironically to artificial gender construction, the pointing is done with their own authority. It is precisely this lack of authority that is most troubling in the construction of Isherwood's Sally who, in the realm of camp performance, is more similar not to the female stars mentioned above, but to parodic drag versions of these stars, which have traditionally been produced by male, not female, homosexual culture. The problem is the varying access and political advantage of this kind of camp for feminist as opposed to male gay concerns, in that what is often sent up or parodied is female, not male, sexuality. Part of this can be explained in that in the social construction of gender, women's roles and costumes (except for occasional aristocratic excesses such as the court at Ver-

[74] Andrew Ross, *No Respect*, 157.

sailles) have been more exaggerated and likely to cross into excess and overstatement, as seen in the self-conscious excess of Mae West's production of herself as spectacle. But the character of Sally Bowles, I have maintained, is produced and parodied against another "actualizing background" which displaces the power of the parody back to male authority, or even male hostility. Indeed, Leo Bersani has suggested that all male camp parody may paradoxically both help deconstruct gender images and also give "vent to the hostility toward women that probably afflicts every male (and which male heterosexuals have of course expressed in infinitely nastier and more effective ways)."[75]

Like the carnivalesque grotesque that is a traditional part of camp humor, Sally is the character who repeatedly makes a spectacle of herself, whether in her grand entrances and shocking announcements or with her painted green fingernails and odd costumes: "Everybody stared at Sally, in her canary yellow beret and shabby fur coat, like the skin of a mangy old dog" (44). As a sexual construction, she often shows the seams: "She had very large brown eyes," the narrator relates upon first meeting Sally, "which should have been darker, to match her hair and the pencil she used for her eyebrows" (22). This construction of Sally also suggests how the relationship of women to camp parody exists as a similar problem in Bakhtin's descriptions of the female carnivalesque, with his image of the senile, pregnant hag. What feminist readers find most promising and frustrating in this use of the grotesque body is its ambiguous positioning within male culture. Whereas Bakhtin represses the gender-specific impact of this model, the feminist reader is apt to recognize in this image the traditional stereotypes of both the aging female body and the biology of pregnancy as repulsive.[76] That is, the carnivalesque, like camp, works in more than one way as transgression but also delineation of sexual boundary, specifically in its use of the grotesque body in relation to female sexuality. Warhol's drag queens and Wa-

---

[75] Leo Bersani, "Is the Rectum a Grave?" *October* 43 (1987): 208. Mark Booth, considering this question in *Camp*, admits that the camping-up of "female" excess is marked by a good deal of hostility: "The effeminate man is a caricature of the traditionally feminine woman, belittling her and exaggerating the artificial elements in her personality to the extent that they become ludicrous." In spite of this, Booth argues that "it would be easy to overemphasise camp's misogyny, which in most cases is tempered by a great affection for women" (97–99). Booth also points out the differences in aim between feminism and camp: "Feminists seek to abolish or to minimise their marginal status, while the camp try to make a virtue of marginality" (56–57).

[76] Mary Russo makes this argument in "Female Grotesques: Carnival and Theory," in *Feminist Studies, Critical Studies*, ed. Teresa de Lauretis (Bloomington: Indiana University Press, 1986), 213–29.

ters's Divine come to mind here, but in the case of Sally Bowles this ambivalence is evident in the oscillation between the narrator's comic and hostile physical descriptions of this character. Although the green fingernails and mangy coat may only suggest Sally's eccentricity, she is described at other times in much harsher terms: "I noticed how old her hands looked in the lamplight. They were nervous, veined and very thin—the hands of a middle-aged woman. The green finger-nails seemed not to belong to them at all; to have settled on them by chance—like hard, bright, ugly little beetles" (29). When Sally first suspects she is pregnant, she drinks so much that "sometimes her eyes looked awful, as though they had been boiled. Every day the layer of make-up on her face seemed to get thicker" (46). It is not difficult to find in these passages traditional Western cultural dread of female biology. Certainly this play of the grotesque, as comic and/or threatening, is climaxed by Sally's pregnancy, abortion, and, most of all her subsequent expression of a wish for the child—thus the threat to enact the grotesquery of pregnancy. This is the conversation that most dramatically interrupts the text, sending the narrator out of the city and beginning the break in his relationship with Sally.

The pregnancy is also the occasion for another kind of ambivalent use of camp, which can be seen in the shifting status of melodramatic discourse in this text. Sally and the narrator laugh together at the cinema when confronted with the story of Great Love, Home, and Children because they are equally outsiders to this ideology. But Sally's pregnancy and abortion radically underscore the difference in their marginal positions. When Sally essentially retells the story of Great Love, Home, and so on as a lie to impress the nurse at the hospital, she reveals that, unlike Chris, she actually has a stake in this story, and that in fact she can imagine only one other story, being " 'looked down on and pitied as the poor betrayed girl who gets abandoned by her lover' " (53). Instead, in the lie she fabricates, Chris is the father, and the abortion is only a short-term delay of family and recuperation into the mainstream: " 'So I told her we were most terribly in love but fearfully hard up, so that we couldn't afford to marry, and how we dreamed of the time when we'd both be rich and famous and then we'd have a family of ten, just to make up for this one' " (53–54). Both versions of the story—the betrayed poor girl and the impoverished lovers—are melodrama, which Peter Brooks, Tania Modleski, and others have identified as the discourse that takes women's stories seriously. As the scene at the cinema suggests, it is also the discourse most vulnerable to camp parody. Sally's postabortion regrets are thus also the demarcation of a certain kind of boundary; because, as a woman capable of pregnancy, Sally has a stake in the story of Great Love, Home, and Children which is located outside the ironic discourse that would transform it as parody. However, this also leaves the character no discourse that can be taken seriously, and again reveals the problem of a location of female subjectivity.

The Sally Bowles story illustrates, then, how the ironic distancing of camp, a particular positioning of the spectator, is not necessarily an empowering one for the position of the sexual woman as spectacle if it does not wholly interrupt the phallocentric discourse in which she is articulated. Moreover, Sally's ambivalence as a camp construction becomes even more problematic in relation to the exaggerating, posturing, threatening political problem that is the subtext of *Goodbye to Berlin*: Nazism. Just as the narrator represents a linguistic and phallic norm against which Sally is drawn and disavowed as body and threat, a parallel dynamic operates in regard to the narrator's relationship to the other developing spectacle in these stories, the rise of the Third Reich.

Here, too, the narrator is positioned not only as objective observer but also as political norm against which Nazism is characterized as morally and physically grotesque. The Nazi *Jodlerin* Frl. Mayr, who makes the anti-Semitic remark about doctors and abortions, is a caricature of the heavy Bavarian lesbian/Nazi, the particular female grotesque that would become a postwar stereotype made classic in Lina Wertmüller's *Seven Beauties* (1975). She is described by Isherwood's narrator with specific physical detail: "The muscles of Frl. Mayr's nude fleshy arms ripple unappetisingly," he tells us (9). In the next scene she listens with sadistic glee as the Jewish woman downstairs is beaten by her boyfriend because of Frl. Mayr's fraudulent interference (11). In "On Ruegen Island," the story immediately following "Sally Bowles," the Nazi menace is the "ferrety" doctor at the beach who uses scientific justifications for putting away non-Aryans and all "criminal" types, including the young working-class Otto, perhaps because of his homosexuality (89). In the final two sections of *Goodbye to Berlin*, "The Landauers" and "A Berlin Diary (Winter 1932–3)," the hints of grotesquery erupt into actual violence as the narrator witnesses anti-Jewish riots and harassment, sees Nazi street violence, and loses his friend Bernhard Landauer to Nazi persecution.

The relationship of the Sally Bowles character to the emergence of Nazism is based on much more than her mindless anti-Semitic remarks, though this is certainly weighty evidence of Sally's alignment with the threatening political Other against which the narrator is positioned. Two other factors in the structure of *Goodbye to Berlin* are also relevant here. First, though the sketches are not presented in strict chronological order, there is a progression from the first "Diary" section of 1930 to the last "Diary" of 1932–1933, and the interweaving events of the stories in between are chronologically related. "On Ruegen Island," for example, is clearly the story of the intervening months immediately after Sally's abortion and the narrator's return to Berlin in "Sally Bowles." In this structuring, it is also clear that the two stories "Sally Bowles" and "The Landauers" overlap, or are parallel stories; thus Sally can make her cameo appearance in the latter story in order to shock Natalia with her sexuality and her anti-Semitism. This intertextual relationship, and the connecting narrative event of Sally's meeting with Natalia, underscores the parallel relationship of the narrator's witnessing of two threatening phenomena—Sally Bowles and the development of Nazism and anti-Semitism. Though the Jewish persecution may certainly have been the most obvious sign of the development of Nazism in Berlin, it is also the element most closely connected to Sally's most unflattering characteristics: her political apathy/ignorance, as seen in her bored response to the political funeral (48–49), her tendency to stereotype and exaggerate, and her language which aims at effect rather than meaning. In an incident in "The Nowaks," Isherwood specifically demonstrates this latter characteristic as anti-Semitic strategy. Frau Nowak engages in some clichés about her Jewish tailor that obviously reflect anti-Jewish propaganda, but she does not understand the implications of what she is saying: " 'When Hitler comes, he'll show these Jews a thing or two. They won't be so cheeky then.' " When the narrator points out what might actually happen "when Hitler comes" and removes her neighbor altogether, she seems startled—though, ironically, for entirely selfish reasons: " 'Oh, I shouldn't like that to happen. After all, he makes very good clothes' " (117).

This gap between surface effect (or performance) and meaning is the second major link between the camp parody and comedy of "Sally Bowles" and the positioning of Nazism in the last two sections of *Goodbye to Berlin*. The escalating violence becomes progressively unreal as history and comprehensible only as spectacle—like film spectacle, in fact, overdramatic, staged, not to be taken seriously. When the narrator learns of a street shooting that had taken place while he was at Bernhard's lawn party, he understands its impact as particularly cinematic and even comic in its combination of high drama and incongruity: "I thought of our party lying out there on the lawn by the lake, drinking our claret-cup while the gramophone played; and of that police-officer, revolver in hand, stumbling mortally wounded up the cinema steps to fall dead at the feet of a cardboard figure advertising a comic film" (177). Like a Hollywood gangster, the policeman falls against a cardboard backdrop; but here, the backdrop, an advertisement, is part of a "real" scenario publicizing a popular illusion. Yet the drama on the street exceeds the drama of what is shown on the screen. The boundaries of illusion/reality are deliberately conflated here, but the problem is that the illusion business of the Nazis, like the illusion business of cinema, seems too overblown and even self-parodic to be taken seriously. In the next sequence, the narrator tries to warn Bernhard that the Nazis are not merely comic and overdramatic. However, the menacing letter that Bernhard has received is couched in too many clichés of Hollywood gangsterism to be taken seriously: " 'We are going to settle the score with you and your uncle and all the other filthy Jews. We give you twenty-four hours to leave Germany' " (178). Bernhard's response is to laugh.

The narrator cautions Bernhard that there is more to the Nazis than comic overdramatization: " 'The Nazis may write like schoolboys, but they're capable of anything. That's just why they're so dangerous. People laugh at them, right up to the last moment . . .' "(179). The subsequent description of the Nazis in this story confirms the narrator's opinion of their effect. The SA boys in uniform stand outside a Jewish department store to urge a boycott: "The boys were quite polite, grinning, making jokes among themselves. Little knots of passers-by collected to watch the performance—interested, amused or merely apathetic" (183).

In the final sketch, "Berlin Diary (Winter 1932–3)," Isherwood makes an explicit connection between the dynamics of spectatorship and the development of the Third Reich. Describing the fascinated crowds watching the obviously fake wrestling match at the fairgrounds, the narrator concludes, "The political moral is certainly depressing: these people could be made to believe in anybody or anything" (190). But the positioning of spectatorship involves more than gullibility, as the next sequences make clear. Witnessing shootings, riots, and the harassment of Jews on the street almost daily, spectators grow progressively more numb, passive, less surprised. During one incident in which a crowd sees a young man beaten by the Nazis, the narrator notices that "they seemed surprised, but not particularly shocked—this sort of thing happens too often, nowadays" (201). The cushioning of this "shock" is directly related to Benjamin's concept of the shocks of modernity in relation to the camera; a particular mode of perception has developed, and what has become incomprehensible as politics or history is comprehensible as the witnessing of a certain kind of spectacle or image.

In this last "Diary," brief, separate incidents are described without connecting narrative, like separate shots or photographs. In the final paragraphs, which describe the narrator's last day in Berlin, the pleasant sight of the Kleiststrasse seems to contradict history: "The sun shines, and Hitler is master of this city." Specifically, the city is located not in real time, but as its own representation: the people and streets have "striking resemblance to something one remembers as normal and pleasant in the past—like a very good photograph." The concluding sentences are a more explicit denial of history: "No. Even now I can't altogether believe that any of this has really happened . . ." (207).

The portrayal of the strategies and discourse of Nazism as performance rather than meaning, as the triumph of image over language, is not simply an imposition of Isherwood's cinematic imagination or of later cinematic conventions. However, this same dynamic of spectatorship makes possible the passivity and denial that is evident in Isherwood's conclusion and that will mark the subsequent adaptations of Goodbye to Berlin . As the stories of Nazi atrocities grow more explicit in the decades after the war, the response grows progressively numbing: "Even now I can't altogether believe that any of this has really happened." But unlike past historical atrocities and disasters, this one not only is recorded by thousands of cameras, but also gives those cameras a bewildering range of subject matter: on the one hand, rows of skulls at the death camps; on the other hand, the choreography of the SS and the glittery displays at Nuremberg. Considering the latter's convergence with the stylizations of mainstream cinema, it was perhaps inevitable that the sexual politics of that cinema figure prominently in representations of the Nazi threat as Other and utterly disavowed; thus in the 1972 Fosse film, Sally Bowles is part of the spectacle onstage that "mirrors" the swastika arm bands in the audience.

Isherwood's construction of Sally is a great deal more subtle and more complex than the character in the Fosse film. Located as she is in the comic, parodic strategies of camp, this character is certainly no straightforward, mirror image of the history Isherwood witnessed in the 1930s in Berlin. As the fellow exile from bourgeois respectability, the self-conscious exploiter of patriarchal power structures, this character suggests the play and resistance evident in the image of Jean Ross in Spender's photograph. But she is also positioned as the threat of image over language, in an uneasy parallel with Nazi strategy, and like the threat of Nazism, her power must be disavowed as Other. Isherwood's project to produce "good heter stuff" thus crosses larger, multiple cultural projects dealing with sexual and historical anxieties.

Chapter Three

THE COLD WAR AGAINST MUMMY

VAN DRUTEN'S I AM A CAMERA

A
LTHOUGH ALL THE Sally Bowles postwar adaptations are
marked by contending aims and strategies, John Van Druten's 1951 Broadway comedy *I Am a Camera* is unique in the
kind of radical splits that characterize even its intended audience, so
that a careful reading of this text inevitably plays contradiction upon
contradiction, raising multiple political questions not easily answered
in a feminist context. On the one hand, Broadway Sally marks the
limitations of female sexual freedom for 1950s mainstream theater,
the comic whore playing at the same time as Audrey Hepburn's vir-
ginal Gigi in the other hit of the season, in the traditional good girl/
bad girl dichotomy of the era. On the other hand, Van Druten's play
leans toward an impatient dismissing of that dichotomy; this Sally
Bowles could also be the emergent sexually independent heroine
whose refusal of respectability at the play's closure brought cheers
from the audience. But what the audience was cheering may not have
been female sexuality so much as a comic transvestite enactment of
sexuality, a comedy and liberation made possible specifically by the
repression or elision of maternity, the displacement of motherhood
throughout a play in which—to borrow a phrase from Mark Booth's
Camp—Mummy is the root of all evil.

The camp reading of this play is no clever interpretation from
hindsight but rather was central to Van Druten's 1950s following,
which was likewise radically split. Van Druten had always been associated with popular and mainstream work. In addition to his successful Broadway play writing (*I Remember Mama*, 1945), he was one of
the screenplay writers for MGM's *Gaslight* (1944) and the director of
Rodgers and Hammerstein's stage hit *The King and I* (1951). However, Van Druten's Broadway work also had associations that were
less mainstream. "Admirers of John Van Druten's plays are a cult,"
one contemporary critic complained about *The Voice of the Turtle*
(1943): "This world is full of two kinds of people—the Van Drutenists
and the others."[1] According to Alton Cook, the "cult" is tolerant of

---

[1] Alton Cook, "Van Druten's Latest Play Has Premiere," *New York World-Telegram* (9
Dec. 1943).

Van Druten's willingness, especially in his early plays, to privilege dialogue over plot, cultivating character rather than event onstage. But the "cult" was more specific than Cook suggests. For Van Druten was among the few 1940s and 1950s playwrights whose "straight" work was able to be read as secretly gay, able to be reread if one knew the codes. *The Voice of the Turtle* and *Bell, Book and Candle* (1950) are the two Van Druten plays that were particularly susceptible to these double readings. The first, which is about a one-night stand that happens by coincidence, was read as a story of the "straight" soldier who becomes accidentally involved in a pickup. The second, with its background of a secret witch cult in New York City, was read as a story about gay culture—another kind of "secret cult" in the early 1950s.[2] *Bell, Book and Candle* yields a good deal of subversive comedy under such a reading, with its constant discussion of how witches can "pass" as normal: "He'd never suspect, darling," a character explains at one point. "Not in a million years. No matter *what* I did. Honestly, it's amazing the way people don't. Why, they don't believe there *are* such things." Another character, purportedly doing research on the subject, claims, "You won't believe this, but right here—all around you—there's a whole community devoted to just 'that.' . . . They have their regular hangouts—cafés, bars, restaurants." Can they be recognized? "Like a shot. . . . It's a something. A look. A feeling. I don't know. But if one were to walk in here right now, I'd know."[3]

I Am a Camera was similarly double coded to please both the mainstream and the marginal audience at a time when a Broadway character could not openly identify an alternative sexual preference. So the Van Druten text gives us the loner who is obviously but covertly gay, befriending the kooky and decadent Sally Bowles, whose "decadence" could be read in other ways by a knowing spectator. But if "decadence" is the code for gay identity, then the apparent heterosexuality and promiscuity of the Sally Bowles character sends into spin a variety of displacements and repressions. The interesting questions here surround the extent to which Sally Bowles's "eccentricity" is coded as gay male rather than heterosexual female eroticism, and the extent to which that eroticism is further displaced as hostility toward motherhood—not only Sally's possible pregnancy and mother-

[2] William Hoffman notes these double readings in his introduction to *Gay Plays: The First Collection* (New York: Avon, 1979), xxii. Van Druten's work is also discussed along these lines in Kaier Curtin's *"We Can Always Call Them Bulgarians": The Emergence of Lesbians and Gay Men on the American Stage* (Boston: Alyson, 1987), 251–52 and in Michael Bronski's *Culture Clash: The Making of a Gay Sensibility* (Boston: South End, 1984),117.

[3] John Van Druten, *Bell, Book, and Candle*, final version, 1950, New York Public Library, Billy Rose Theatre Collection, 11, 46, 48.

hood, but also its more blatant representation as the character Van Druten invented as nemesis of both Sally and Christopher: Sally's mother, Mrs. Watson-Courtneidge, who must be eradicated in order for Sally's sexual freedom to triumph.

The interruption of a formidable Mummy in this text marks a major departure from the plot of the Isherwood story, in which Sally only mentions an heiress Mummy who is safely back in England and would never know of her daughter's exploits. In the three acts of Van Druten's comedy, Sally Bowles has an abortion, is wooed and jilted by a wealthy playboy, and then is nearly dragged home (back to England) by the larger-than-life Mummy who arrives in Berlin threatening to restore Sally to virtuous middle-class life as a marriageable Miss Watson-Courtneidge. The appeal of the play in 1951 was precisely its resistance to the conventional courtship plot of Broadway comedy which would surely have steered Sally into happy marriage by the final curtain. From a feminist perspective, the conventionality of early 1950s theater is of particular interest in that the theater functions as a major public discourse in articulating female subjectivity. The conventional courtship comedies of that time (for example, Anita Loos's *Gigi*, Damon Runyon's *Guys and Dolls*) and heterosexual melodrama (for example, Tennessee Williams's *The Rose Tattoo*) can be seen as part of a wider discursive positioning in an ideology that Betty Friedan would later name as the Feminine Mystique. More recent cultural studies have revealed that the era's positioning of women was neither as monolithic nor as uniformly repressive as Friedan's white middle-class model implies. Certainly the very appearance and popularity of the Sally Bowles character in this era point to more complex and contradictory articulations of female sexuality. Some of this can be evidenced in the contrast between the two most prominent emerging Broadway actresses of the 1951–52 season and their respective hits. The newly discovered Audrey Hepburn was the star of *Gigi*, the fairy tale of the fantasy virgin child-woman who succeeds in corraling the desirable playboy into monogamy and marriage; Julie Harris, on the other hand, who had won the critics' hearts the year before with her debut in *The Member of the Wedding*, now played the promiscuous Sally Bowles, who could make grandeous conclusions about the sexual etiquette of bringing a man back to one's room after a date: "I do think one ought to go to the man's rooms, if one can. I mean, it doesn't look so much as if one was sort of expecting it."[4] Whereas the triumph of Gigi, who was being trained to be the professional courtesan, is her entry into respectable marriage, the

[4] John Van Druten, *I Am a Camera* (New York: Dramatists Play Service, 1955), 17–18. All page numbers cited in the text are from this edition.

triumph of Van Druten's Sally is her repudiation of respectability and her resolve to continue her sexual adventures throughout Europe.

These two Broadway characters signify not only the range of theatrical discourses constituting female sexuality in the early 1950s but also the gap between the mainstream public discourse concerning women in that era—the domestic, submissive family woman, specifically, the mother—and the emergent discourse of the eroticized, decidedly nonreproductive woman that the fashion industry would gradually emphasize and fetishize. The same issue of *Life* that profiles Julie Harris as the hot star of the Isherwood adaptation also features an introductory piece on the new Hollywood "starlet" Marilyn Monroe (specifically referring to her previous public exposure on a girlie calendar), as well as a whimsical story of girls at a Catholic high school who went to considerable effort to procure "modest" prom gowns in a fashion season in which strapless and backless gowns were all that could be found.[5] That is, the wartime pinup/girlie magazine genre was gradually interpenetrating something as mainstream as the fashion industry in the gradual 1950s conflation of sexuality and consumerism. A review of advertisements in mainstream magazines such as *Life* and *Time* shows a radical split between representations of the wholesome, motherly housewife and the bare-shouldered evening-gown goddess who looks back at the camera in a sultry testament on behalf of liquor or luxury cars. As historian Peter Lewis notes, "A decade which venerated both Dr. Spock and Marilyn Monroe was not a simple one."[6]

As both theater and history, *I Am a Camera* was marked by similar confusions of what story it was supposed to tell, even aside from the gay subtext that further complicates its reception. Directed as well as written by Van Druten, the play enjoyed a successful and profitable run of nearly nine months and was named best play of the 1951–1952 season by the New York Drama Critics Circle. But its reception among critics was ambiguous, partly because of its refusal to produce the conventional hero and the conventional heterosexual narrative. Julie Harris as the unconventional heroine, however, was an overwhelming success. Her refusal of bourgeois life in the third act was played and received triumphantly: "The first-night audience cheered with joy," reports Isherwood.[7] Yet 1951 critics were uncomfortable about how to situate the comic/triumphant story of Sally within the 1930s Berlin milieu which, even if played down in Van Druten's pro-

---

[5] "Hollywood Topic A-Plus" and "Quest for Propriety," *Life* (7 April 1952): 101–4 and 44–45.

[6] Peter Lewis, *The Fifties* (London: Heinemann, 1978), 42.

[7] Christopher Isherwood, *Christopher and His Kind*, 62.

duction, was consistently remarked upon as the "ominous world" or "sinister background" of the play. Within this context, one critic said of Harris that "one does not know whether to congratulate her for making us forget the nature of the material or to scold her for turning it into something superficial."[8] The seriousness suggested here is a reminder that this text is also poised in extratextual tensions of a Cold War in which concepts of good and evil, heroes and villains, were being sharply delineated at the same time that a coherent narrative of a heroic postwar United States failed to emerge. Given these problems, this version of the character Sally Bowles reveals a number of converging issues having to do with the hero's story in drama, the theatrical space for female sexuality, and specific postwar anxieties about a culture's imagining of itself (the character Christopher as the passive, innocent observer of sinister world politics) and its imagining of female sexuality, especially in relation to motherhood.

In adapting the Sally Bowles story, Van Druten faced a number of constraints in producing not just "good heter stuff" but a popular, monetarily successful Broadway play as well. In 1951, Isherwood was in great financial difficulty, and he attempted a dramatization of his Berlin novels with Lesser Samuels and Speed Lamkin. When this project collapsed, Isherwood's friends Alec and Dodie Beesley appealed to Van Druten. The playwright had been a friend of Isherwood's since their acquaintance in England in the 1930s, when Van Druten had supplied for him the corny movie plot embedded in *Prater Violet*. Several sources report that the "Sally Bowles" dramatization was presented to Van Druten as a "challenge" ("I bet you can't write a play about Sally Bowles"), which he undertook immediately, completing the text within a few weeks during the spring of 1951.[9] Thus the 1950s Sally Bowles, like the 1930s original, was constructed specifically as a mainstream, commercial project, but with considerably more pressure to conform enough to theatrical standards to produce a hit.

The "challenge" to Van Druten lay specifically in the popularization of a Sally Bowles in a mainstream theater whose current heroines were Gigi, Anna from *The King and I*, and an updated but nonetheless eventually submissive shrew in a revival of *Kiss Me, Kate*. The problem was theatrical convention, not censorship. Unlike the cinema, theater in the United States was not subject to a censorship code prohibiting subject matter or plots, even though there had been pres-

[8] Harold Clurman, review of *I Am a Camera, The New Republic* (24 Dec. 1951): 22.

[9] These details are discussed in the Brian Finney biography, *Christopher Isherwood*, 208, and in Iain Johnstone and Jenny Rees, "Bowles Players," 54.

sure in the late 1930s from the Catholic Church to impose such a code through New York City's Commissioner of Licenses. Broadway's relative freedom sprang partially from the vicissitudes between written script and the variations of any individual performance, as well as from the comparative sophistication of audience (urban, adult, middle to upper class) as opposed to the much wider audience of cinema. Given this smaller audience, transgression was less of a threat to the authorities. In addition, distinctions between "legitimate" theater and traditional forms such as burlesque and vaudeville remained flexible. Mae West, for example, was able to perform on Broadway in her own burlesque plays in narratives that had not been possible in Hollywood since the Production Code went into effect in 1934. Though they were not as popular as her early films had been, the West plays and revivals were still seen occasionally through the 1950s. Between 1949 and 1951, there had been short revivals of *Diamond Lil*, which reviewers welcomed precisely because West could "make sin seem very funny and sex somewhat hilarious,"[10] a feat that would not be possible in American film for another decade. Even though the New York penal code had the power to prohibit theatrical productions suggesting "perversion," this code was frequently challenged or disregarded, though the issues at stake were usually homosexual rather than heterosexual.[11] Thus Van Druten was free not only to use the abortion plot but also to provide a narrative in which the promiscuous woman is not punished at the end—freedoms he would certainly not have had in 1951 American cinema.

However, the "censorship" of Broadway productions tended to be internal and closely attuned to a general sense of public morality. The representation of promiscuity was usually limited to melodramatic suffering (Tennessee Williams) or eventual accommodation into domesticity and romance, as was the case in Van Druten's own earlier successful drama *The Voice of the Turtle*, in which (even if a gay audience was rereading the characters), the soldier's one-night stand develops into serious commitment and eventually marriage. One reviewer of the latter play admits that the plot line in fact verges on the border of the unacceptable but argues that the story is handled with enough "good taste" to "disarm any squeamish members of the audience who may be inclined to feel a trifle shocked by the frankly sexy theme of the play."[12] Generally, though, the narrative of the soldier

[10] Ward Morehouse, "Sin, Sex and Mae West," *Sun* (7 Feb. 1949).

[11] These details concerning the history of censorship on Broadway can be found in Kaier Curtin, *"We Can Always Call Them Bulgarians,"* 211–24.

[12] Wilella Waldorf, "John van Druten's Latest: 'The Voice of the Turtle,' " *New York Post* (9 Dec. 1943).

on leave and his casual affair won reviewers' sympathy, demonstrating a growing worldliness and permissiveness that perhaps are related to the social impact of wartime experience: the rise in illegitimate births during the war, the increased divorce rate afterward, and the sexual experience of the generation of men overseas in the armed forces.[13]

What Friedan describes as "the feminine mystique" was part of the idealistic postwar social discourse of the family that emerged in response to these wartime disruptions and aimed at a repositioning of men and women alike. Women, however, were far more radically targeted, partly because of the specifically maternal discourse that was greatly popularized through the Ferdinand Lundberg-Marynia F. Farnham 1947 best-seller, *Modern Woman: The Lost Sex*. The "lost sex" argument insisted on motherhood as the normative regulator of culture, simultaneously idealizing maternity and blaming all the world's problems on bad mothering. The impact of Lundberg-Farnham is particularly relevant to *I Am a Camera* and will be discussed at length further on. But it is important to point out here how this discourse and set of representations—images of the happy, white, middle-class housewife—contended not only with postwar social trends, but also with contradictory representations of women within popular culture. By 1950, the percentage of women in the work force was 31.4; a full 35 percent of mothers worked outside the home by 1955. And whereas women's magazines consistently addressed and articulated the content mother at home, Freidan also describes the eruptions and contradictions within the "mystique" often found in those same magazines in fantasies and romances suggesting the possibility of sexual adventures outside marriage—that is, the simultaneous eroticization of that housewife.[14] The postwar "woman question" is powerfully encapsulized by Lundberg and Farnham themselves in an introductory chapter suggesting the greater range of choices for women following the war: "Should they wear low-cut gowns, sleeveless dresses, one-piece bathing suits, 'shorts,' trousers, petticoats, tight sweaters at work, corsets or high-heeled shoes? Is it all right for them to go about bare-legged in public? Are they to be permitted to smoke, to drink, to move about freely, at all hours of the day and night, in public places? Should they be allowed in saloons?"[15] At the very cultural moment that was situating woman back into the home to rescue her as

---

[13] John Costello persuasively makes this argument in *Virtue Under Fire: How World War II Changed Our Social and Sexual Habits* (New York: Fromm, 1987).

[14] Betty Friedan, *The Feminine Mystique*, 1963 (New York: Dell, 1970), 250–51.

[15] Ferdinand Lundberg and Marynia Farnham, *Modern Woman: The Lost Sex* (New York: Harper, 1947),4.

"the lost sex," the American woman was facing a barrage of potential sexual and social freedoms often centered specifically on the public appearance of the female body—bare legged or in trousers, smoking or drinking in saloons—and soon wholly sexualized in representation through Hugh Hefner's bourgeois formulation of pornography, *Playboy* as philosophy and magazine, in 1953.

Perhaps the emergence of this permissiveness, even given the strong conservative discourses contradicting it, accounts for the fact that nowhere do reviewers of *I Am a Camera* refer to the hypothetical "squeamish members of the audience" who had possibly been present eight years earlier. Even the critics who read the Sally Bowles character as a prostitute had no moral objection to the play, nor objection to the abortion sequence (referred to discreetly in the reviews as an "illegal operation"). But the play also leaves traces of the nervous vicissitudes concerning female sexuality evident in the cultural contradictions. How seriously sensual/sexual could Sally Bowles be on 1951 Broadway? While Van Druten may have constructed a transvestite Sally that wholly undermined a mainstream representation of sexuality, there is considerable evidence that he also felt the need to inscribe the character successfully into a range of discourses acceptable to mainstream theater of the era. First and foremost, the play reveals a traditional structure in which Sally's goals and ideals are clearly subservient to the "hero's," uninteresting as he may be, and in which his moral insight and authority are validated in proportion to his ability to deal with the female obstacles in his path, in yet another rerun of *Oedipus Rex*.

In spite of the enormous critical attention given to the Sally Bowles character as played by Julie Harris, the story is not formally hers at all but rather enacts the more familiar portrait of the artist as a young man. At the beginning of *I Am a Camera*, the character Christopher Isherwood (played by William Prince in the original production) is struggling to write his impressions of Nazi rioting in Berlin. But he has been in the city for six months, has barely written a word, and the only two sentences with which he is pleased are the ones that give the play its title: " 'I am a camera, with its shutter open, quite passive. Some day all of this will have to be developed, carefully printed, fixed' " (10). Unlike Isherwood's *Goodbye to Berlin*, the Van Druten play has a much tighter and more conventional structure; the three acts of the play, in which Christopher meets and is progressively more involved with Sally Bowles, show him in gradually escalating levels of engagement and positive action, leading up to his motivation and decision to write his story, thus confirming him as reliable authority, and author of Sally's story as well. But even this developing-artist narrative was considerably looser than that of most Broadway plays of the time. In his introduction to the Dramatists Play Service edition, Van Druten writes about his problems in having *I Am a Camera* produced: "Too many people found the play plotless, pointless and leading nowhere" (5). But as an experienced and popular playwright, Van Druten knew how to utilize the conventions of popular theater even if he was willing to loosen them considerably with Isherwood's material. Accordingly, he builds around the unpredictable Sally character a number of predictable devices, such as a romantic subplot and a melodramatic positioning of anti-Semitic politics: the wealthy Jewish character Natalia from "The Landauers" in *Berlin Stories* is courted by the gigolo Fritz Wendel, who actually falls in love with her and becomes willing to admit his secret—that he, too, is Jewish!—and willing to court her despite the hostile political climate. Van Druten also provides an opportunity for Christopher to be "heroic" by denouncing Nazism and even getting involved in a street fight in which he tries to protect Natalia from Nazi harassment. Finally, this text gives us a closure that validates the play's action as having given Christopher both material and motivation to leave Berlin and become a serious writer.

Although this trajectory validates Christopher as "heroic," it also conforms to the demands of gender in the oedipal dynamic as described in feminist theory. The male agent is the maker of meaning and culture, and the feminine is designated as that which is impervious to change, as obstacle, space, or materiality. The temptations and monsters that Christopher faces in order to become a writer (which also is inscribed within the text as "becoming a man") are clearly female; beyond the distractions and potential motherhood of Sally Bowles, Van Druten adds not only Sally's stuffy mother from England but also a third surrogate mother, landlady Fräulein Schneider, to represent a kind of mindless, populist fascism. From all this, Christopher will emerge not just as survivor, but also as the writer/photographer who will later tell the tale, putting into order the threats of both female sexuality and fascism and promising to organize Sally herself into representation.

In act 1, in which Sally's happy promiscuity is stymied by the discovery of her pregnancy, Christopher comes to the rescue by paying for the abortion. At the end of that act, he speculates that the whole episode is something to forget about after a few drinks, but then he questions its triviality, and so reveals his first step in the direction of more serious introspection: "And we won't believe or remember a thing about it. Either of us. (*Starts to put the cigarette in his mouth. Then he stops and looks at the door.*) Or will we?" (39). Act 2 is mostly the story of his involvement with Sally and Clive, the wealthy American who promises to take them on a reckless world tour but who jilts them shortly before they are supposed to leave. Christopher seriously characterizes Clive's temptations as "the Devil's" (61) and after the jilting, urges Sally to "repent" with him, drinking and partying less, so that he can start work on his writing. But Sally is clearly not serious about such a resolution, and the curtain falls on their estrangement. Chris is no longer able to laugh at Sally's jokes about herself: *"The laughter dies. She tries again, it fails. They move slowly away from each other"* (63).

The concluding act introduces a new complication for Sally, which is resolved as the other plots—Christopher's writing crisis and the ongoing romance between Natalia and Fritz—come to closure as well. Both Natalia and Christopher are accidentally caught in an anti-Jewish demonstration in which Natalia bravely makes a speech and is then injured along with Chris, who gets bloody fists defending her. Meanwhile, when Sally's mother, Mrs. Watson-Courtneidge, arrives in Berlin to fetch her daughter, Christopher is forced to play the role of Sally's fiancé so that Sally will appear respectable. The turning point of this farce occurs when the mother attacks Christopher as a no-good drifter and would-be author who involves himself wrongly in foreign politics. Sally defends him, but she also confirms his textual authority with an extratextual reference to the "real" Isherwood: "He's a very fine person. . . . And he's an artist. Well—potentially. All artists need time. He's going to write a wonderful book one day, that'll sell millions of copies, or a lot of short stories all about Germany or something. . . ." (80). Shortly after this confrontation, Sally gets rid of her mother and denounces the bourgeois life-style Mrs. Watson-Courtneidge had wanted to impose on her. But in the meantime Christopher has been sufficiently inspired to leave Berlin and begin serious writing about what he has seen. Moreover, he has apparently learned lessons to "live by," as well: "But now I've got to put it all down—what I think about it. And live by it, too, if I can. Thank you for the idea about that book, Sally. The short stories. I think maybe that will work out" (82). He urges Sally to go back to England with him, but Sally claims she has a man or job on the Riviera. Besides, she confesses, it is her nature to drift along, not to have stability: "You're a writer. You really are, I'm not even an actress, really" (83). Sally departs for adventure, leaving Chris to watch her from the window. "The camera's taken all its pictures, and now it's going away to develop them," he says. "I wonder how Sally will look when I've developed her?" (84).

The validation of Christopher as authority and writer, which had been the dynamic of Isherwood's story "Sally Bowles," is obviously at work here, too, at least in a structural analysis. The argument about Christopher's writing being "not snappy enough," the episode borrowed from the original story, occurs just before the appearance of Sally's mother in act 3. Whereas the narrator's revenge in "Sally Bowles" was the joke on Sally's sexuality, the revenge in the Van Druten play is more curiously focused on female and maternal identity. After Sally insults Christopher's writing and storms out, he gives the speech about "the awful, sexual flair women have for taking the stuffing out of men," as in the Isherwood story. But in this adaptation, Sally's immediate punishment is to be faced with her identity as powerless daughter in the face of the monstrous motherhood that haunts the text: "Chris, something awful's happened. Guess who I met on the stairs. I met Mummy" (68). In the Van Druten play, the validation of Christopher as writer is further pushed to the forefront with the play's ending becoming the literal beginning of the embedded text, *Goodbye to Berlin*. By the time the play appeared on Broadway, Isherwood had a solid enough reputation in the United States (though, ironically enough, not for his Berlin stories), that Sally's prediction of his future success supports the trajectory of a "true" story of Isherwood and Berlin, while reinforcing her own randomness and insubstantiality: "I'm not even an actress, really." Again, the closure reinscribes the anxiety of ascertaining written text over body, materiality, and motherhood.

Even more problematically, this trajectory of the writer emerging from the temptations or complications of female sexuality converges with the antifascist critique climaxed by Chris and Natalia's encounter with the Nazi toughs in the street. Chris's ability to oppose Nazism is obviously part of his development away from the passivity he shows in the early scenes of the play. Anxiously tending to his wounded hands, Chris immediately imagines amputation. His hypochondria is a running joke throughout the text, but the joke also fits into the castration anxiety/writing anxiety of the larger dynamic:

> CHRISTOPHER: (*Looking at his hands.*) You know, I wonder if I shouldn't take these Band-Aids off, and put on some iodine. I could get gangrene.
> NATALIA: No, Christopher, you could not.
> CHRISTOPHER: You never know. Then they amputate your hands. And you can't write or type any more (75–76).

This is immediately followed by Christopher's second anti-Nazi stand, his argument with his landlady, Fräulein Schneider, who recites anti-Semitic propaganda about the Jewish danger to Germany, concluding that Germany "must come first." Christopher's response is to push into her face the same fist that had been wounded in his fight: "Suppose I push this in your face. (*Thrusts his fist near Schneider's face, and she retreats.*) Because Germany must come first—and I'm strong enough to do it, and to hurt you? What does that prove?" (77). The stage gesture reinforces Christopher's new stature and empowerment, his move from passivity to the ability to "thrust" and shortly thereafter to write. As if to confirm the character's newfound potency (as male/writer/anti-Nazi) in the last act, Christopher is given a final stage gesture suggesting a frustrated-but-"real" relationship with Sally. Her exit line after their final embrace is "I do love you." When she is offstage, Christopher replies: "I love you, too, Sally. And it's so damned stupid that that's not enough to keep two people together" (84). So their lack of sexual interest in each other is ascribed to vague general circumstances—a hint that love is "not enough to keep two people together" in the world of the 1930s, perhaps, or in modern times—but that otherwise there would be a serious relationship here.

Overall, the positionings of anti-Semitism and anti-Nazism in regard to the play's characters create a disturbing sexual gestalt. Schneider's anti-Semitism is itself a startling development in act 3, in that she had thus far been characterized as the lovable, bawdy mother, nurturing and fussing, but specifically sexual, full of references to her "saucy" past (11) and to her enormous bosom—which is another odd, running joke in the play. On the other hand, it is the asexual Natalia who stands up to the Nazis "like Joan of Arc" and is able to speak out against them eloquently: "Yes, she got quite fierce," says Christopher. "She made a speech. She was almost like Joan of Arc. I was quite astonished" (74). In regard to the anti-Semitism of the background, the narrative has three of the four young people make specific changes that motivate them toward some kind of political action which is also narrative closure: Fritz decides to tell Natalia he is Jewish; Natalia turns into Joan of Arc and makes her speech; Christopher fights Nazis, stands up to Schneider, and becomes a writer.

Among the young people, only Sally Bowles is left out of the antifascist trajectory, and in the sign system of female sexuality onstage, she is aligned much more with Schneider than with Joan of Arc/Natalia. That sign system is itself excessive in this play, as can be seen in photographs of the original cast and production. Whereas the three men vary less in typecasting and costuming, the latter tending to signify class distinctions, the women onstage are heavily coded to signify distinctions of both class and sexual meaning. Schneider's housedress fits loosely over breasts that are huge to the point of grotesquery, recalling the problematic carnivalesque hag. References to Schneider's figure throughout the play point repeatedly to the "joke" of the older, unmarried woman whose body nevertheless develops into the maternal. She herself cheerfully refers not to her breasts but to "the bosom. . . . It is like carrying a suitcase. *Two* suitcases" (11). Olga Fabian as Schneider is attractive enough to carry off a flirtatious manner even as she takes the discursive position of being the surrogate mother who is past or outside of sexuality: "Once I was sweet. Sweet as a sugar cake. Now I am sweet like a fat old bun" (12). The other, "real" mother in the text, Mrs. Watson-Courtneidge, is dressed in tweeds and cape, emphasizing class and playing down sexuality altogether. She demands at once a denial of sexuality and an understanding that it is something of which only men are capable and guilty. "Sally has been very good about you, Christopher," she says at one point concerning Sally's evident life-style. "She has continued to deny everything that I am absolutely sure has taken place. I think that shows a very fine character" (79). Van Druten uses the word *lady* in his introduction and stage directions three times to describe how Mrs. Watson-Courtneidge should appear (8, 69), and this coding positions her in distinct counterrelationship to Fräulein Schneider. The two daughters of the text are likewise parallel extremes. Natalia wears a high-necked suit and sports an enormous, schoolgirlish bow over her chest. All her hair is tucked beneath a small helmetlike hat. This hat had an especially severe effect on the facial features of actress Marian Winters as it emphasized her thinness and plainness: the virgin and Nice Girl, the Gigi of the text. Sally is the most heavily coded/costumed of all four. She wears a low-cut, tight black sheath, split a few inches up the front, with transparent net sleeves, and a long, bright red scarf is tied loosely around the décolletage; she carries a long black cigarette-holder and, according to stage directions, has "*a page boy's cap stuck jauntily on one side of her head. Her finger-nails are painted emerald green*" (15). In the course of the play, she at one point appears in a slip worn under a dressing gown; when she sheds the gown, she casually dresses in front of Christopher, pulling on her skirt and stockings during the scene in which they argue about the article he has written for her (66–67).

All four women characters represent stereotypes of female sexuality and class so heavy-handedly as to be caricatures or parodies, but the ideologeme of the narrative works against the sexual comedy, or at least creates a moralistic hierarchy of discourses concerning sexuality and politics. In the face of a dangerous politics—specifically fascist and anti-Semitic—the young writer and his friends move from passivity to action, from disengagement to commitment. What they reject is, first, the mindless prejudice of the working-class mother figure; Christopher complains in frustration that he cannot even argue with Schneider because he has "intelligence" whereas she has "just been listening to things"(77). Second, they reject the right-wing elitism of the bourgeois mother; Mrs. Watney specifically deplores Christopher as one of those "drifters who call themselves authors, never write a word, and then vote Labor on the slightest provocation" (80). If that is the thrust of the play, so to speak—and a far more didactic one than in Isherwood's original story—then Sally Bowles is particularly suspect as the character who, like the two bad mothers, is essentially the same at the end as she had been at the beginning—the female element impervious to change. What Isherwood claimed to admire about the character, that "even the greatest disasters leave a person like Sally essentially unchanged"[16] becomes far more ambiguous in the context of Broadway theater conventions that demand certain kinds of closures and political positions. Christopher must take the superior moral position and go back to England (away from the Continent that will be rapidly occupied by the Third Reich). As for Sally—"She'll just go on and on, as she always has—somewhere," Christopher concludes in the play (84). Like the fascism represented in the text, Sally is a material force or continuing, immutable dynamic as opposed to the organizing/writing male/human/antifascist.

Yet even though 1951 critics were often disturbed by the problems of this narrative, its comedy at odds with its didacticism and grim historical background, the most obvious gap—or perhaps the most promising space—within the play is the difference between this moralistic and linear narrative about the hero and the much more interesting dynamic of the character Sally Bowles, both in terms of the performance by Julie Harris and the positioning of the character as disruption and even subversion of the hero's story. The casting of Harris in this role opens a variety of contradictions not evident in the narrative described above, privileging the play of masquerade and the exposure of femininity as theater, which then undermines the elaborate sign system of gender that the play otherwise hierarchizes. And the success with which Harris apparently upstaged the play itself—the overwhelmingly unanimous praise accorded her performance—may reveal multiple ideological splits that complicate the oedipal, antifascist scenario described above—for the issue of motherhood that is so frequently brought to the forefront in this text both suggests traces of the predominant social discourse concerning the constitution of womanhood in the early 1950s and reveals a distinct resistance against that discourse.[17]

[16] John Lehmann, *Christopher Isherwood*, 29.
[17] This chapter focuses on Van Druten's production, which starred Julie Harris, because her performance came to be closely associated with Van Druten's character and because, with her performance in the film version, Harris achieved the reputation in

Just the year before the Van Druten play, Julie Harris had achieved fame on Broadway in her debut as the androgynous, tomboy adolescent Frankie Addams in *The Member of the Wedding*. Drama critics of the Van Druten play invariably referenced her earlier tomboy performance. Subsequent publicity, especially after her rave reviews for *I Am a Camera*, emphasized her boyishness; the *Life* "Close-Up" describes her as looking like "a twelve-year-old boy who has been taking Lionel Strongfort's body-building exercises for a long time with no success. She is 26, very small (5 feet 4 inches, 105 pounds) and her silhouette is almost flat."[18] Thus some of the most frankly sexual lines recited on Broadway in 1951—for example, Sally's speech declaring "I had a wonderful, voluptuous little room—with no chairs—that's how I used to seduce men" (25)—are considerably qualified by an actress who still looks like the tomboy in disguise. Later, Isherwood remembers Van Druten explaining, " 'If you have a great actress, type-casting is unimportant.' "[19] However, the casting of Harris was not simply a variation on typecasting but a much more radical casting against type, especially considering the other popular Broadway actresses of the era who played more conventionally attractive heroines and who would have portrayed a more seriously sexual Sally—Jessica Tandy, Ann Sothern, Janis Paige, Dolores Gray, Ann Crowley, Lilli Palmer.

The excessive costuming and accessories of Harris likewise have a substantially different effect than if they had been worn by one of these other actresses. Harris in the elaborate scarf, see-through sleeves, and split skirt represents, not the cultural "sexy woman," but a joke about that very representation. Likewise, the play's repeated references to Schneider's "bosom," as well as the exaggerations of Schneider's figure, set up an odd joke in its final reference to Harris. Natalia's huge bow tie explicitly covers most of her chest to confirm the absolute virginity of her character, whereas Sally's red scarf gives a peek a boo effect to her low-cut sheath. But the latter effect of se-

---

later interviews and reviews as "the" 1950s Sally Bowles. However, other actresses played the role in concurrent productions in other cities and on the play's 1953 tour, among them Barbara Baxley, Lee Grant, and Rita Gam; Dorothy Tutin played the role in the London production. Unlike the film version's definitive text, the performance texts and conditions involved here are multiple. Because much of my argument in this chapter is centered on the casting of Harris as an important production condition, I need to point out that the performance of other, more traditionally "feminine" actresses would substantially affect the way in which the play makes meaning, and could considerably alter the text/performance dynamic described here.

[18] Robert Wallace, "Close Up: Julie Harris," *Life* (7 Apr. 1952): 156.
[19] Iain Johnstone and Jenny Rees, "Bowles Players," 54.

6. Broadway play *I Am a Camera* (1951). Julie Harris's costuming and poses self-consciously mimic "sexiness."

ductiveness can only be a joke on Harris's slightness.[20] So Sally's flirtatious references early in the first scene to "bosoms" are less sexy than ironic. Telling Christopher he can visit her anytime in the room across the hall, she says that if either of them feel low, they can "just sob on each other's bosoms. (*Sally and Christopher meet in front of couch. He gives her drink.*) I say, Fräulein Schneider's got a big one, hasn't she? Like an opera singer, or that woman in the music halls who can make hers jump." About the latter possibility, Chris offers that "We might train her" (24). Suddenly the imagining of the female body as grotesque—literally as spectacle—overcomes what would otherwise be seductive stage business: the move to the front of the sofa, Sally's bold talk about "bosoms." Is this a nervous, misogynous disavowal or a more ambiguous displacement of the assignation of meaning of the female body, a reminder that Sally's excessive costuming and excessive talk continue to disclose her masquerade as "woman?"

The question here is particularly relevant in that the overdressing of Julie Harris's boyish figure can easily be read as a type of cross dressing rather than as masquerade. Both issues have been of interest to feminist theory in regard to their relative possibilities for empowerment, with one argument suggesting that "masquerade" may acknowledge femininity as "mask" or "non-identity," but that transvestism at least makes possible another kind of sexual identity.[21] However, transvestism can work either as a subversive or as a reactionary dynamic, depending on the text and the context of reception; it can destabilize the sign system of clothes/gender/identity or can work as a nervous reaffirmation of sexual difference—that is, male-female cross dressing can fetishize female sexuality in yet another strategy of disavowal.[22] The medium of theater itself is a factor here; Barbara Freedman has argued that the theater, unlike film, has tra-

[20] This is especially ironic in light of the virtual obsession with female breasts in 1950s popular culture, when in film, for example, "Whole careers were built on breasts," as Peter Lewis says of Jayne Mansfield, Jane Russell, and Great Britain's Diana Dors: "Never in this century at least had so much respect been paid to mammary development," *The Fifties*, 49–50.

[21] Mary Ann Doane makes this case in "Film and the Masquerade: Theorising the Female Spectator," *Screen* 23 (1982): 74–87. Doane, like others discussing this question, is responding to Joan Riviere's theory that all "womanliness" is a "masquerade" grounded in resentment of male sexual power. See "Womanliness as Masquerade," *Psychoanalysis and Female Sexuality*, ed. Henrik M. Ruitenbeek (New Haven: College and University Press, 1966), 209–20.

[22] Annette Kuhn makes this distinction in *Power of the Image* (London: Routledge, 1985), 49–57. For an example of cross dressing as destabilization, see Caryl Churchill's feminist drama *Cloud Nine* (New York: Methuen, 1984), in which the family mother is played by a man, the black servant is played by a white man, and the little boy is played by a woman in order to emphasize gender and racial constructions.

ditionally played freely with such signs as costume to indicate the instability of gender. In the framing device of *The Taming of the Shrew*,
she points out, the character in the original productions would have
been a boy playing a page playing a girl in a play watching a play,
epitomizing this kind of instability.[23] These questions are in fact applicable to Harris in the Van Druten play, in that they hinge on
whether or not she was able to carry off with wry self-consciousness
a brilliant triple disguise: a woman playing a boy playing a woman.
Van Druten's introduction to the play heavily suggests his own inclination toward this characterization when he describes how the character Christopher must be more amused by than attracted to Sally:
"He is deeply fond of her, but he is never physically attracted to her,
nor does he find her romantic. It is essential to establish this in the
first scene. His line of 'I think you're wonderful, Sally' must be read
as if it were spoken by a youngish man to a bright and impudent boy
of twelve" (7).

Of course, on the one hand, it is exactly the coding of Sally as a
"boy of twelve" that must be displaced so that the attraction of the
other man is not developed in the narrative. This possibility of a
cross-dressed, transvestite Sally—the sexual woman who is secretly
the "impudent boy of twelve"—further complicates the reading of
the play and further undermines the "straight" politics and narrative
of antifascism and portrait-of-the-artist-becoming-a-man. On the
other hand, even if the boyishness of Harris may undermine the artifices of sexual construction, it may also serve to placate male anxiety
about the force of female sexuality—a sexuality that, in the character
of Sally Bowles, would have been otherwise too threatening for the
1951 stage.

Van Druten's construction of Sally reveals the traces of this threat
and the need to mollify Sally's sexual impact. For example, Isherwood reports that there was a joint decision to play the promiscuity
with deliberate ambiguity: ". . . when Julie Harris was rehearsing for
the part of Sally in the American production of *I Am a Camera*, John
van Druten and Christopher discussed with her the possibility that
nearly all of Sally's sex life is imaginary; and they agreed that the part
should be played so that the audience wouldn't be able to make up its
mind, either way." Thus, Isherwood explains, the volatile line about
seducing men by not having chairs in the room was delivered by Harris with "exquisite ambiguity."[24] Admittedly, such a performance

---

[23] Barbara Freedman, "Frame-Up: Feminism, Psychoanalysis, Theatre," *Theatre Journal* 40 (1988): 375–76.

[24] Christopher Isherwood, *Christopher and His Kind*, 61.

would mitigate moral objections to the play, positioning the character carefully within postwar ambivalence between permissiveness and conservatism. This ambivalence illustrates, as well, the possible gaps between narrative and performance; an audience that "wouldn't be able to make up its mind, either way" was in fact seeing a story that included an abortion and a sugar daddy, Clive, pointing to a sex life that is much more than imaginary.

Another textual device that concedes to ambiguous cultural and generic demands about female sexuality, and that seems prior to the casting of the androgynous Harris, is the articulation of Sally as child or childlike, a variation of the whore-with-the-heart-of-gold in that real innocence can be ascertained in spite of sexual behavior; or female sexuality can be disavowed, with the assurance that in the neutrality of childhood there is no threat of "lack." In his 1972 memoir, Isherwood sums up the stage-play Sally as being "cuter and naughtier" than his original.[25] Van Druten, in his introduction to the play, makes it clear that this is his intention but claims that Isherwood himself suggested this characterization in a letter: " 'She is a little girl who has listened to what the grown-ups had said about tarts, and who was trying to copy those things' " (6). Van Druten claims that he thus tried to create a double-sided Sally Bowles, giving her "flagrant conversation, and her total absence of any moral values on the subject of sex," but also giving her the stage props of childhood: a teddy bear that she brings with her when she moves into Christopher's room and a terrible painting of a kitten awakening in heaven (6).

This conflation of eroticism and childlike innocence in representations of women was a major 1950s deployment of female sexuality, evident, for example, in the Hollywood invention of "sex kittens" on the model of Marilyn Monroe and in the specific kind of fluffy, childlike, "kittenish" heroine that Betty Friedan finds in women's popular fiction of the decade.[26] This dynamic at work in *I Am a Camera* is a noticeable variation of the original Isherwood construction of Sally Bowles. Shortly after the abortion sequence, for instance, Van Druten provides a short dialogue in which Sally appears to be genuinely surprised at Christopher's description of social values concerning sex, the traditional belief that lovemaking is supposed to be "something rare and special" instead of casual and trivial:

SALLY: Oh, goodness, is it? Yes, I suppose it *is* supposed to be. Oh, is *that* why people say it's wrong to do it when you're not married, or terribly deeply in love?

[25] Ibid.,62.
[26] Betty Friedan, *The Feminine Mystique*, 30–49.

CHRISTOPHER: Yes, of course it is.

SALLY: Well, why didn't anyone ever *tell* me?

CHRISTOPHER: I expect they did, and you didn't believe them (42).

The later appearance of Sally's mother, and Sally's immediate response of appearing chaste and respectable for her, wholly explodes the notion that Sally could have been brought up in a bourgeois British home without ever having heard or believed conventional ideas about sexual behavior. Yet Van Druten asserts in his introduction that the above dialogue be played without irony: "When, in Act II, Scene 1, she sees some truth in the virtues of love and fidelity, she sees them, really and truly, for the first time. Her line of 'Oh, goodness, is it?' should have the flash of a sudden new realization" (6–7). In light of her later submissive discourse with her mother, it becomes evident that Sally's "surprise" in this scene is derived not as much for the effect of comedy as for an accommodation to the pressure to produce a popular character palatable for 1951 Broadway constitutions of the sexual woman.

Yet according to the 1951 reviews, it was not Julie Harris but rather Audrey Hepburn in *Gigi*, who was playing the childlike seductress that season. There is considerable evidence that Harris, whose performance was described as dynamic, energetic, stunning, distinguished, played Sally in a grand, comic theatrical style rather than as the child/siren written by Van Druten. Critical response to the play often pointed to the difference between Van Druten's script (generally considered mediocre, or at least problematic) and Harris's performance of it. "Julie Harris Held Better Than Play," the review for the *Journal American* was headlined. Isherwood biographer Fryer reports that "Neither the Beesleys nor Christopher were wildly enthusiastic about the play in script, but it was a quite different matter on stage. It opened in Hartford, Connecticut, on November 8, 1951, with Julie Harris in the lead. It was she who made the play."[27]

Harris's transformation of the play and the character Sally Bowles has received most comment from Isherwood himself. His initial meeting with Harris during Van Druten's rehearsal had been set up as a publicity gimmick, but Isherwood claims he was genuinely moved. "This was Sally Bowles in person. Miss Harris was more essentially Sally Bowles than the Sally of my book, and much more like Sally than the real girl who long ago gave me the idea for my character," he explains in the introduction to *The Berlin Stories*. His description of the evolution of this character is marked by both a materialist awareness of various textual conflations and a contradictory

<hr>

[27] Jonathan Fryer, *Isherwood*, 241–42.

idealism about "creatures of art." It also situates Sally and Harris as safely "unlovable": "I was dumbfounded, infatuated. Who was she? What was she? How much was there in her of Miss Harris, how much of Van Druten, how much of the girl I used to know in Berlin, how much of myself? It was no longer possible to say. I only knew that she was lovable in a way that no human could ever quite be, since, being a creature of art, she had been created out of pure love."[28]

In his 1972 memoir, Isherwood gives more credit to Harris than to her various cocreators, claiming that "Julie contributed much of herself to the character." This later recollection is additionally interesting for its conflicting descriptions of Harris as "vulnerable" and as the bohemian "Joan of Arc"—an especially odd comparison in that the Van Druten text uses this description for Natalia in the scene where she takes her stand against the Nazis. It also reiterates the character as unlovable/untouchable: "She seemed vulnerable but untouchable (beyond a certain point), quickly moved to childlike delight or dismay, stubbornly obedient to the voices of her fantasies; a Bohemian Joan of Arc, battling to defend her way of life from the bourgeoisie." In the same passage, Isherwood reads the conflict between Sally and her mother as the story of the play. When her mother intends to take Sally back to England, he says, "the battle appeared to be lost," and Sally's change of costume signaled defeat: "In token of her humiliation, she wore a frumpy expensive British coat which her mother had made her put on. She looked as miserable as Joan of Arc must have looked when she was forced to stop dressing as a man." To some extent, the Joan of Arc reference reinforces Isherwood's original, partially androgynous conception of Sally Bowles, the desire crossed with her namesake, Paul, perhaps followed through by Van Druten's idea of Sally as the twelve-year-old boy. But the transvestite effect also converges with the revolt against respectability described here by Isherwood as the virtual trajectory of the play: "Then, in the last scene, Julie entered in the costume she had worn throughout most of the play—a black silk sheath with a black tam-o'-shanter and a flame-colored scarf, the uniform of her revolt. Seeing it, one knew, before she spoke, that her mother had retired routed from the battlefield. The effect was heroic. Bohemia had triumphed. The first-night audience cheered with joy."[29] Though Isherwood's reading of Sally as the androgynous Joan of Arc may be an imposition of an inclination to see female sexuality as cross dressing, there is little doubt that contem-

[28] Christopher Isherwood, *Berlin Stories*, vii.
[29] Christopher Isherwood, *Christopher and His Kind*, 62.

porary critics similarly read the play as a story of Sally's triumph rather than as portrait-of-the-emerging-artist Christopher.

If so, Van Druten's careful balance of sexuality with childlike innocence is wholly subverted not just by Sally's triumph over her mother's middle-class mores but by the play's ending as well, which launches Sally into happy and eternal promiscuity—the code here, perhaps, for other kinds of freedom. In the last scene, Christopher describes to Sally the advantages of "going home" with him, where his family will help with money and where he will get a regular job. The choices laid out for her in this scene are as binary and relentless as those in contemporary magazine photos and stories: utter conformation either to home/maternity/family or dangerous, glamorous eroticism. Sally describes her upcoming Riviera rendezvous with a Yugoslavian film director with "a long, black beard"—"I've never been kissed by a beard before"—who has "exciting" if vague ideas for filmmaking in South America. Christopher, alarmed by these reckless plans, offers her the cultural alternative: "Oh, Sally, *must* you? Must you go on like this? Why don't you go home, too?" Her reply is brief: "And be Miss Watson-Courtneidge again?" (83). That is, the alternative is to become not just her mother's daughter but actually to become her mother, the one who uses the "real" name designating class, family, money. In her next explanatory speech, refusing Christopher's offer to take her home and take care of her, she makes clear that she is not even a "career girl" but rather an adventurer who specifically resists stability in favor of "excitement"—presumably, sexual excitement:

> SALLY: It wouldn't be any good, Chris. I'd run away from you, too. The moment anything exciting came along. It's all right for you. You're a writer. You really are, I'm not even an actress, really. I'd love to see my name in lights, but even if I had a first-night tomorrow, if anything attractive turned up, I'd go after it. I can't help it. That's me. You know that really, don't you?
>
> CHRISTOPHER: Yes, Sally, I'm afraid I do (83).

What is fascinating about this exchange, in regard to Christopher as the play's putative hero/writer/antifascist, is that his position has been wholly conflated with that of Mrs. Watson-Courtneidge through the signification of "home" as stability, fidelity, conventional morality. In the larger representation of history in the play, "home" is also the enemy of German fascism and anti-Semitism. And in the play's self-referentiality, "home" is the entire symbolic order through which the play articulates itself: the "real" Christopher Isherwood retreats from the hazards of fascist Germany in order to become the great writer.

In spite of this overdetermination of the signified, however, Sally Bowles's resolute resistance of "home" is what clearly endeared her to the 1951 audience just as it made Christopher's more "homey" character forgettable in comparison. The Cold War Sally Bowles, then, may in fact have been—at least in her Broadway incarnation— the transvestite foot soldier, the bohemian Joan of Arc, in a subversive battle against the Happy Housewife later described by Friedan.

Yet the most troubling element of the 1951 *I Am a Camera* consists perhaps not of the bohemian triumph of Sally in tension against the hero's authority and antifascism, but its simultaneous convergence with the narrative's hostility toward the maternal, a hostility that is embedded not just in the plot line but also in the sign systems of costume described above, including Sally's rejection of her mother's "frumpy expensive British coat." Although Mrs. Watson-Courtneidge emerges as a rather stereotypical stuffy, upper-class mother, she is also a quotation from a much larger comic tradition that Lucy Fischer describes as the matricidal dynamic of mainstream comedy. Though Fischer is concerned with the narratives and representations of film comedy, her observations are particularly relevant to the elisions and repressions of the maternal in the Van Druten play. In the genre of the comic film, she tells us, "The figure of the mother is largely absent, suppressed, violated, or replaced. Thus, the genre urges us to Throw Momma from the Train."[30] Hostility toward the maternal, Fischer warns, is part of the larger problem of the positioning of woman in comedy, where she tends to vanish or diminish like the Lily Tomlin character in *The Incredible Shrinking Woman* (1981). In Sally Bowles's speech proclaiming what should be her independence, her freedom from respectability, this very self-diminishment is evident: Christopher has identity, he is "really" a writer, but as for herself— "I'm not even an actress, really." Yet the alternative for Sally within the text is another kind of vanishing act. When she is wholly under the control of her mother in the previous scene, Christopher protests that she has become invisible, as it were, through symbiosis: "Sally, don't. Don't let her! . . . You're disappearing, right in front of my

[30] Lucy Fischer, "Sometimes I Feel Like a Motherless Child: Comedy and Matricide," in *Comedy/Cinema/Theory*, ed. Andrew Horton (Berkeley and Los Angeles: University of California Press, 1991), 60–78. Arguing that the comic genre has been "obscured and appropriated by the masculine erotic" (64), Fischer points out that this dynamic is a patriarchal subversion of ancient comedy's genesis in female fertility rites. In the film tradition described by Fischer, the comic trajectory often portrays a motherless domestic scene, or even foregrounds a maternal scene without mothers in order to assuage multiple anxieties concerning maternal power as threat to male sexuality. In other scenarios, the threat of maternity circulates as a hostile joke throughout the text.

eyes" (78). The powerful mother has become the magician who can put the sexual daughter under her tweed cape and transform her into the conformist: "I hope the girl you knew *is* disappearing," Mrs. Watson-Courtneidge replies (78). Sally's mother is the only character in the play who is wholly unsympathetic. The only character not originating in Isherwood, she is profoundly stereotypical—very much a familiar construction from a comic tradition inimical to the maternal figure.

Van Druten's *I Am a Camera*, unlike any of the other adaptations, postulates Sally Bowles's freedom and sexuality in a directly inverse relationship to her identity as daughter. The narrative clearly requires a disavowal of the mother as the condition of the daughter's eroticism; the abortion sequence, in reinforcing this dynamic, reveals that the threat of daughterhood is actually the possibility of the woman's own motherhood. So although Mrs. Watson-Courtneidge does not appear until act 3, she operates in a ghostly and threatening absence in the first two acts. She is the person to whom Sally must write lies about life in Berlin (61); she is the parent that Sally perceives as the opposition to a liberating father (24–25); and she represents the specific ideology that Sally claims to have escaped (63). Significantly, Mrs. Watson-Courtneidge as the "real," biological mother is also the confining, antisexual alternative to a sexual, imaginary mother who is one of Sally's lies. When Fritz Wendel gives his initial, tantalizing description of Sally Bowles to Christopher, he hints that her seductiveness is a French trait passed to her through her mother: "Hot stuff, believe me. Ultimately she has a bit of French in her. Her mother was French" (14). Later Fritz reveals his belief that this is the cause of Sally's frankly sexual language: "You English are so *reticent*. . . . If Sally did not ultimately have a French mother, she would not talk about it, either" (28–29). In the original Isherwood story, Sally tells the same lie to Fritz and also admits the truth to the narrator, in a much more minor incident. The amplification of this same incident in the Van Druten play illustrates how the maternal discourse has become privileged enough seriously to inflect the narrative. For here, Sally's punishment for her lie is the appearance and oppression of Mummy herself.

Explaining this lie in the Van Druten play, Sally tells Christopher she thought it would be "impressive" to have a French mother: "I suppose it's like tarts calling themselves French names to excite men" (25). As this suggests, the French mother is a patriarchal construct and part of the male social/sexual order in which Sally has complete complicity. The invention of a male-constructed sexual mother is a significant alternative to Sally's real mother, whom she claims to "worship" even as she disclaims any likeness to her, predictably identifying herself instead with her father, who in turn represents career, mobility, freedom, and—as the play later reveals—sexual freedom as well: "Mummy's a bit county, but she's an absolute darling. I simply worship her. I'm afraid Daddy's side of the family comes out in me. You'd love Daddy. He doesn't care a damn for anyone. It was he who said I could go to London and learn acting" (24). Accordingly, in act 3 Sally is able to use her father as coconspirator to get rid of her mother, playing a joke on him that she knows he will "forgive" because together they approve of infidelity toward the mother: "I got a friend in London to send her an anonymous telegram telling her Daddy was having an affair. That sent her off in a mad whirl. But Daddy will forgive me. Besides, it's probably true—and I don't blame him" (81).

As the father-identified woman (or the impudent twelve-year-old boy), Sally often takes on male discourse and male prerogatives that are especially outrageous considering the boundaries of female discourse and behavior evidenced by Natalia and Mrs. Watson-Courtneidge. Sally's sexual mobility and casual infidelities, for example, are traditionally male privileges in the culture from which she has emerged. In the course of the play, Sally's sexual interests move rapidly and without remorse from Klaus to Clive to the bearded Yugoslavian. She shares with the male characters a discourse in which there is an assumption that relationships with the opposite sex are a series of opportunities or strategies. Like a fellow adventurer, Sally eagerly asks Fritz whether he knows Natalia is a virgin (23). She also gives advice about his tactics with Natalia that sounds more like talk from one-of-the-boys than from another woman: "I should think his best way with a girl of that kind would be to make a pounce" (23). Likewise, Sally's frank discussion with Christopher about Schneider's bosom is typically male in its objectification of the female body: "I say, Fräulein Schneider's got a big one, hasn't she?" (24). If Sally is comic precisely because she is a male impersonator, then the comedy again depends on the female absence traced by Fischer as a convention of the modern comic narrative: the possibility that the comedienne is funny because of her attempt to be like a man.[31]

Whereas Sally takes on the discourses and mobility of masculinity in order to remain the bohemian Joan of Arc, her mother is positioned as the opposition and threat to this kind of freedom. This is

[31] Ibid. Fischer contends that the sexual woman in the comic narrative is either eliminated, repositioned as the object of male jokes, or is present in the only mode available to the comedienne: as an imitation man, a transvestite joke about female desire for the phallus.

particularly made clear in the sequence in which Sally and Christopher decide, temporarily, to reform their lives. Sally's mother is named specifically as part of the ideological standards by which their own lives are "wrong" in comparison:

> SALLY: What's wrong with our way of life?
> CHRISTOPHER: Just about everything. Isn't it?
> SALLY: I suppose so. Not getting work. Not even trying to. That operation. The lies I've written Mummy. The way I haven't written home at all for weeks now (61).

Specifically, the "lies" to "Mummy" have been lies about marriage and stability: Sally has told her that she is sharing quarters with Christopher because they are engaged. The true story—the way of life that they here describe as "wrong"—is that she and Christopher have violated the most basic laws of both family and state by their refusal to be gainfully employed and their refusal to form the nuclear family. (And again, considering the protagonist's repressed gay identity, the "lies" and cover-up are displaced as hers.)

Yet in the ensuing scene, Sally balks at the idea of actually changing her life, much to Christopher's dismay. Sally insists that a life of adventure—sexual adventure—is still her most promising route to a good future: "Why, I could go to a party tonight, and I could meet the most wonderful man, who'd make all the difference to my whole life, and my career" (63). Christopher's disapproval of this is no surprise. In the ideological ideal that they both recognize as the antithesis of their rebellious, "wrong" life-style—the ideal of family, home, and motherhood—Sally would have a great deal less freedom than he would. She immediately talks about imprisonment: "I'm going to be quite different. But there's no reason I shouldn't go out. I don't have to shut myself up in prison" (63). Her angry response to his disapproval is especially interesting in that Chris is immediately conflated with Mummy: "You're almost as bad as my mother. She never stopped nagging at me. That's why I had to lie to her. I always lie to people, or run away from them if they won't accept me as I am" (63).

This particular "Mummy," who materializes as the most imprisoning aspects of mainstream ideology, may in fact also be, along with Sally's transvestism, another private homage to camp sensibility in the Van Druten play. In the "Mummy Is the Root of All Evil" chapter in *Camp*, Mark Booth outlines the function of the stereotyped bullying mother in what he calls camp's natural affinities to adolescence—the sense of exclusion from the "real" adult world and the resentment toward fascination with prescribed sex roles. In "modern folklore," says Booth, a boy's development into homosexuality in particular is linked to the stifling, "formidable" mother who is thus a stock camp figure.[32] One could argue that this is the Mummy configured by Isherwood in his account of his angry, adolescent rebellion against heterosexuality. "Girls" are what ideology "commands" him to desire: "My mother endorses them, too. She is silently brutishly willing me to get married and breed grandchildren for her. Her will is the will of Nearly Everybody, and in their will is my death."[33] The Mummy of the Van Druten play certainly bears some relationship to this stereotype of homosexual resentment and reveals that Sally's later triumph over respectability—over Nearly Everybody—is rooted in these marginal as well as mainstream conditions. It also points to the moments in the text and performance when Sally as transvestite is far more central to the play's gay subtext than Chris himself, whose option for stability becomes situated as the threat of the respectable Mummy in this scene and in the closure.

The threat of the maternal or Mummy and the significance of Sally's original lie (the French mother) are also central to *I Am a Camera*'s other major event focused on motherhood, the abortion. Like the lies grounding the truth about Mummy, this narrative event also foregrounds lying. First, Sally admits that she lied to herself about her pregnancy, "pretending it wasn't true" (31). She also lies to Schneider about how the baby's father jilted her: "It's I who doesn't want him, Fräulein. I don't ever want to see him again" (33). When the abortion is being discussed and planned, an entire comic scene is built around the untimely arrival of Clive, to whom everyone lies about what is going on (35–38). Sally also plans to falsify the conditions of the abortion: "And you know, I think perhaps you had better come with us," she tells Christopher. "We'll say you're the father. I think it looks better to have him along" (35). That is, Sally's claim that she lies only to people who "won't accept" her life-style actually reveals that she often lies to maintain the status quo concerning female behavior and middle-class values. The lies undress the transvestite, in effect, revealing the truth of the body underneath, and disclosing the "lie" of the double masquerade: here is the woman who is disguised as the impudent boy parading as the woman. But the naked, vulnerable female underneath must nevertheless be clothed in the protective falsehoods of the socially acceptable woman.

Most of all, Sally's lies concerning the abortion support the major lie that the play must maintain, that Sally as the erotic woman is neither mother nor daughter, that the maternal can be successfully

[32] Mark Booth, *Camp*, 87–89.
[33] Christopher Isherwood, *Christopher and His Kind*, 12.

eluded/elided so that sexual freedom is possible. But sexual freedom here is imagined on strictly patriarchal terms and constructions, as is made clear by the invention of the French mother, a mother who has no biological claims, who can never actually materialize to confirm the materiality of both childbirth and resemblance, but who instead exists as pure pornographic sign, the possibility "to excite men." In the scene just previous to the offstage abortion, Christopher admits that the abortion is a way to deny "the facts of life." Thinking aloud after the other characters have exited, he is significantly given some stage business that suggests fetishization as yet another disavowal of "the facts":

> CHRISTOPHER: (*Sally's slippers in his hand.*) And this is the kind of thing we used to make dirty jokes about at school. The facts of life. And here we go to prove they're not true, or that you can dodge them. (*Drops the slippers.*) And then we'll get pounds and pounds spent on us for dinner. And drink too much. And try to believe that none of it matters anyway (38–39).

In the previous scene, the possibility of Sally as a mother is in fact treated like his "dirty jokes." Here Sally glibly recounts that she got herself expelled from school by claiming to be pregnant: "And the headmistress said that a girl who could even think of anything so disgusting couldn't possibly be let stay on" (25). Sally's response to her real pregnancy is likewise revealed in terms of a joke, something "degrading," but also a confirmation of a truth otherwise disavowed, an imposition of "old rules." Because this speech occurs just after Schneider has assured her that an abortion is possible, the referent here—the "it"—slides in meaning among the abortion, the pregnancy, and a third "it" that seems to point to the more general conditions of female sexuality:

> CHRISTOPHER: It'll be all right, Sally, I know it will. The other girl was all right.
> SALLY: There's something so *degrading* about it, as well as dangerous. Oh, damn! Isn't it idiotic? All the men I've had, and there have been quite a lot, and this has to happen to me. It's awful, too, when you think about it, that there's something alive inside of you, that you can't have. That you mustn't have. It's like finding out that all the old rules are true, after all (34–35).

Although the referent to "it" slides here from the pregnancy to a larger female biological joke that seems to have been played on Sally, there is likewise an odd play on the phrase "that you mustn't have." In the sense of "having a baby," giving birth, this play creates a strange contradiction with the next sentence; the "old rules," so to speak, would mandate that she would in fact "have" the baby. But the gap between these sentences is the gap between the "rules" of the maternal—the recognition of the entire spectrum of female sexuality—and the law of the fathers in which Sally has lived and according to which the maternal can not only be denied and disposed of, but which also recreates a kind of sexuality necessitating that denial. As the self-identified daughter of the father, Sally has had access to the institutions and privileges of the symbolic; when her mother arrives on the scene to reclaim her into narcissistic symbiosis, Sally's opportunities and sense of self rapidly diminish. She metamorphosizes from the impudent boy of twelve to the incredible shrinking woman—submissive, passive, homebound. Her snappy, assertive language becomes nostalgic and clichéd: "Mummy's quite right, Chris. She really is. I ought to go home. To my past, and my roots and things. They're very important to a girl" (78).

The frustrations of this trajectory—Sally's disavowal of her mother and her alignment with paternal perogative, her grim choice between maternal confinement or patriarchal transvestism—are situated in the larger patriarchal scenarios that have been described psychoanalytically by Nancy Chodorow, among others. Although Chodorow's analysis seems to be limited by its model of the traditional, middle-class family structure, that model seems to be the basis of the fictional family in the Van Druten text. Chodorow describes the crisis of identity/boundary/symbiosis unique to girls because of a girl's greater continuity with the preoedipal maternal relationship. Because the female symbiotic bond is later not as completely severed as the male's, the issue of identity with the maternal can become defensive: "An oedipal girl's 'rejection' of her mother is a defense against primary identification, hence her own internal affair as much as a relational affair in the world. . . . what she is doing, in splitting her internal maternal image, is attempting by fiat to establish boundaries between herself and her mother."[34] In this struggle, the father is likely to emerge as the symbol of independence and separation. Chodorow makes clear, however, that this dynamic is reinforced by family and cultural organization. The father enacts separation from symbiotic merger not simply biologically, but by virtue of capitalist work habits and sociology as well. Chodorow suggests that there has not been enough study of historical shifts that have changed parenting habits over the past fifty years, even though throughout these shifts of history and

[34] Nancy Chodorow, *The Reproduction of Mothering: Psychoanalysis and the Sociology of Gender* (Berkeley and London: University of California Press, 1978), 124.

changes in the family, women remain primary nurturers and caregivers for children.[35]

But we do know that considerable cultural pressures emerged in the United States immediately after the war years that foregrounded the issue of motherhood in a public discourse, a discourse that reinforced the dynamic described by Chodorow. Whereas the paternal was situated as the active, independent economic support of the family, the maternal was situated as the home-confined emotional support. More than that, maternity became the site of a struggle involving not just definitions of sexual difference but also ideological and psychological pressures and resistances concerning what Chodorow calls the reproduction of mothering.

A key element in this discourse and controversy—the single source quoted most often in 1950s popular texts promoting and defining motherhood—was the Lundberg/Farnham pseudo-Freudian cure-all, *Modern Woman: The Lost Sex*, which illustrates how mystification of motherhood can operate as the underside of brutal misogyny. Attacking "modern woman" as the major postwar social problem, this text makes the argument that feminism parallels fascism as twin neurotic conditions characterizing modernity. Typifying all revolutionary activity as essentially neurotic (hence feminism's connections to both fascism and Marxism), Lundberg/Farnham then pinpoint maternal care as the single and overwhelming factor in neurosis; if the basis of all history is the childhood home, then the "principal instrument" of neurosis/unhappiness is the woman, either in her refusal to be maternal or in her faulty mothering. The refusal of woman to acknowledge her true nature, motherhood, and the subsequent "masculinization of woman" is thus responsible for all twentieth-century evil—or what Lundberg/Farnham call "unhappiness": feminism, fascism, alcoholism, juvenile delinquency, and so on, as defined in a series of appendices to the text. The chapter detailing the specific types of neuroses caused by specific lapses in mothering is titled "Mother and Child: The Slaughter of the Innocents."[36] In other popular texts of the era, the mystification of motherhood reveals its aggression against women in other ways, as in the hostile pop Freudianism of Philip Wylie's *Generation of Vipers*, which discloses its matricidal tendencies openly: ". . . I have researched the moms, to the beady brains behind their beady eyes and to the stones in the center of their fat hearts." Like Lundberg/Farnham, Wylie's theory of

[35] Ibid., 215.

[36] Ferdinand Lundberg and Marynia Farnham, *Modern Woman*, 298–321. See also 48–71 on the connection between women and "The Ghostly Epidemic" of neurosis, and appendix III, "Facts and Statistics Reflecting Unhappiness," 387–412.

"Momism" concludes that the world's problems—including World War Two—spring from motherhood: "Our society is too much an institution built to appease the rapacity of loving mothers. . . . Even while the regiments spell out 'mom' on the parade grounds . . . it is the moms who have made this war."[37]

This connection of the perils of modernity and modern woman's failure as mother (an eerie echo of the fascist sexual politics in Otto Weininger's *Sex and Character*) was manifest in alarming ways in 1950s articulations of "the woman problem." Lynn White, Jr., then the president of Mills College, addressed the issue of women's education in his treatise *Educating Our Daughters*. White suggests that contemporary college education fails to address women's real needs as future wives and mothers; a more suitable curriculum in women's colleges would center on family, the home, and culinary arts: "Why not study the theory and preparation of Basque paella, of a well-marinated shish kebab, lamb kidneys sautéed in sherry, and authoritative curry." This curriculum is directly tied into international politics, for only radical individualism and concern with the private sphere, he argues, will save us from totalitarianism. Accordingly, if a woman's "housekeeping extends merely into the local school board and park commission but not to the United Nations itself, her housekeeping is vain."[38] The progressive response to White, Mirra Komarovsky's *Women in the Modern World: Their Education and Their Dilemmas*, argues against White's most blatant antifeminism and presents the case for a curriculum for women that is wider than paella and authoritative curry; but it, too, assumes that "the educated and the gifted housewife . . . is doing the most important job in the world." Specifically, she concedes that good motherhood is the single most important factor in child rearing, although "the father's contacts" with the child should ideally be of high quality, too. The result of this division of parenting in much postwar discourse on maternity is the positing of an essential womanhood as redeemer of modernity. As Komarovsky notes: "An appeal is currently directed to women to redeem our overcompetitive and conflict-ridden world through the exercise of the distinctively feminine virtues."[39] While Komarovsky concludes that men had better share in that challenge, too, other contemporary texts leave the responsibility completely to the maternal. Agnes E. Meyer's popular autobiography, *Out of the These Roots: The Autobiography of an American*

[37] Philip Wylie, *Generation of Vipers* (New York: Rinehart, 1942), 192, 203–4.

[38] Lynn White, Jr., *Educating Our Daughters: A Challenge to the Colleges* (New York: Harper, 1950), 78, 108–10, 105.

[39] Mirra Komarovsky, *Women in the Modern World: Their Education and Their Dilemmas* (Boston: Little Brown, 1953), 292, 297–98, 300.

Woman, includes a fierce antifeminist chapter that ends with this appeal: "For as mother, woman represents the focal point of time and eternity and the perpetual triumph of life over death."[40]

Given this discursive context, and the singularity of Sally's mother in the Van Druten play as opposed to all the other adaptations, Mrs. Watson-Courtneidge seems to materialize from specific historical conditions that, in Macherey's terms, are the latent issues reworked in the text. In these latent conflicts, the mother is all-powerful, all-threatening, all-to-blame—and simultaneously privileged with an almost hysterical frenzy. She is the focal point of time and eternity, but she is also fierce biological and psychological necessity; Lundberg/Farnham specifically describe the childless woman as nonorgasmic, the unmarried woman as dangerously "distorted."[41] In an era that situates motherhood as both cause and cure of universal neurosis, the vanquishing of Sally Bowles's Mummy must have been a particularly powerful kind of exorcism. Little wonder that the crowd cheered to discover that Sally could discard the monster/magician's tweed cape and maintain herself as motherless child beneath. But the price of that enactment of freedom is a disavowal of the maternal that, at its most hostile, reveals a continuation of Wylie's misogynist Momism. When Sally angrily accuses Christopher of being "as bad as my mother," the reference could just as well be Wylie's mom-monster, with beady eyes and heart of stone. The Van Druten play seems to make the misogynist gesture in helpless response to the misogynist offstage space.

Like the moms whom Wylie specifically compares to Hitler both for their treachery and nostalgia for the great family past,[42] the mothers in *I Am a Camera* are positioned in a disturbing relationship to the text's antifascist critique. The vanquishing of Mummy is parallel to the vanquishing of Schneider, who simply disappears from the text after Christopher explodes against her anti-Semitism in the next-to-last scene. Mrs. Watson-Courtneidge appears immediately after this argument and expresses a more subtle kind of anti-Semitism; when Christopher reports that he hurt his hands in a fight concerning Jews, she asks loftily, "Why were you fighting about *them*?" (78). She then makes it clear that problems concerning "*them*" should be of no interest to the rest of the world. Criticizing Christopher as the dangerous, leftist drifter, she tells him, "You live in foreign countries, and you let yourself get involved in obscure political issues that are

---

[40] Agnes E. Meyer, *Out of These Roots: The Autobiography of an American Woman* (Boston: Little Brown, 1953), 357.

[41] Ferdinand Lundberg and Marynia Farnham, *Modern Woman*, 271, 296.

[42] Philip Wylie, *Generation of Vipers*, 193–94.

7. Broadway play *I Am a Camera* (1951). The triumph of Sally (Julie Harris) is the vanquishing of motherhood and Mummy (Catherine Willard), much to the pleasure of Chris (William Prince).

no concern of yours" (80). Although it was communism rather than German fascism that was of political concern in 1951, this characterization of Watson-Courtneidge (as the 1930s isolationist who would let Hitler's agenda go unchecked) works to reinforce the essential villainy of Mummy—and seamlessly perpetuates the cultural discourse of faulty motherhood as the source of the world's ills.

This historical reference—the representation of an isolationist attitude in the play's era—foregrounds the question of which history, exactly, is being portrayed here. Anxiety concerning German fascism and anti-Semitism has been conflated with anxieties about voracious, monstrous motherhood that seem more directly related to postwar issues in American culture than to prewar Berlin. Yet the issues here, I would argue, are more circuitously connected. As described in my first chapter, the sexual politics and practices of the Third Reich were obsessively focused on motherhood, not just in the institution of "pure" Aryanism, but also as an inevitable result of the absolute sexual polarizations by which a "natural" order could emerge. This Nazi sexual agenda so much resembles that described in *The Modern Woman* that Lundberg/Farnham address the issue themselves in defense. Although the Nazis "ordered" women back into the home, they explain, nothing was "accomplished" except the increased birthrate, the "multitude of obvious neurotics that was Germany of the Third Reich." In contrast, they point out, their own agenda is not to "order" women into the home, but to "attract" them there: "If, however, women could be *attracted* into organizing their lives more closely around the home and spheres of nurture, an important step would have been taken in making the home a place where children might grow up into well-balanced adults."[43] In spite of this differentiation of method, Lundberg/Farnham then plot out their own ideal agenda, which is strikingly similar to the earlier fascist one: childless women would be gradually eliminated by law from some public spheres; they should not be allowed to teach children, for example, "*on the ground of theoretical (usually real) emotional incompetence*" (italics theirs). Mothers would receive cash subsidies for each child; women would "naturally" be drawn to the "nurturing" professions as opposed to the more "masculine" areas of business, law, mathematics, technology. And the ensuing population problem would be solved by "imposing public controls to prevent the breeding of certain strains."[44]

Although Lundberg/Farnham's proposals represent an extreme of postwar sexual politics in the United States, the romanticization of motherhood in public discourse nevertheless duplicates the Third Reich's ideology of a "natural" sexual order as the beginning of a better world order. The mandate for a pure, essentialist motherhood that would save the world from totalitarianism is a continuation of the Nazi totalitarian doctrine of the sacred maternal; Mother's Day in the Third Reich was officially connected to a celebration of the Aryan heritage. Even the contradictions within the American postwar motherhood discourse—the hostility and misogyny most blatantly evident in Wylie—parallel the misogynous roots of the Reich's cultivation of pure womanhood.

Van Druten's *I Am a Camera* both reworks and resists these condi-

[43] Ferdinand Lundberg and Marynia Farnham, *Modern Woman*, 364.
[44] Ibid., 364–65, 370–71.

tions and anxieties, both duplicating and disavowing German fascism in its contentions and in its tension of narrative and performance. The imprint of 1950s ideology is most evident in the play's conventions of comedy, the aesthetic structure that works to disavow or malign the maternal. Yet the victory over the maternal, Sally Bowles's final resistance not just to domesticity but to the constraint of male narrative as well, is a subversive choice in 1951 American culture. Unlike the film version of this play, in which Sally Bowles is finalized as a joke, to reappear in another narrative, Van Druten's version has Sally "just go on and on, as she always has—somewhere" (84), Christopher says. Could the dynamic stage performance of Julie Harris actually be contained by Christopher's closure, his assertion of final control as storyteller/photographer? "The camera's taken all its pictures, and now it's going away to develop them. I wonder how Sally will look when I've developed her?" (84). Ironically, the language here reinforces one last displacement of the maternal, a male wish to "develop" Sally as his own creation.

The reviews and subsequent discussions of the play show little interest in Christopher's story. The rave reviews for Harris's performance and energy onstage further undermine the text's claim that this play is the Sally "developed" by Christopher Isherwood. This is not, after all, the story of Gigi, whose triumph is almost flawlessly consistent with a Lundberg/Farnham agenda: the triumph of domesticity, the bachelor as the unhappy man who must be appropriated into marriage. Although both plays were soon made into films, it will be the story of Sally Bowles, not of Gigi, that will be updated for adaptations in the next three decades, to replay a fascination with the sexually free cabaret singer, but also to replay the fascination with the story's fascist background and the operations of both as irresistible spectacle.

Chapter Four

SALLY, LOLA, AND PAINFUL PLEASURES

THE FIRST ON-SCREEN SALLY BOWLES

CONSIDERING THE ORIGINS of the character Sally Bowles as the "good heter stuff" of the cinema-loving Isherwood, the eventual film adaptation of *Goodbye to Berlin* seems to spin the project full circle, as the character who had been constituted as body, materiality, and spectacle replays that dynamic literally through the visual apparatus of cinema. Although the Broadway play also materialized the character physically, I have argued that the foregrounding of artifice may have allowed the performance of the androgynous-looking Julie Harris to work subversively within the multiple perspectives of theatrical space. But the 1955 film version of *I Am a Camera* controls the spectatorial vision more rigidly. Although film spectatorship is itself a multiply determined process that operates within historical, psychoanalytical, and intertextual dynamics, it is nonetheless directed by a camera gaze more restrictive than the gaze of the theater audience. The camera can privilege bodies with close-ups and specific framings; it can fetishize by what it discloses as well as by what it chooses to hide. Though Julie Harris played Sally Bowles in both the stage and screen productions, her presence as body and sign is constituted quite differently in the latter because of the visual apparatus and mediations of cinema.

Perhaps the most obvious mediation is the camera's ability to constitute or at least posit Julie Harris as a seriously sexual woman through camera angles and framings that do not disclose the actress's actual smallness and slightness. Sally Bowles is filmed within the conventions of mainstream cinema, which feminist film theory has argued is both fetishistic and disavowing; in her low-cut nightclub costume, for example, Sally is framed three-quarter length so as to center the heart shape of her gown just above her breasts. In a long sequence occurring when Sally has moved into Chris's room and into the bed behind the curtains, the camera plays out a lingering obsession with what can and cannot be seen of her body; underclothes are thrown from behind the curtains, Sally's head and arm poke out with the suggestion that she is otherwise nude, and she walks around

8. *I Am a Camera* (1955). The early sequences establish the sexiness of Sally Bowles (Julie Harris) through visual jokes: the discovery of flimsy underwear by the landlady (Lea Seidle) and the quilt that keeps slipping off Sally.

wrapped only in a bed quilt which in one shot supposedly slips, teasing the viewer with what Chris (Laurence Harvey) has seen.

In short, there is less opportunity in the film version for the casting of Julie Harris to work as a subversive dynamic that can comment ironically on the construction of female sexuality. Instead, the editing and framing contribute to the standard cinematic coding of the sexual woman. Sally's sexuality on-screen is purely costume, gesture, stylized postures. Rather than suggesting the possible mutability of transvestism, the film instead constructs femininity as masquerade, a layering of accoutrement and disguise. Director Henry Cornelius had originally talked to both Elizabeth Taylor and Jean Simmons about playing the part of Sally;[1] because these more "attractive" leading la-

[1] This detail about casting comes from A. H. Weiler, "By Way of Report" (*New York Times*, 20 June 1954): sec. 10, p. 5.

dies—by Hollywood standards—had at least been considered, the camera work and costuming (or disguising of Harris) may have had to be particularly excessive as overcompensation, a way for the text to insist on a sexuality not obvious in the less glamorous actress. The first third of the film is literally riddled with visual jokes and "sexy" references (underpants found on the chair, the bed quilt that threatens to slide off, a peek at her garters), as if the director were anxious to establish the sexual attraction of the character who was billed as the "wanton" Sally Bowles.[2]

No matter who played Sally, it is clear that her story was outside the guidelines of mainstream film in the United States in the 1950s, though Van Druten had worked on a film script and hoped a Hollywood production was possible. Correspondence in the case files of the Motion Picture Producers and Distributors Association (MPPDA) shows that Joseph I. Breen, chief of the Production Code Administration, warned that the story line of the original Van Druten play contained several elements strictly prohibited by the code, including the abortion incident and unacceptable (sexually frank) dialogue. Breen also quotes the code itself on the play's most blatant violation, as he sees it: " 'Pictures shall not infer that low forms of sex relationship are the accepted or common thing.' "[3] Shortly thereafter, Breen's office received the Van Druten film script and deleted so much of its story and dialogue that Van Druten dropped the project altogether.

But even though an American production was discouraged, a film project of *I Am a Camera* was possible in Great Britain specifically because of a recent change in the censorship code there. British films had previously been awarded certificates of approval classified A and U (adult or universal/family); then in 1950 an X certificate was devised by the British Board of Film Censors to designate films that would be objectionable to any but an adult audience. Most critics agree that the X rating was utilized to indicate truly frank sexual material on the screen only after a long, hesitant process of financial experimentation, and it did not actually make an impact until later in the decade. Nevertheless, the new certificate is what made possible the filming of *I Am a Camera*. British producer John Woolf bought

[2] This was the characterization of Sally used in a prerelease piece in the *New York Times Magazine*. In this same article, a photo of Harris as Sally is juxtaposed with a George Grosz 1930s cartoon, with the claim that Grosz had been an inspiration for the "mood" of the film. See "Grosz is a 'Camera,' " (24 July 1955): 2.

[3] Letter to Joseph Sistrom of Hollywood, 18 May 1953, Motion Picture Producers and Distributors Association Case Files, Herrick Library, Academy of Motion Picture Arts and Sciences (hereafter MPPDA).

the screen rights and obtained Henry Cornelius, a successful director of film comedy, who in turn lined up John Collier—with whom he had previously worked for Alexander Korda—as screen writer.

Cornelius was at the time enjoying a particularly successful reputation as the director of the 1953 hit *Genevieve*, which itself had required some negotiation with the censors in order to obtain a U certificate. This film is about two couples—one married, one not—in an antique-car race, the destination of which is a weekend at a hotel in Brighton. While the dialogue contains several innuendoes about the plans of the unmarried couple once they reach the hotel, strategies of comedy conveniently interfere to ruin the plans by having one of the women (Kay Kendall) pass out after too much champagne. Raymond Durgnat praises the Kendall character as "exceptional" among otherwise misogynist portrayals of the sexually free woman in British film who is usually "the glittering frisky popsy." Kendall, he argues, at least was able to suggest a likable human being with some intelligence and character.[4] Although Kendall's character is notable in contrast to the later treatment of Sally Bowles, the film is, ironically, most interesting in comparison to American Production Code–approved texts for its treatment of sexuality not in relation to the "popsy" and her frustrated boyfriend, but to the married couple. It is the latter who are the object of the film's most obvious double entendre and who have the frankest lines of dialogue about their intentions in their double bed (which itself would have been prohibited by the code). Generally, the popular success of *Genevieve* illustrates a relative sophistication about sexuality in British film which the Production Code in the United States would prohibit for almost another decade. The material of *I Am a Camera*, however, was considerably more risqué even by British standards, and Cornelius and Collier made a number of changes to produce a script that "soft-pedaled" Sally's promiscuity, according to the filmmakers. The writers felt it necessary, for example, to alter the pregnancy/abortion sequence by having Sally change her mind about the abortion and accept motherhood, and by later having the pregnancy turn out to be a false alarm. Julie Harris com-

[4] Raymond Durgnat, *A Mirror for England: British Movies from Austerity to Affluence* (London: Faber, 1970), 183. The best known British "popsy" or sex symbol of the 1950s, on the other hand, was Diana Dors, the glamorous screen actress in the tradition of Marilyn Monroe. See Christine Geraghty's essay "Diana Dors" in *All Our Yesterdays: 90 Years of British Cinema*, ed. Charles Barr (London: British Film Institute, 1986), 341–46 for a more thoughtful examination of how Dors self-consciously manipulated her own image as vulnerable child or as commodity. Far from being the mindless "popsy" of many of her films, suggests Geraghty, Dors often portrayed characters caught in specifically class-oriented conflicts.

mented during the shooting, "There's no denying that in the film Sally is seen through slightly rose-colored glasses."[5]

British censorship was not all that the filmmakers had to deal with. Though the film could be made and distributed in Great Britain, the producers also realized that the larger, more profitable market was the United States, and the adaptation from the play was also aimed at being able to obtain a Production Code approval overseas, a project that in the long run failed. When the film came to the United States, critics in the trade journals proclaimed that its dialogue and situations were "the raciest ever used in a picture."[6] In fact, however, except for the pregnancy scare and references to the abortion, many of the situations in the film are stock ploys from both American and British comedy. Much of the comedy is derived from the convention of the self-proclaimed bachelor whose life is invaded by a "madcap" woman (in the tradition of 1950s comediennes such as Lucille Ball or Mitzi Gaynor, and later in the multiple Rock Hudson–Doris Day romances). In a framing device that opens and closes the film, "Christopher Isherwood" is the successful postwar London writer who arrives at a literary cocktail party to discover that the writer being honored is his old friend from his prewar Berlin days, Sally Bowles. In the flashback that makes up the film narrative, Chris tells the story of how, in 1931, he found Sally singing (rather poorly) at a Berlin nightclub and was obliged to take her home with him because she had nowhere else to go. In explaining to her that the setup is strictly a gentlemanly arrangement, he provides the comic/sexually teasing stock situation of the unmarried couple forced to spend a night in the same room, as in *It Happened One Night* (1934) and *I Was a Male War Bride* (1949). The example of "racy" dialogue that was quoted consistently in critics' previews and reports in trade journals is one of Sally's lines when she arrives in Chris's room: "What shall we do first—have a drink or go to bed?" she asks. Even though the context makes it clear that Chris will sleep on the sofa, the sexual innuendo spoken so casually by a woman apparently strained the bounds of the standard sharing-the-room scenario, and the line was quoted incessantly in the prerelease discussions and in later reviews.

[5] Stephen Watts, "On Shooting a 'Camera,' " *New York Times* (23 Jan. 1955): sec. 2, p. 5. Ironically, this change in the abortion plot resulted in a fierce complaint from another *New York Times* writer, Bosley Crowther, who claimed that it resulted in the most "distasteful" part of the film because Sally's explanation (about miscounting her days) "is literally too embarrassing to repeat." "The Anomoly of a Code" (14 Aug. 1955): sec. 2, p. 7.

[6] "Distrib Fears 'I Am a Camera' May Be Too Candid to Win Prod'n Code Seal," *Variety Daily* (23 June 1955).

The film text apparently attempted to temper Sally's story by imposing the running comic line of the prim professorial-type bachelor being shaken and "persecuted" by the sexual young ingénue. When Sally proposes that they set up a platonic kind of housekeeping together so that Chris can better attend to his writing, the predictable catastrophes occur with Sally's adventures and calamities. As in the stage play, the appearance of the wealthy Clive makes possible for Sally and Chris a grander style of living for a short while; their supposedly comic decadence is illustrated in a bizarre "wild party scene" organized around Chris's recovery from a hangover.[7] After Clive jilts them in the midst of their preparation for their world tour together, Sally discovers she is pregnant, and Chris feels driven to do some inspired writing in order to pay for the abortion. Just as he obtains the money, though, Sally shocks him by announcing she has changed her mind, intends to keep the baby after all, and plans a happy marriage and family with him. The "comic" nightmare that ensues (the bachelor trapped!) is suddenly interrupted by Sally's realization that the pregnancy had been a false alarm, and that she is in fact leaving Chris for new adventures. But the trapped-bachelor ploy is resumed again in the final scene following the flashback: Sally reappears twenty years later and once again threatens to take possession of Chris's life and sanity as she drags him away from the cocktail party. The pregnancy/abortion narrative, then, is funneled into the "comic" story of the threatened bachelor, supposedly to appease the censors on both sides of the Atlantic. Instead, the maintenance of the comic mode—Sally is never punished, never repentant—was exactly what prevented the American film industry censors from approving the film.

The controversy concerning the MPPDA censorship actually made the film a minor American cultural event of the mid-1950s, a test case for the power and effectiveness of the Production Code seal. As a successful—and uncensored—stage play that was adapted into an "objectionable" film, *I Am a Camera* entered a debate that had just previously been fought by Otto Preminger with his 1953 film *The Moon Is Blue*, similarly adapted from a successful play. The William

[7] The "wild party" sequence apparently made an impression on the American audience. It was featured in a two-page photo spread in *Life*, "Wildest Movie Binge" (8 Aug. 1955): 35 and likewise praised by *Time* as a sequence that "should go down in movie history." See review of *I Am a Camera* (15 Aug. 1955): 58ff. Herman G. Weinberg, in "Before the Putsch," *Film Culture* 1 (1955): 25, claimed that the episode, "as happens seldom on the screen, is really wild." Perhaps what impressed these reviewers was the representation of several intoxicated people on the screen at once, including Sally Bowles.

Holden/Maggie McNamara vehicle, made notorious by the use of the word "virgin" and the topic of virginity in innuendo, was denied a Production Code seal and therefore not booked at mainstream theater chains which had the policy of showing only code-approved films. But because of the great amount of publicity involved, it went on to become a box-office success on the art-house circuit. Advance publicity about *I Am a Camera*'s potential problems with the MPPDA system—a series of press releases to *Variety* and the *New York Times* in the months preceding American release—suggests that the film's distributor, Distributors Corporation of America (DCA), may have hoped for the same reverse effect; *The Moon Is Blue* became a standard reference in the debate and news reports. Nevertheless, after the code seal was actually denied to the Cornelius film by the MPPDA on July 21, 1955, a few weeks before its scheduled American release, the DCA requested an appeal on the decision in order to enable wider distribution. The appeal was denied, but as the publicity surrounding the case escalated, it became clear that *I Am a Camera* would be enormously profitable even in limited bookings, as American audiences lined up in hope of seeing a "racy" film.[8] Because most state censors passed the film, and because the result of the controversy was an even bigger audience, the MPPDA came under heavy criticism in this case, which may have influenced the revisions of the code in 1956, revisions that included allowances for reference to abortion. The distributors took advantage of the controversy, meanwhile, by explicitly advertising it: ads and lobby cards featured Walter Winchell's comment that the film "makes the dialogue in *The Moon Is Blue* sound like a nursery rhyme!"

This discussion of Cornelius's *I Am a Camera* has already introduced two very different explanations of how the film makes meaning. On the one hand, in describing the camera's constitution of Julie Harris as Sally Bowles, I am referring to film theories that privilege individual spectatorship, the apparatus as enunciation, the operations of suture, and the psychoanalytic dynamics that have been especially useful for feminist film theory. On the other hand, in situating the film within its institutional and commercial context, examining the impact of censorship on its mode of production and reception, I am not only privileging the space outside the text but also suggesting a different approach to spectatorship by positing a spectator who is part of the vast network of culture that has previously offered read-

[8] See "DCA Prez Fred Schwartz Asks Major Prexies Overrule Code, Help Him Get 'Camera' Seal," *Variety Daily* (29 July 1955): 1ff. and "Despite Lack of Code Seal, 'Camera' Grosses 300G in Ten Key City Dates," *Variety Daily* (13 Oct. 1955): 1ff.

ings and positionings of the film. The visual apparatus of cinema makes spectatorship a unique problem in reading; as my discussion of Isherwood's original "Sally Bowles" made clear, however, the wider problem is how to read texts both as semiotic systems and as historical productions. Similarly, I am most interested here in the points of intersection between these two approaches, the issues that converge and that provide avenues of dialogue in order to acknowledge the multiple ways in which a text makes meaning. Inevitably, any reading privileges certain elements of the text to the exclusion of others; but insofar as possible, I am attempting to avoid a denial of either the textual or contextual operations. Instead, I am interested in their interaction, in their play in the dynamic of cultural and cinematic codes. This interaction includes the discourse surrounding the film's release, not only the advertisements but also the prerelease publicity, critical response, and in this case, the Production Code dispute, all of which position the film for its contemporary audience within a given framework of expectation and meaning.[9]

In the case of Cornelius's *I Am a Camera*, these cultural discourses in the space outside the film are particularly significant in regard to the text's constitution of the Sally Bowles character and female sexuality. Because the film project of *I Am a Camera* was initiated and carried out in conditions of censorship and prohibition, and because the resulting censuring and advertising of the film in turn privileged the "raciness" of the text, then the constitution of the Sally Bowles character is specifically tied up with 1955 conceptions of what constituted the kind of female sexuality that was considered *literally* threatening to the public. This threat was specifically articulated by the powerful Legion of Decency, whose rating system was intended both to boycott certain films and to protect public morality, which explained that *I Am a Camera* received a Condemned rating because it "offends Christian and traditional standards of morality and decency."[10]

Recent film theory has illustrated that censorship is an especially rich point of interrogation between elements of film text and cultural context. Once censorship is construed not simply as a constraint or prohibition but also as part of an interrelated process of the "play" of

[9] For an extended study of this contextual theory of cinema and spectatorship, see Barbara Gail Klinger, "Cinema and Social Process: A Contextual Theory of the Cinema and Its Spectators" (Ph.D. diss., University of Iowa, 1986). For an example of two potentially disparate readings—contextual and psychoanalytical—that come into focus, see Lucy Fischer and Marcia Landy, "*The Eyes of Laura Mars*: A Binocular Critique," *Screen* 23 (1982): 4–19.

[10] "Legion of Decency Nix on 'Camera' is Appealed to Cardinal Spellman," *Variety Daily* (15 Aug. 1955): 1ff.

power, in Foucault's terms, then it is easier to theorize a textuality that is not handicapped by a text-context dualism.[11] The ensemble of practices involved in *I Am a Camera*, for example, reveal particular consequences of institutional and cinematic codes. With the constraint of having to "soft-pedal" the sexuality represented in the film, conventions of visual comedy, even slapstick, are deployed, as well as the comic scenario of the helpless, harassed bachelor, which in turn sets up a cinematic dynamic of an odd, comic masochism. Unlike all the other adaptations, this film constitutes Sally's sexuality as a series of jokes that emerge not from camp humor but from mainstream codes of film comedy.

This film also points to particular crises or tests of the constitution of sexuality at a certain historical moment. The critical response that this film was the "raciest" of its time, while certainly an exaggeration for the sake of publicity, provides a useful historical gauge of how the character Sally Bowles functioned in 1955 as a cinematic sign. Passages of film texts that come under scrutiny as objectionable provide a justification for privileging those passages because they point to specific anxieties and contentions concerning morality or politics.[12] In the case of Sally Bowles, those passages serve to point out how this character was configured within the context of an ongoing controversy concerning the public enunciation and representation of female sexuality. The irony of this testing of representation is that the visual spectacle of Julie Harris as sexual could only be constructed by careful editing and framing; except for the MPPDA's objection to a close-up of Sally's underwear found on a chair, these visual jokes and references were never the site of the film's controversy.[13] Instead, the controversy centered on dialogue—what could be said and implied in public about female sexuality—and on the situation of a pregnancy scare and the possibility of abortion. Other current films in release were certainly more explicit about extramarital sexual relations— Katharine Hepburn's implied adultery in *Summertime* (1955) or the question of fidelity in *The Seven Year Itch* (1955)—and certainly far sexier—Cary Grant and Grace Kelly's fireworks scene and double en-

[11] This is Annette Kuhn's argument in *Cinema, Censorship and Sexuality, 1909–1925* (London: Routledge, 1988).

[12] Lea Jacobs persuasively makes this case in "The Censorship of *Blonde Venus*: Textual Analysis and Historical Method," *Cinema Journal* 27 (1988): 21–31. Also see Jacobs's extended discussion of censorship in relation to constitutions of female sexuality in *The Wages of Sin: Censorship and the Fallen Woman Film, 1928–1942* (Madison: University of Wisconsin Press, 1991).

[13] Letter to Fred Schwartz of Distributors Corporation of America from MPPDA's Geoffrey M. Shurlock, 2 Feb. 1956, MPPDA.

tendres in *To Catch a Thief* (1955) or Ava Gardner's sultry performance in *The Barefoot Contessa* (1954).[14]

Although Breen had quoted the Production Code in censuring *I
Am a Camera*'s portrayal of "low forms of sex relationship" as "the
accepted or common thing," later MPPDA correspondence with the
film's distributors specifies the objectionable lines and scenes: Sally's
line about having a drink or going to bed; her comment about not
being "exactly what some people consider a virgin," and later her
claim that she has reformed and is "practically a nun"; all references
to an abortion; Natalia's claim that if necessary, she would live with a
man before marriage; and Sally's flaunting of the panties found on
the chair. To make the film acceptable, explained Breen's successor,
Geoffrey Shurlock, there would need to be "a proper voice for morality to present concretely the wrongness of Sally's life," perhaps an
off-screen comment by the Laurence Harvey character.[15] In short,
the MPPDA was insisting that female sexual activity cannot be explicitly spoken of, cannot be joked about, and could only be represented
as morally wrong (as explicitly stated, for example, by the Katharine
Hepburn character at the end of *Summertime*). Significantly, in *The
Moon Is Blue* it was virginity rather than alleged promiscuity that was
at issue with the industry censors. That is, in both the Preminger and
Cornelius films the issue of sex is defined as the status of female sexuality, its potential pleasures or choices, represented not visually (the
most we see of Sally's sexual activity is an occasional kiss with Clive)
but present as a self-articulation. For surely the impact and scandal
of Sally's line "What shall we do first—have a drink or go to bed?" is
the scandal of female desire, desire without coyness and outside of
the more circuitous discourses of flirtation. Sally is not only able to
name her condition—"not exactly what some people consider a virgin"—but also to place it satirically within the range of sexual options
available to women by later claiming herself to be "practically a nun."
What is at issue here, too, are the codes of comedy discussed in my
previous chapter in relation to the stage play; if Sally's line about the
drink or bed is funny because she is taking on male discourse and
male options, the censors in 1955 were not amused.

According to *Variety*'s report of the film's sneak preview in New
York, *I Am a Camera* "caused eyebrow lifting" among the general pub-

---

[14] Distributors Corporation arranged a special screening of the film for several hundred invited guests and afterwards gave them a questionnaire that cited these particular films as examples of what was currently acceptable for the MPPDA. The audience
by a large majority agreed that *I Am a Camera* deserved Code approval. See Henry
Hart, "Economic Censorship," *Films in Review* 6 (1955): 507–10.

[15] Letter from Geoffrey Shurlock to Fred Schwartz, 2 Feb. 1956, MPPDA.

lic over some of the same things that concerned the MPPDA. In addition to the dialogue about a drink or bed and the reference to virginity, the other controversial line of Sally's, according to the preview audience, is her reply to the question of why she wears green fingernail polish: "To attract men. I like to feel their eyes running up and down me like mice."[16] However, critical response to the film and its controversial nature varied considerably. Although the dialogue was often cited for its unusual "honesty" and candor in being "adult," some critics agreed with the MPPDA that the film is too "raw" for general movie audiences. *Variety* had little sympathy for Sally, characterizing her as falling "somewhere between a nympho and an amateur prostitute" who borders on "idiocy." *Time* was enthusiastic, calling it "brimful" with "sex," but *Commonweal* chided the "vulgar and embarrassing" abortion discussion, as did the *New York Times*.[17] This range of American critical response reveals that the 1955 film construction of the Sally Bowles character touched on sensitive cultural issues that were very much in process, unsettled, and contending with an emergent permissibility concerning what could be said and what could be represented in a mainstream medium on the topic of sexuality.

In contrast, the film's reception in Great Britain suggests how strongly audience expectations qualify and shape not just what is institutionally permissible but what kind of reading will ensue as well. After five years of experience with the X-certificate films, but more importantly, within a recent film history in which sexual desire does not have to be codified with elaborate flirtatiousness or coyness ("Make love to me," the wife on the bed asks outright in the U-certificate *Genevieve*), the British audience was far less directed to focus on the film's sexual representations. Although advertisements in the United States emphasized the film as one that tested the limits of the forbidden—the "raciest" dialogue ever, "The Most Delightful Double Exposure Since Adam and Eve," the comparison to *The Moon Is Blue*—the public discourse surrounding the film at the site of its origin was much more varied. British advertisements sold the film as a kind of Marx Brothers comedy (a comparison in fact made by some critics in regard to the film's party scene), touting it as "the gamiest

[16] "Distrib Fears 'I Am a Camera' May Be Too Candid to Win Production Code Seal," 1.

[17] For a sampling of these diverse opinions, see Weinberg, "Before the Putsch"; also reviews of of *I Am a Camera* in *Variety* (4 Aug. 1955) and in *Time* (15 Aug. 1955): 58ff.; Philip Hartung's review in *Commonweal* (9 Sept. 1955): 565; and Bosley Crowther's review in the *New York Times* (9 Aug. 1955): 29.

and wackiest picture of the year."[18] The dailies, of course, could not ignore the film's censorship debate in the United States and were eager to sensationalize the film's presentation of Sally, often emphasizing her shocking behavior as it had to do with alcohol as much as with men. Often, garish headlines ("DOES IT SHOCK YOU TO SEE A GIRL LOOKING LIKE SHE'S SOZZLED?" "SAUCY SAL—THE X GIRL") were followed by articles explaining that the film was more silly than sexy.[19] But in lengthier and more serious reviews, particular interest was vested in the film as an adaptation of the Isherwood story, and critics often expressed disappointment that Isherwood's concerns about German fascism were not sufficiently represented. The Cornelius film seems to "miss the point of the original material" concerning "social and economic insecurity," said the critic for *English*. The review in *Sight and Sound* likewise situated the film as an adaptation from both Isherwood and Van Druten, characterizing it as "a knock-about farce quite incidentally supposed to take place in Isherwood's Germany." The *Times* gave the film a lukewarm review but mainly criticized it for not dealing enough with the historical background, and the *Daily Film Renter*, conceding that it is an "adult" film, also expressed surprise that the "corrupting politics that rotted Berlin life of the time make but a cursory appearance." The *New Statesman* expressed irritation about the awkward portrayal of Isherwood, and though admiring Julie Harris's performance, regretted that this Sally Bowles is "lost" to "the Isherwood reader."[20] In short, an entirely different set of concerns appears in these readings, revealing very different priorities concerning history and literary origin.

The comparatively heightened sensitivity to the historical issue— the film's subdued references to the growing Nazi threat—is no surprise. Unlike the United States, Britain was still feeling the impact of

---

[18] In contrast, theater ads in the United States punned on the camera in the title and the possibility of what might be seen. "The Most Delightful Double Exposure Since Adam and Eve," the ads read. See the *New York Times* (5 Aug. 1955): 15 and (7 Aug. 1955): sec. 2, p. 4. The appeal to voyeurism was even more specific in the accompanying graphics: two photos of Sally's body, one cropped at the neck showing her wearing a low-cut, very short dress which, with her legs crossed, revealed the tops of her stockings; the other photo is cropped at the waist, showing her leaning over to lift her skirt and adjust a garter.

[19] Leonard Mosley, "Does it Shock You to See a Girl Looking Like She's Sozzled?" *Daily Express* (19 Aug. 1955); Donald Zec, "Saucy Sal—the X Girl," *Daily Mirror* (14 Oct. 1955).

[20] See reviews of *I Am a Camera* in *English* 11 (1956): 20; David Robinson's review in *Sight and Sound* (Winter 1955/56): 150; the review in the London *Times* London (17 Oct. 1955): sec. C, p. 3; Leslie Wood, "The New Films," *Daily Film Renter* (14 Sept. 1955): 4; and William Whitebait, "Sally in Whose Alley?" *New Statesman* (22 Oct. 1955): 508.

the recent war in material ways; sugar and tea continued to be rationed until 1952, butter and meat until 1954. A great number of Britons had just moved from the unattractive prefabricated temporary housing built quickly after the war or were living in areas newly reconstructed since the bombings. Nor was reconstruction complete; 1954 photos show children in Birmingham playing in leveled bomb sites. Significantly, the Cornelius film in fact opens in what is presumably contemporary London, so that the flashback to Weimar Germany has particular historical impact. A here-and-now is quickly established, a "safe" modern-day London from which a darker previous time is remembered. Laurence Harvey as Isherwood is specifically privileged as a "historical" observer; the transition shots between the contemporary scene and the flashback show him posed at the window looking out on the streets of London and then, as he explains in the narration, onto the streets of 1931 Berlin, on New Year's Eve. Even "New Year's Eve" signals a marking of history that is ominous from the point of view of the diegetic contemporary London—but also for the specifically adult (X-certificate) audience to whom the film is directed. Nineteen thirty-two would be the last full year of the Weimar Republic and would thus mark the beginning of a political development that had had enormous impact on the 1955 adult spectator in Britain who was still living with the material evidence of the Third Reich. Little wonder there was disappointment that Isherwood's story of the rise of Nazism had been almost completely submerged in the story of Sally Bowles.

Yet the very insistence of the historical framing device in this film and the substitution of the story of Sally for the story of Nazism therein suggest another dynamic at work engaging both historical and sexual issues. The story of a distant and hazardous past turns out to be the story of a sexually free, would-be nightclub singer who is entirely at home in "decadent" Berlin—represented visually as a series of smoky, noisy bars and Nazis on street corners and represented in the narrative through the subplot of the anti-Semitism complicating Fritz Wendel's courtship of Natalia. On the one hand, this narrative seems to be situated in the completely safe and victorious world in which both Nazism and cultural/female decadence have been defeated. Sally is encoded first as only a memory, even an occasion for nostalgia, a character contained in the narrator's story. But there is a virtual eruption of a "real" Sally at the end of the film, and though this is coded as part of the comedy of the harassed bachelor, Sally's reappearance is a threat that seems to be simultaneously sexual and historical; whereas all else has changed (Chris is the mature, successful writer; the Nazis have been defeated), Sally is the wild element of

Weimar Berlin that is startlingly omnipresent. The film strains to distance itself from an evil past, supposedly resolved by the war itself, which operates here as an entirely unreferenced event, but an event logically necessary to make possible the transition from Nazis-in-the-street Berlin to the tidy world of the London literary cocktail party. Yet that world is neither safe nor reliable. It has been infiltrated by women, for one thing, and its stories about itself seem to resist the neat closure its tellers would prefer. Even its story about a clear demarcation between corrupt prewar Berlin and safe, innocent London slips with Sally's appearance.

There is good evidence that the conflation here between historical and sexual anxiety is grounded in the gender debates and anxieties of the 1950s in Great Britain, which in many ways resembled those in the United States during this era. The British work force was in fact infused by women between 1951 and 1961, so that the percentage of married women who worked rose from one in four to one in three. At the same time, popular discourse continued to portray women as essentially domestic and maternal, playing down woman's work as not "real" work while emphasizing her attractiveness as a consumer. Not surprisingly, as in the United States, the female presence in the work force precipitated a host of cultural stratagems that encouraged women to reassume their "proper place."[21] One of the most powerful of these stratagems was the circulation of arguments presented by a text that is very much the British equivalent of *Modern Woman*. This is John Bowlby's 1953 guidebook on motherhood, *Child Care and the Growth of Love*, with its warnings about what it coined "maternal deprivation." Though not as radical in its recommendations as Lundberg/Farnham, this text similarly argues that maternal care of children is the single most important factor in determining the child's later mental, physical, and social development. The role of the father is posited minimally, though Bowlby concedes that "fathers have their uses" as providers of "economic and emotional support" for mothers. Like *Modern Woman*, Bowlby's text points to faulty motherhood as the source of all modern ills, because the child "deprived" of continuous maternal care is the future social offender: "Deprived children, whether in their own homes or out of them, are the source of social infection as real and serious as are carriers of diptheria and typhoid."[22] The rise of both divorce and illegitimate births in Great

---

[21] For an extended description of this situation in relation to British cinema, see John Hill, *Sex, Class, and Realism: British Cinema 1956–1963* (London: British Film Institute, 1986), 7–18.

[22] John Bowlby, *Child Care and the Growth of Love* (1953; Harmondsworth, U.K.: Penguin, 1959), 12–13, 181.

Britain since the war are twin targets of Bowlby's argument, pointing to the more general cultural alarm about growing postwar permissiveness. The divorce rate in Great Britain, for example, had quadrupled by 1950 from its prewar yearly average. Generally, then, just as cultural pressure increased to keep women contained as full-time mothers within the nuclear family, statistics on employment and divorce show the opposite trend.

The case is not simply that the maternal anxieties that can be traced in the "matricidal" comedy of the Van Druten stage play are once again in evidence in the film. "Mummy" has vanished from the Cornelius text, but the potential motherhood of Sally Bowles remains a problematic issue, epitomized in a shocking iconographic treatment of Sally as a beast-mother and in Chris's "nightmare" scene in which he imagines Sally in infinite reproduction of herself. The anxieties focused on motherhood and female sexual power are both articulated and complicated through particular cinematic codes: first, an alignment of the camera gaze with a male gaze that is posited as author and authority; and second, within a positioning of the spectator in a problematic psychoanalytic dynamic that, given the film's historical references, operates to reinforce the film's political ideology concerning the English "survivor" of Weimar Berlin.

As is true of Isherwood's original Sally story, Cornelius's *I Am a Camera* is based on a joke about texts and sex, authors and authority. Because of the comic narrative of the bachelor/intellectual versus the show girl that attempted to "soft-pedal" the play's more disturbing sexual themes, this adaptation is far more focused on the anxiety of the young writer than the stage play had been, and even more centered on the female threat to author/authority than Isherwood's story. Moroever, the cinematic apparatus establishes this authority with particular force, in that the camera gaze is literally Chris's in key scenes, reinforced by a deep, authoritative voice-over that relays and controls the narrative, and that suggests a trustworthy unity of character as shots are matched to this voice.[23] The film begins with a shot of Laurence Harvey striding assertively toward the camera while the voice-over proclaims, "My name is Christopher Isherwood," identifying himself further as writer and "confirmed bachelor." The latter is surely a cue to the film's comic convention that will require an even-

[23] As Mary Ann Doane points out, the voice-over is a powerful strategy in the "homogenizing" of mainstream film: ". . . the voiceover commentary places the image by endowing it with a clear intelligibility," thus ensuring a "oneness" which "is the mark of a mastery and a control." "The Voice in the Cinema: The Articulation of Body and Voice," in *Narrative, Apparatus, Ideology*, ed. Philip Rosen (New York: Columbia University Press, 1986), 345.

tual romantic attachment no matter how much the "bachelor" resists. To a certain extent, then, the grave authority of his voice and demeanor is already undermined by the mode of comedy. But his continued voice-over narration is a powerful assertion of Chris's control of the narrative, especially in conjunction with the film's multiple eyeline shots confirming that we see what he is seeing.

In addition, the self-introduction as real-life Christopher Isherwood gives the narrator and the character Chris much more authority than the character had had in the stage play. The status of his celebrity, as the opening scene makes clear, is not simply as writer but specifically as male writer. At the literary cocktail party, his voice-over tells us with disdain: "A gaggle of female journalists was in evidence, from which I gathered some lady's murky memoirs were being foisted on the public." The scene clearly inscribes male writing and writers as serious and "real" (they wear glasses and dark suits, they gather quietly to listen to Chris's story) and female writers and texts as frivolous (the women laugh and clink their wineglasses noisily in the next room). The publisher's cocktail party, Chris tells us, is usually for "the more dubious items on their list." He warns us that "the more worthless the book, the more they need alcohol and noise to launch it." Thus Sally's triumph—the fact that she has a text of her own, that she has succeeded in Chris's territory—is seriously undermined because it is positioned in a literary world in which women writers are their own dubious joke. Ironically, throughout all the adaptations, this is the only narrative suggestion that Sally Bowles could possibly tell her own story, a possibility immediately extinguished in the same scene, when an insert shot reveals the book cover (illustrated with a sketch of a woman flashing a leg in a sexy come-on) and then continues with Chris's narrative. The book's title, *The Lady Goes on Hoping*, presumably suggests that the resolution or "hope" of her story is her eventual "end" in matrimony—the event toward which the film's narrative has in fact been poised with the introduction of the "confirmed bachelor." Sally's own text, then, turns out to be the standard Sally Bowles iconography. Rather than getting the story in her own words, we get Chris's story of Sally, told from what is posited as his obviously superior position, the observing "camera," as he calls himself in his flashback.

Because this text involves the visual apparatus that can literalize Isherwood's original metaphor, the dynamic that had been apparent in the Isherwood story dominates the film text and accounts for many of the major changes in John Collier's adaptation. Sally as body and materiality, surface and spectacle, both threatens and is recontained by a symbolic order that can speak itself with authority and organize itself with the power of language. Chris's voice-overs control the narrative by matching spoken text to shot; what he says is reinforced by what is seen. In contrast, the emptiness of Sally's language—a feature of all the Sally Bowles texts—is reinforced by the contrast between what she says and what the camera shows. When Chris appears in a particularly silly jungle outfit with knickers and safari hat, she gushes that he looks "marvelous, absolutely irresistible." When he takes her to the expensive Russian restaurant, she takes on the lofty discourse of the upper class and begins to babble to the equally impoverished Chris about how they will be "doing a lot of sailing" in the coming spring—while the camera focuses on Chris's shocked expression. Because her language is so full of hyperbole, Sally sounds equally unreliable when she tells the truth: she tells Chris in the same scene that he is insensitive, a bad writer who has no understanding of women, and the camera shows Chris responding with a condescending smile. In general, the structure of shot-countershot that is used here for comedy also works to undermine Sally's status, reliability, and authority.

Chris's self-description in the film as the objective cameralike eye is presented as a historical necessity. Because of the grimness of the encroaching Nazism of those days, he explains, he "took refuge in a convenient phrase" and "ducked the issue" by becoming the "camera, quite detached." As one of the objects of his vision, Sally's first appearance is in a show girl act, the scenario that Mulvey claims is the cinematic overdetermination of the dynamic by which the male gaze controls female spectacle. Chris is positioned as a member of the audience, in what has become the traditional location of the leading man observing the desirable woman. In turn, Sally first appears in shots that are eyeline matches for what he is seeing. Thereafter, the visibility of Sally's body constitutes the running joke about her threat to Chris as writer, a joke set up in their initial conversation in which he tells her that his writing excludes sex from his life: "You need not be afraid of me. There's no room for that sort of thing in my life. You see, I have work to do, very important work." Though Sally agrees not to interrupt his "important work," this is also the occasion of her famous line about having a drink or going to bed, followed by a scene in which, as Chris tries to fall asleep on the sofa, Sally flings clothes and underwear, piece by piece, from behind the bed curtain. And though this scene is part of the comic tradition of the supposedly chaste couple sharing the room (borrowing, in fact, from the more famous curtain divider of *It Happened One Night*), what is at stake here is not virginity (Sally has casually referred to her lack thereof) but an intellectual/sexual virginity necessary for the male writer, a guard against pollution by female sexuality.

As body and spectacle threatening the "important work" of writing—which itself is valorized throughout the text by the status of a "real" Christopher Isherwood who wrote about a serious historical crisis—Sally is aligned with the visible and the subsequent fetishizations of what-can-be-seen in relation to her body in these first scenes. Her underwear flies through the air and is discovered in Chris's chair; her head and arm peek from the curtains; the bed quilt she is using for a robe "slips" from around her. When she reaches out from behind the bed curtains to find the light switch, her arm makes a teasing come-hither gesture to the sleeping Chris; and when Natalia in the next scene makes a serious speech about unemployed Germans who "do not have clothes to cover them," Sally pops her head out of the curtains to exclaim that she is one of the unclothed. In two different scenes, Sally lifts her skirt in front of Chris in order to adjust her garter strap in the stock allusion to secret female space.

At one point in the film, when Chris's writing is going badly, Sally volunteers to help out, suggesting that he improve his characters by giving them distinguishing physical features or making them inherit a great deal of money. "Oh, talk about something you understand," he retorts. "Don't be stupid." But what Sally is actually suggesting as a construction of character duplicates how she herself is constructed in the film text, as body and materialism, the uncontrollable matter and life force in opposition to control, order, rationality.

Because of mainstream cinematic demand for a sexy, masculine leading man, the conflation of authorship/masculine sexuality is far more central in the *I Am a Camera* film than it had been in the stage play. The most overt identity of Chris's writing with his sexual ability occurs in the same scene in which Sally attempts to give him literary advice. This is, in fact, Chris's only heterosexual move in the film. Depressed about his writing and supposedly drinking too much wine with dinner, he responds inappropriately to Sally's comforting hug and pounces on her, with the implication that despite his writer's block, he is not entirely impotent. This scene is also a partial remedy for what Isherwood would describe in later interviews as the chronic problem with the Sally/Chris relationship in the 1950s adaptations. Chris had to be represented both as handsome narrative hero and also as someone who does not have a sexual relationship with an attractive, available woman. In this scene, Sally backs away, explaining lamely, "I know I talk like a fool very often, but . . ." This response sets up another rhetorical premise that is perhaps similar to Van Druten's attempts at making Sally's promiscuity ambiguous: Sally may not really be as promiscuous as she seems, and therefore it is not really odd that her relationship with Chris is chaste.

The scene in the Russian restaurant both confirms Chris's identification of sexuality with authorship and makes possible the shift in sexual power that permits his continued role as chaste protagonist. When Sally attacks his writing ability, he responds by attacking her sexual ability, and a strange argument ensues that pits his supposed talent against her supposed attractiveness. Masculinity and the ability to write are positioned in hostile opposition to female sexuality. Chris presumes that accusing Sally of "inadequate sex appeal" is a fair rebuttal of her accusation of inadequate writing ability, which is also for him sexual ability or male authority. Chris is instantly proven wrong in this scene as Sally immediately uses her flirtatious skills to attract and pick up the wealthy American Clive (Ron Randell), whose own masculinity is proven in another way: he picks up the tab for everything and subsequently becomes Sally's lover.

With the addition of money as another signifier of masculine sexual power, this arrangement serves both to strain and to decenter the actual "romance" of the text. Sally is certainly the film's most interesting, dynamic, and attractive character. Her position as threat to written text and anti-intellectual is positioned within the trajectory as a supposedly good-natured joke about the "popsy." Chris, then, should be her leading man, her romantic interest. Instead, the film provides Clive as lover, a caricature of masculinity, puffing his fat cigar and sporting an intellect roughly on the level of the foxtail Sally wears around her neck. Ironically, Clive's limitations are precisely the signifiers that allow Chris to remain the protagonist of his own story. Once again, the superior camera/observer views a freakish or inferior subject, this time the materialist American. Associated purely with physical indulgence, Clive is a fitting mate for Sally, who is pure matter, pure image. In the restaurant scene, she and Clive epitomize consumership, the devouring of the physical world. Even as a caricature of masculinity, Clive is nevertheless aligned with Sally against Chris's writing. When he later jilts them both, Sally defends him against Chris and his "precious book" by saying emphatically of Clive and with obvious contrast to Chris: "He was a *man*." Together, she and Clive make a powerful obstruction for Chris's pursuit of his "important work," his writing. "I could have written a masterpiece," Chris says later, had it not been for the interventions of these two friends.

As opposition and threat to language and authorship, Sally is aligned with the visual and specular in several specific ways. Even before Sally appears on-screen, Fritz describes her power as visual; she won his heart, he says, because she gave him "the look of the eyes."

When Sally meets him again at the cabaret, she claims she remembers him because of his own eyes. Later, she explains her delight at having men's eyes run up and down her body "like mice." This acknowledgment of the gaze as sexual dynamic is repeated in the song she sings at the cabaret, celebrating not just love at first sight, but love based entirely on sight:

> I saw him in a café in Berlin,
> The kind of place where love affairs begin.
> I only saw the lamplight on his hair.
> He stopped and picked his hat up from a chair.
> A minute later, he paid the waiter,
> And when I dared to look again he wasn't there.
> Never ask me how or why,
> That I can't explain,
> I can't forget him, I never met him,
> I only saw him in a café in Berlin.

This song, the melody of which recurs throughout the film as Sally's theme, is a reference to the film quotation that may be most direct in the cabaret scene, but that also functions in the narrative strategy of the Cornelius film. "I Only Saw Him in a Cafe in Berlin" is a German song that was introduced to Cornelius by Marlene Dietrich because, Cornelius said in an interview, "it has the flavor of the Thirties."[24] As I discussed in my first chapter, the influence of Dietrich and her German connection to the 1930s is due to the impact of her role in Von Sternberg's *The Blue Angel*, a powerful precedent in the film tradition that uses the cabaret show girl as an iconographical representation of Weimar "decadence" and the rise of fascism. The Dietrich character, Lola Lola, from that film is in many ways a precedent for the Sally Bowles of the Cornelius text: the vital, sexually charged opposition to the bookish professor, the material threat to the realm of the written text and the schoolroom. In the traditional reading of this film, the professor's schoolroom, the social order, is disrupted and its representative, the professor himself, destroyed by the attraction to female sexuality, which seems to function in Lola like a blind, devastating force. Whereas feminist readings of Dietrich and this film may reveal more complicated dynamics, it seems to me that the more reductive and binary interpretation—the intellectual versus the show girl—is the basis of the cultural allusion here. The visual dynamic of *I Am a Camera* is also similar to that of *The Blue Angel*. Like Lola's inner dressing room—from which underpants similarly are tossed—

---

[24] Stephen Watts, "On Shooting a Camera," 5.

9. *I Am a Camera* (1955). For her Berlin cabaret performance, Sally Bowles (Julie Harris) wears a sequined tuxedo-like costume recalling Marlene Dietrich's performance tuxedo in *Blonde Venus* (1932).

the bed curtains in Chris's room become the secret female space to which the film alludes with hints of the garters, panties, slipping bed quilt. The materialization of female sexual threat literally lands on Professor Rath's shoulder and in Chris's chair.[25]

Though the "ruin" of Chris in *I Am a Camera* is diverted into a comic trajectory, his torments at the hands of Sally similarly shift the power dynamic in this film. As Chris's tidy male order and world gradually collapse, his suffering escalates into a "comic" frenzy that is virtually hysterical, and that operates in a more complex dynamic than simple repression or disavowal. In the narrative as told by Chris to his colleagues, Sally's entrance into his life signaled chaos, loss of discipline, and loss of control. His "pure bed" is appropriated as secret female space, his books are replaced by Sally's kooky stage props, and women's undergarments appear on his desk chair. Significantly, his actual loss of control is physically enacted in scenarios of regression and humiliation as he slips further and further from detached bachelorhood and as Sally grows more and more powerful in her performances in front of the camera and Chris. On the one hand, Chris's voice-overs and position as "camera-eye" watching Sally continue the dynamic by which he has control of the gaze; through Chris's perspective, for example, we see Sally lift her skirt to adjust her garters before she leaves Berlin. Yet a considerable shift in power occurs between Sally's cabaret performance, when Chris regards her with superiority and even pity (and when she is positioned as the most traditional object of the male gaze), and the later famous "wild party" sequence, in which Sally presides as crazed, queenlike mistress of ceremonies while a helpless, infantilized Chris is physically overtaken—literally wrapped up and carried around, groaning, in the background. The spectacle of female sexuality offering itself up to the male gaze has been replaced by an elaborate spectacle of male suffering. This is a remarkable reversal of the cinematic dynamic involving the fetishization of the female body, the construction and disavowal of Sally as body/materiality versus the superiority of male language and text, a dyamic that usually operates as a sadistic punishment or repudiation of female eroticism. But in this film, an opposing dynamic is also at work, privileging the "comic" punishment and suffering of the male protagonist at the hands of a powerful woman. While the camera has aligned the spectator with Chris as the voyeur in relation to Sally, this spectator position has shifted from

[25] See Peter Baxter's study of this phenomenon in *The Blue Angel* which concludes that the fascination and fear of hidden female space is the repressed text of the Von Sternberg film: "On the Naked Thighs of Miss Dietrich," 18–25.

dominating gaze to pleasurable suffering—from sadism to maso-chism.

It is true that the elaborate punishments and humiliations of Chris are always situated within the codes of mainstream comedy. These include the familiar scenarios of the stuffy professor flustered by the sexy, "madcap" siren; the prim bachelor suddenly turned into house-maid; the introvert victimized by the "crazy" who involves him in em-barrassing public situations. But it is also true that in each case, spec-tatorial pleasure is achieved through the viewing of suffering imposed by the controlling woman, and that Chris's humiliations greatly undermine his sexual and authorial power. The early scene at the cocktail party establishes Chris as voyeur (looking out the win-dow) and authority (the successful writer looking back at history), but he is displaced from these positions fairly early in his narrative, when he becomes the spectacle of humiliation. Immediately after Sally's sexual threat is established in the first-night sequence with the bed curtains and underwear, it operates to embarrass Chris in front of his landlady, his friend Fritz, and his upper-class pupil Natalia. Chris's more severe humiliations begin when he proposes to "set up house-keeping" with Sally in a platonic way that would enable him to do his writing, thus supporting his identity as author and head of a patri-archal household. Sally promises to cook, clean, and darn his socks—but she promises this as she poses and dances dramatically with a large feather fan. In the next shots, it is Chris we see in an apron, washing dishes and scraping messes from the stove while a well-dressed Sally waves good-bye and rushes away. In the following shot, Chris admits that he is a failure as a writer.

As Chris loses his authority, his body literally begins to go out of control. In one scene shortly before the appearance of Clive, Chris develops an imaginary crippling disease which he presents to Sally and Fritz like a child looking for an excuse not to go out with his parents. He complains that he has "locomotor ataxia . . . a form of paralysis," which he demonstrates by crossing his leg, hitting his knee, and failing to get the usual reflex action. He literally cannot "get it up." The "paralysis" is quickly cured by Fritz, who points out that Chris had aimed at the wrong spot. But it is the first time that Chris shows an inclination toward a more blatant spectacle of suffering, the acting out of pain in front of Sally, who is in fact paralyzing his ability to write.

The appearance of Clive, and Sally's subsequent romance with him, escalate Chris's humiliations and suffering. In the restaurant scene, he cringes and pleads with Sally, trying to tell her he does not have the money to cover the check, while she devours everything she sees. Just as he is accepting the fact that he will take the punishment, so to speak, and go to jail for it, Sally picks up Clive who in turn picks up the check. Chris accompanies the new couple around town for the night, but the sequence ends with an embarrassing rejection; he tries to follow them into a taxi which drives off without him, leaving him alone on the street.

The most bizarre humiliation sequence, and the most obviously masochistic, begins then with Chris's ensuing hangover, which he deliberately interprets as a serious disease because, he says, he was "furious with Sally." But his enactment of revenge rapidly develops from fantasy to fact as he literally loses all control and actually does suffer. Sally and Clive wrap him up like a baby and carry him off to Clive's hotel, where he is subjected to painful "cures," beginning with the arrival of a stern German doctor armed with a huge rectal thermometer. Chris's cry of pain is heard by Sally and Clive in the next room, in the film's first shot that does not include Chris; his control as narrator is suddenly undermined with a view that cannot be the "camera eye" of the writer at the literary cocktail party. Furthermore, Sally and Clive are now positioned, with the spectator, as witnesses overhearing the offscreen suffering, so that Chris's position has been reversed from narrator to object.[26] With this total physical control, Sally and Clive now also control what was supposed to have been "Chris's story about Sally," to paraphrase the narrative as set up by Chris for his writer friends. Having appropriated the camera gaze, these two characters arrange what turns out to be the narrative's strangest detour and most excessive spectacle when they decide both to invite in several more specialists and to plan a huge party to cheer up the patient.

The famous "wild party" sequence is orchestrated with the suffering of Chris at the hands of increasingly sadistic doctors, while the suite fills up with drunken revelers and Sally merrily presides over a festival of pain. Chris is pummeled by a huge, rough masseur; boiled and frozen by a suspicious pair of hydrotherapists; and finally electrocuted by a ghoulish doctor who resembles a Medieval torturer. Throughout, Sally literally dances with glee as Chris fills the air with screams of pain and becomes a particular kind of comic spectacle— helpless, infantile, on display to a jeering audience. The perverse eroticism of the sequence is only thinly concealed; at one point a cu-

[26] Mary Ann Doane suggests in "The Voice in Cinema: The Articulation of Body and Voice" that the pleasure of overhearing is "not unlike the voyeurism often exploited by the cinematic image" (342).

rious audience surrounds his bed as he is stripped, and his groans during the massage are unmistakably sexual.

Although the regression of the scholarly writer to helpless victim is part of the comic trajectory, the reversal of power that reaches an exaggerated pitch in this sequence invokes a larger issue in feminist film theory. Psychoanalytic accounts aligned with Mulvey's political utilization of Lacan theorize that the performing woman in the film text must be "controlled" within the narrative and by the apparatus, through demystification, punishment, or fetishization. But because this theory posits a wholly powerful and subjugating male gaze, it does not account for the power and authority that a character such as Sally retains even if her sexuality is fetishized. For instance, it does not deal with the woman-as-spectacle who herself claims the power of the gaze, as Sally does quite literally even before she becomes the viewer of Chris's suffering: at the end of the earlier nightclub act, she takes a monocle out of her blouse and pops it into her eye socket in an odd gesture that might be a prop for her song about love based on sight, but that is a literal return of the audience's gaze upon her. More generally, as many scholars have pointed out, in theorizing the trajectory of the classic cinema as essentially sadistic toward female sexuality, this account of narrative and spectatorship is limited in its capacity to describe the pleasures of this cinema for female spectators.

In acknowledgment that the dynamics of spectatorship are far less monolithic than originally described by Mulvey, theorists have more recently been interested in the ways in which spectatorship and identification operate in more complex, often bisexual operations.[27] One alternative point of entry into this problem, and one that is particularly relevant to both Sally Bowles films, shifts the question from (male) sadism to the question of masochism; and although male masochism in particular has received a good deal of attention, the psychodynamics of masochism can perhaps be applied to female spectatorship as well. Whereas the arguments of and responses to Mulvey center on pleasure as *mastery* of lack, the arguments around masochistic theory center on the primacy of pleasure-in-being-mastered. One basis for this argument for pleasure-in-unpleasure is based on Freud's descriptions of the primary and secondary processes' interaction that postpones pleasure or gives it a "circuitous" route through negation and repetitions of loss-scenarios.[28] The other, preoedipal

---

[27] See Tania Modleski's summary of this debate in her introduction to *The Women Who Knew Too Much*, 9–13.

[28] Kaja Silverman reads Liliana Cavani's *The Night Porter* along these lines in "Masochism and Subjectivity," *Framework* 12 (1983): 2–9. Silverman suggests here that patri-

basis, and a source of both keen interest and fierce debate for feminist scholars, is Gilles Deleuze's study *Masochism: An Interpretation of Coldness and Cruelty* (1971), which is deployed in Gaylyn Studlar's theorization of a "masochistic aesthetic" in her study of Von Sternberg's Paramount films with Marlene Dietrich. The controversies surrounding this approach concern the overall political implications of a theory that privileges the relations of powerful motherhood against the helpless infantalized subject. That is, while Mulvey's theory (of the sadistic trajectory) illustrates how the dynamics of cinema reinforce patriarchal power structures, a theory of masochism based on the powerful, preoedipal mother suggests a politics in which phallic power is disavowed and considerably diminished. Cornelius's *I Am a Camera* and the later film adaptation, Fosse's *Cabaret*, are significant test cases for this debate, not only because a masochistic trajectory is clearly involved in each, but also because the political situation of each is so closely embedded in the sexual politics. How does male masochism function in a narrative in which what is being disavowed is the ultimate Fatherland? In both films, the powerful, sexually charged Sally Bowles figure overwhelms the more passively situated young man who indeed seems to enjoy his suffering; and the question in each case is the metonymic use or transformation of female sexual power within a narrative concerning another kind of passive positioning, the witnessing of the rise of the Third Reich.

Studlar situates the oral mother in the preoedipal realm in which the father is entirely absent, and the mother represents not the threat of castration, but the possibility of imminent separation and lack-of-boundary—symbiosis—which is both alluring and threatening. The scenario of masochism thus recreates a "heterocosm" in which the female is a powerful, idealized figure, and in which pleasure operates ambivalently on two levels. It originates in the mother who represents both the "dread" of devourment and the promise of "blissful incorporation," and there is additional ambivalence in the identifications made in this scenario, the continual shifts between pain and pleasure, separation and merging. As a result, Studlar writes, masochistic desire tends to be polymorphous, diffuse, and not polarized along rigid lines of gender: "Through the mobility of multiple, fluid identifications, the cinematic apparatus allows the spectator to experience the pleasure of satisfying the 'drive to be both sexes.' "[29] Studlar points

---

archal culture indeed produces texts in which the female subject often takes up the powerless, masochistic position, but the pleasure of those texts resides in identification not with the dominator or subjugator but with the suffering and passivity.

[29] Gaylyn Studlar, *In the Realm of Pleasure: Von Sternberg, Dietrich, and the Masochistic Aesthetic* (Urbana and Chicago: University of Illinois Press, 1988), 35. This urge "to be

out that masochism as defined by Deleuze encompasses a broad range of narrative possibilities, including the witnessing of the primal scene, oral fantasies of devourment or abandonment, and the oedipal triangle.

Although Studlar's theory avoids the rigid binary positionings characteristic of analyses based on Mulvey's Lacanian model, it has come under attack precisely because it does not deal with the less ambiguous and less pleasurably flexible positionings of women in film that are of political concern.[30] No matter how much ambivalence exists between male "dread" of and "ambivalence" toward women, the consequence continues to be a sadistic and dominating positioning of men toward women in mainstream cinema.[31] The sexual dynamics of Cornelius's *I Am a Camera* are similarly complicated by both sadism and masochism, as my analysis already suggests, and the introduction of the Cornelius film into these particular arguments can perhaps point to some specific interfaces of the psychoanalytic dynamics of spectatorship and other, contextual concerns of my study: censorship and postwar readings of fascism.

In particular, *I Am a Camera* may illustrate how a textual dynamic can be reframed, as it were, by cultural practices and allusions. On the one hand, the paradigm of a "masochistic aesthetic" is a particularly useful description of the power shifts in this text. The Chris character, for example, never regains his early (sadistic) mastery as the superior camera eye once Sally has had an impact on his narra-

---

both sexes" that is rooted in the desire and dread of symbiosis is also deeply ambivalent, but the cinematic apparatus provides the "dream screen" which "permits the spectator to relinquish body-ego and superego control" (189). Studlar's subject is the Dietrich/Von Sternberg Paramount films in which Dietrich "is not the passive object of a controlling look" but rather "looks back or initiates the look . . . akin to the powerful oral mother's return of the child's gaze" (48). The male characters in these films, meanwhile, "often play out the conflict between identity and desire, superego and ego, repression and perversion" (57).

[30] In "Masochism and Male Subjectivity," *Camera Obscura* 17 (1988), Kaja Silverman objects to Studlar's argument as "a determinedly apolitical reading of masochism, which comes close to grounding that perversion in biology" (66 n. 51). Silverman's own interest in masochism here resides in how the male masochist theatrically enacts a larger "cultural subjectivity" as one whose meaning comes from the Gaze of the Other. Silverman, too, is interested in Deleuze, particularly in Deleuze's contention that what is punished for the male masochist is his resemblance to the father, particularly in the simultaneous yearning for and fear of the dominating oral mother. But she claims that Deleuze's own methodology betrays him—that is, that his refusal to acknowledge the place of the paternal shows exactly how much phallic power resides in this dynamic (57).

[31] Tania Modleski makes this argument in *The Women Who Knew Too Much*, 11. See also Modleski's critique of Deleuze in "A Father is Being Beaten" (71).

tive, except for a brief period which is then subject to a comic reversal. Instead, Chris is progressively more dominated and more out of control, while the codes of comedy concerning the reluctant bachelor also require him to be eventually "overwhelmed" (indeed, devoured) by the leading lady, as he is in the last scene. Generally, the character of Sally Bowles as both written in the script and as performed by Harris is far more powerful and engaging than that of Chris, conforming to the loving inflictor of suffering described by Studlar. Yet a great deal of the text's energy goes into the "control" of this power through the assertion of Chris as author and authority—and that dynamic is a social one, not a psychoanalytic one, relying on the extratextual knowledge of Isherwood and his Berlin novel. The major premise behind the film's running joke is also a specific, misogynist premise located in a cultural allusion: the social assumption that only men are "real" writers, the misogynist tradition traced out by Gilbert and Gubar, among others, that the pen is the penis and serious writing is a legacy of the fathers. In addition, the extratextual elements involved in the pleasures of the text involve a specific history, as well. This is a narrative that allows Chris self-righteously to punch a Nazi storm trooper in a conflation of male and moral authority, whereas the sexual authority of Sally is increasingly aligned with the dubious politics of Berlin. So although Studlar's theory is perhaps most useful in acknowledging Sally's power in the psychodynamics of the text, it also needs to be augmented by the acknowledgment of these extratextual resistances (as well as the textual authority ascribed to Chris) which in fact reveal more hostile political positionings of female sexuality.

In accounting first for the psychoanalytic sources of spectorial pleasure, I have pointed out the shift that occurs from the early fetishizations of Sally's body-as-spectacle to increasing focus on the spectacle of the sufferings and humiliations of Chris, a shift perhaps cued by Sally's previous "return of the gaze" during her cabaret performance when she popped the monocle into her eye socket and smiled back at the audience. The next narrative shift, the decentered romance of Sally and Clive, provides many elements that Studlar describes as central to masochistic fantasies: the primal scene, the oedipal triangle, fear of devourment by the oral mother. The Clive romance furthermore provides the key element of phallic disavowal for Chris; he can take the punishment, so to speak, but the guilt belongs to the sexual father. In the restaurant scene in which Clive makes his first appearance, Sally literally becomes the devouring mother, eating and drinking everything in sight, proclaiming a large and seemingly infinite "hunger." Though Sally has been coded as the sexually active woman so far in the text, the relationship with Clive is the first time Chris and the film audience actually witness heterosexual activity, with Chris in the position of the helpless, excluded child. Chris's immediate response the following morning is his literal infantalization when he is wrapped in sheets and carried away to the film's ultimate masochist spectacle, the party scene, which closely conforms to Studlar's description of the "spectacle of decorative and erotic excess that displaces conventional narrative 'progress.' "[32] His elaborate suffering in this scene, far from being a "nightmare," as he himself describes it in the voice-over, operates like a masochistic wet dream, as his regression to the infantile is complete and Sally reaches new heights of power and control. He wakes the next morning, he tells us, feeling "like a new man" who "could have written a masterpiece" except for Sally and Clive's distractions. Rather than writing, in fact, as the next two shots reveal, Chris appears as the watching accomplice to their romance. His gaze on them—primal-scene fantasies—is literalized with binoculars which he uses in both shots, at a horse race and at an opera. The latter shot is especially startling; while Chris watches, Sally turns her own opera glasses onto Clive while they kiss. Taking up a gaze of her own in front of Chris's gaze, Sally asserts a powerful kind of control.[33] While Sally continues to make a spectacle of herself, Chris is not the controlling voyeur but a more helpless watcher of a sexuality that he himself can disavow.

This is a sexuality and power that Sally explicitly claims and enjoys. Chris's "comic suffering" is always at the hands of the woman who both names herself as "not exactly what most people would call a virgin" and whose performance and dialogue reveal a frank enjoyment of sex. On the one hand, Chris's masochism would seem to develop from a classic castration-fear scenario. In an early scene, for example, that establishes Chris's nervousness about Sally in his life, she discovers his large tray of pills and vitamins and engages him in a conversation that, in innuendo, teases him about potency. "I bet you wear a belt as well as braces," she comments and then asks if all the pills are meant " to restore your strength or something." When he offers her a vitamin, she replies that she has "rather too much vitality already." But although the defensiveness of Chris's position is clear, it would be much more difficult to argue that spectatorial pleasure resides strictly therein, as compared to the considerable pleasures of Julie Harris's performance, her vivaciousness and sexual "vitality" in contrast to Chris's hypochondria. Even contemporary reviewers who ob-

---

[32] Gaylyn Studlar, *In the Realm of Pleasure*, 134.

[33] As Mary Ann Doane points out in "Film and the Masquerade," "Glasses worn by a woman in the cinema do not generally signify a deficiency in seeing but signify an active looking, or even simply the fact of seeing as opposed to being seen" (83).

10. *I Am a Camera* (1955). Sally (Julie Harris) retains a gaze of her own while Chris (Laurence Harvey) is the passive spectator to her romance with Clive (Ron Randell).

jected to the film on moral grounds, or the British reviewers who found it generally disappointing, agreed that Harris's performance was the film's one saving grace. Thus there is a far stronger argument that spectatorial pleasure here is multiple and diffuse, located ambivalently in both dread and identification, rather than positioned purely at Sally's expense.

Furthermore, what is at stake here, as much as anxiety about Sally's "vitality," is the character's ability to articulate it, which was the specific anxiety of American film industry censorship, and further evident in media discourse that emphasized the "raciness" of the dialogue. The controversial lines quoted in these discourses are Sally's exclamations about her own sexual activity and enjoyment: her acknowledgment of exhibitionism, of feeling men's eyes "like mice" up and down her body; her ability to say the "man's" line about having a drink or going to bed; the puns she shares with Schneider about being chaste/chased. The MPPDA had also cited a line of Natalia's, her assertion—in the face of Sally's obvious sexual activity—that she herself would live with a man before marriage under certain circumstances. Though anxieties about female sexual power are embedded in a variety of ways throughout the text, the censorship controversy hinged on the fact that the narrative fails actually to punish or censure Sally—as the MPPDA explicitly suggested the distributors do in order to make the film acceptable. The MPPDA wanted Chris's voiceover to add a condemnation or in some way be "a general voice for morality . . . condemning and pointing out the wrongness of the heroine's promiscuity."[34] But if such a gesture would contain and make acceptable Sally's sexuality, it would also seriously undermine or completely ruin the comic trajectory; Chris's voice-over cannot be both that of comic victim and that of "a general voice for morality." The comic trajectory itself, I have argued, is a way to make Sally's sexuality acceptable. The most radical mark of Collier's adaptation from the Van Druten text is the imposition of this particular kind of comedy that makes Chris the masochistic "victim" of Sally's "vitality." What Studlar's theory—or any psychoanalytic theory—cannot account for is that the psychodynamics of the text may have particular historical uses. In this case, the masochistic pleasures of the text, which may include pleasure in the sexually powerful, punishing woman, operate as one kind of historical necessity in 1955; if Sally is allowed to speak of her own sexual pleasure, someone has to suffer.

The final narrative shift of *I Am a Camera* considerably complicates the masochistic scenario and most overtly uncovers the film's general

---

[34] MPPDA file memo from Geoffrey Shurlock, 7 March 1956, MPPDA.

misogynist subtexts working in contention with Sally's sexual freedom and power. First, Clive—the phallic father who, in the ideal masochist scenario, is guilty of sex with Sally—abandons them both. An argument follows in which Sally flatly accuses Chris of jealousy because Clive "was a man," implying Chris is not. Chris then sets out to "prove his manhood," but through a particularly masochistic scenario, deliberately provoking some Nazi propagandists on the street and engaging in a fight in which he is clearly outnumbered. Walking away with some bruises, which apparently make him feel much better, Chris is then faced with a much more serious confrontation: the literal affirmation of powerful female sexuality as motherhood. When he returns to his rooms, a meek and frightened Sally announces she is pregnant. The response to this is significant. Chris first offers to marry her, but after an abortion is agreed upon, Chris makes an offer that is much more in keeping with the sexual dynamic of the text. He offers to pay for the abortion by seriously going to work on his writing, thus asserting his own innocence, his disavowal of phallic guilt, as well as reinforcing the paradigm in which "writing" signifies a noble kind of celibacy—and defensiveness against women.

But he can also enact a patriarchal fantasy here that temporarily shifts the dynamic from masochistic passivity to a more active and innately misogynist "control." In the scene in which Sally confesses her pregnancy, Chris has been newly empowered by his fight with the Brownshirts, an empowerment that works seamlessly to put him in charge when he finds a much diminished and uncertain Sally back in the room. In an odd reversal, Sally's motherhood seems to confer upon him an ideal patriarchal fatherhood. He takes control, makes decisions, and does the manly thing, which is working hard to make money for the "family." In the next few shots, Sally brings him coffee and cakes like the good little wife while he does the fatherly job of writing. But the happy-family scenario has only been enacted in order to deny its possibility. His manly job of making money will specifically prevent Sally from actually becoming a mother, prevent her from enacting literally the power and authority that she already embodies as the threat of female sexuality. So the conflation of author/male authority which had been present earlier in the film as the valorization of Chris—a valorization that Sally continually subverted—now operates seamlessly, and apparently with her own cooperation, to position Chris as heroic.

As it turns out, Chris's enactment of the patriarchal hero is a joke, a momentary positioning that is quickly overturned in the final power reversal, in which Sally again takes charge and Chris is left as helpless and suffering spectator to her will and performance. Unfortunately, the terms of Sally's triumph are so explicitly linked to dread of her potential motherhood that it would be difficult to argue here the operation of the kind of benign heterocosm that Studlar finds in the Dietrich films. Chris returns from a successful writing commission, money in hand, to find Sally saying good-bye to Natalia and Fritz, who are now blissfully planning marriage and "millions of the most divine babies," as Sally puts it. The possibility of an infinite female reproduction is both named and disavowed, for this is the same scene in which Chris sends Sally off to the abortionist with his new earnings. But when he returns to their rooms a few hours later, he is shocked to find Sally ensconced there, surrounded by baby clothes and accessories. She has decided to have the baby after all and take him up on his previous offer of marriage.

The iconography of this scene is so startling that it seriously strains against the intended comedy. Sally is literally the beast-mother; she has propped up her foxtail (the variety that has the stuffed head intact) in a bassinet and sings it a lullaby as the horrified Chris looks on. The relationship of beast-baby to monstrous motherhood thus reinforces Sally's positioning to preverbal, material power. Waving her black cigarette-holder while she loftily makes plans, Sally presides over a surreal court, the beast-mother's dollhouse complete with cradle and rattles.

Her motherhood is directly subversive to the "manliness" and male ambition Chris has recently attained; the plans she makes completely ruin his new job prospects. Thus his earliest and greatest fear, that Sally would disrupt his authorship/authority, is realized. At the prospect of baby bottles, Chris races from the room, explaining that "Daddy" needs a bottle, too. In the next shot, Chris has again become the powerless infant, this time rocking back and forth in his bed/cradle as he tries to get drunk. His voice-over narration tells us: "If I dozed for a minute I had visions of a boy like Clive, followed by a string of little girls all exactly like Sally." At this, he bolts up in horror, for this is literally the nightmare of female reproduction; Sally will produce either mindless beasts (Clive), or worse, will reproduce endless replicas of herself, suggesting female sexuality as an endless, mindless, self-reproducing force. So the "comic" tormenting of the professor/bachelor ends in misogynist, specifically matricidal comedy. Significantly, this twist in the plot—Sally's sudden embrace of motherhood—had apparently been made to "soft-pedal" the controversial issue of abortion, so that the pressure of censorship results in the film's most openly hostile misogyny.

In all the other texts, the Sally Bowles character goes through with the abortion, but in the Cornelius film the pregnancy is diverted into

11. *I Am a Camera* (1955). A horrified Chris (Laurence Harvey) watches Sally (Julie Harris) nurture her beast-baby, the foxtail she has propped into a bassinet and surrounded with infant's accessories.

the comic trajectory and becomes another joke. Sally is "not much good at arithmetic," she explains to Chris the next morning. On the narrative level, then, Sally's pregnancy is like Chris's paralysis and rheumatic fever, an imaginary disease. In a gesture that is particularly telling of 1950s representations of women, Sally whisks off her full-length apron to reveal her low-cut nightclub dress underneath and announces that she is leaving town for another adventure. With immense relief, Chris smiles as he watches Sally depart, looking down at her from the window and holding one of the baby rattles that had been purchased for the imaginary infant—who is, of course, Chris himself.

The entire abortion sequence illustrates how the ambivalent aspects of motherhood in the masochistic scenario—Sally as both vitality/fertility and beast-mother, both healthy sexuality and threatening eroticism—can be undermined by other, specifically misogynist agendas. In this case, ambivalence toward the maternal operates seamlessly in codes of comedy about the trapped bachelor and the all-engulfing mother. Even more disturbingly, the masochistic scenarios in this text uncomfortably resemble the aesthetics and theatrics of the very politics against which the film trajectory (or at least its sense of "heroism") is aligned: ". . . situations of control, submissive behavior, extravagent effort, and the endurance of pain. . . . egomania and servitude . . . choreography [which] alternates between ceaseless motion and a congealed, static, 'virile' posing." This description comes not from Studlar but from Sontag in her description of fascist aesthetics in "Fascinating Fascism."[35] It would not be difficult to read many key scenes in the Cornelius film as enactments of this paradigm: the control, submission, and extravagence of the wild party scene; Sally's egomania growing in relation to Chris's servitude; Sally's ceaseless activity in juxtaposition to her elaborate poses with the feather-fan or beast-baby.

The problem here is that the Cornelius film's allusions to German fascism raise alarming questions about representations of history in relation to a comic/masochistic trajectory. Specifically, the fascism that is represented as historical background tends to be duplicated in the operations of the "joke" about the serious writer versus the show girl. This running joke and its enactment within the film convention of woman-as-spectacle have uncomfortable correlatives in the fascist ideology that the film supposedly repudiates. Amplifying Walter Benjamin's description of the aestheticization of politics, Russell Ber-

---

[35] Susan Sontag, "Fascinating Fascism," 316.

man points out the implication of fascist emphasis on spectacle rather than thoughtful reflection and on the priority of repetitious speech (slogan) over written text: "The corollary to iterative speech, in which nothing new can be enunciated, is . . . the spectacular image, which transfixes the viewer without the possibility of understanding." That is, fascist modes of communication work against complex readings: "This is the aestheticization of politics and war as objects of contemplation; they are to be judged in terms of their surface appearance and beauty, not in terms of an interior content, for the spectacle is characterized precisely by its lack of an inside."[36]

Considering Sally Bowles in the Cornelius film as characterized by both an empty, iterative language "in which nothing new can be enunciated," and as "surface appearance and beauty," the film operates in a double paranoia concerning her "lack of an inside." On one level, Sally as surface and theater is constantly juxtaposed to Chris as intellectual and writer. The continual voice-overs give us a Chris with an "inside" with the suggestion that we are hearing a thoughtful reflection or history. Although the voice-overs are always matched with shots of Chris himself, reinforcing his authority as "whole" person, the most startling contrast to this occurs at the end of the film, when the rediscovered Sally whisks Chris away from the party, and her mischievous, slightly hysterical laughter can be heard past the last cut and into the shot of the end title. The result is not only a disavowal of female body (or denial of the illusion of unified self with which the film had privileged Chris), but also an ironic gesture of giving Sally "the last word," as it were—but allowing it to be only noise, no word, no language at all, in a continuation of the film's paradigm of Chris as language opposed to Sally as materiality or as surface emptied of language. On another level, the entire pregnancy and abortion sequence both acknowledges and attempts to disavow Sally as someone whose "inside" is powerful and threatening: the space of her sexuality, the space in which she can conceive. Unlike all the other Sally Bowles texts, the Cornelius film presents the resolution of the pregnancy as a joke—in fact, a joke on Sally's lack of interior sense, or even lack of physical self-awareness—allowing the text to disavow her interior space and entirely resolving Chris's nightmare of female reproduction.

Whereas an elaborate set of defenses and disavowals is addressed to Sally as the sexual threat to Chris, the other threat represented in

---

[36] Russell Berman, *The Rise of the Modern German Novel: Crisis and Charisma* (Cambridge, Mass. and London: Harvard University Press, 1986), 224–25.

the text—the rise of German fascism—is disposed of with curious ease. Early in the film, this threat is specifically mentioned by Chris as the background for his story. He reminds his listeners at the party that at the time when he was in Germany, there were Nazi hoods on street corners "making themselves unpleasant." In the shot that accompanies this voice-over, an eyeline match of what Chris is presumedly watching from his window in Berlin, the street-corner Brownshirts are tripping up and laughing at a man who looks much like Chris, someone coded as an intellectual with briefcase and the inevitable eyeglasses, someone who is a thinking witness to the mindless political spectacle. Chris is posited as the sympathetic norm with an obvious, identifiable Other and enemy, the anti-intellectual Nazi. Yet, whereas the film uses a variety of shorthand representations of "decadent" and restless Weimar Berlin, the only other appearance of a Nazi is the one Chris punches in the face, to his great self-satisfaction, later in the film.[37] The moral Englishman has his opportunity to make his strike against German fascism, which then promptly disappears from the film altogether.

The vanquishing of fascism significantly occurs in the narrative when Chris is as effective as he will ever be—and as "manly"; as in the Van Druten play, antifascism is conflated with masculinity. First, he has just reprimanded Schneider, who is wailing that there is a Jewish conspiracy "to bring the country down." "That's absolute rubbish," Chris replies sharply. Second, he has just angrily broken off his relationship with Sally, who has shown a singular insensitivity to the political question when Fritz comes to explain that Natalia is worried about Nazi threats. Preoccupied with Clive's sudden disappearance, Sally ushers Fritz out the door without taking him seriously, much to Chris's outrage. Third, Chris goes to visit and console Fritz, and offer him the advice that resolves the subplot—that Fritz should admit to Natalia that he is Jewish. When he leaves Fritz, Chris explains in voice-over that he felt he was "in real life again after a long, crazy dream," and this comment introduces the scuffle with the Nazis; afterwards, he tells us in voice-over that he is finally out of his "wretched protective shell" with Sally "off [his] neck." The release from Sally is situated as release from political indifference, indecisiveness, and even cowardice; he is immediately able to solve her preg-

[37] In *A Mirror for England*, Raymond Durgnat points out how this gesture satisfies the audience, too, in Cornelius films that "plump the little Englishman into tight corners and show how, better late than never, he rises to the occasion. In *I am* [*sic*] *a Camera* Laurence Harvey feels much better after punching a storm-trooper in pre-war Germany" (39).

nancy problem, too, with the noble offer to work to raise money for the abortion.

As previously explained, this surge of stereotypical male heroism is quickly reversed when Sally embraces motherhood and Chris is again positioned as her "victim." But my point is that the comic masochism of the text—the "problem" of Sally's vitality/sexuality—is situated in a startling alignment with the historical problem. Sally herself displaces the Nazi enemy who humiliates the bespectacled intellectual in the early establishing shot. Once Sally is disavowed as a "long, crazy dream," then Chris can quickly deal with the "real" enemy on the street, who actually disappears much more easily than Sally, who will follow him to postwar London. The complication in this substitution of Sally as "comic" foe is, as I have suggested, the startling duplication of fascist methodology in the textual enunciation of female sexuality. As I argued in my first chapter, the deeper and long-range problem here is a mainstream cinematic tradition that operates seamlessly in a continuum with fascist sexual politics: the nervous positing of absolute sexual boundaries, the heightening of sexual difference, the illusion of the unified male self against which the feminine is situated as enemy and Other.

The 1955 theater ads in the *New York Times* announcing the upcoming premiere of the Cornelius film featured a cartoon of two hands holding up lacy panties, with the caption "One of the delightful bits of wardrobe in *I Am a Camera*." A reading of this film certainly cannot be reduced to this image, but many of the issues and problems surrounding the film in fact converge on this fetishized gesture and the scene in the film to which it alludes. Fritz and Natalia have accepted the story that Sally's night in Chris's room has been entirely chaste, but the scene ends with Sally discovering her panties on Chris's chair. She smiles and cries out in triumph, while holding them up to the camera for a close-up. The visual evidence, that is, exceeds the story and to some extent *is* the story: fetishization, the threat to male subjectivity, the threat of a female intrusion into and ruin of culture. The chair, after all, is where Chris had sat in a previous scene to do his writing. Even this early in the film, Sally has come across as a far more interesting character than Chris, so that Sally's exhibit of the evidence works as a snide reversal of the traditional post-wedding night exhibition of the bloody sheets. If anything has been surrendered the night before, it is Chris's virginity, not hers, and the female triumph converges with the embarrassment to Chris. But this pleasurable victory comes at considerable cost—the reduction of female sexuality to the lacy panties, the "joke" that it could be threatening.

Moreover, if these panties are also a reference to the famous ones that land on Professor Rath's shoulder in *The Blue Angel*, they also involve a reductive historical reading, Weimar as an oedipal crisis that precipitated German fascism,[38] which will in fact haunt future configurations of Sally Bowles.

[38] Patrice Petro in *Joyless Streets*, continuing her argument on gendered readings of this era, claims that the popular use of Dietrich (along with Louise Brooks) as a figure of Weimar female sexuality is a "convenient" way "to project a reading of male subjectivity in crisis," because Dietrich was "typically featured in films where male characters are brought to their doom as a result of their uncompromising devotion to a feminine ideal" (159). Because Dietrich emerged onscreen relatively late in Weimar history, Petro suggests that her use as sexual embodiment of Weimar says more about a "fascination" in scholarship than about Weimar women (160).

Chapter Five

(NAZI) LIFE IS A CABARET

SALLY BOWLES AND BROADWAY MUSICAL

CONFRONTING SALLY BOWLES about her indifference to the political crisis around her in Weimar Berlin, the writer-protagonist of Joe Masteroff's 1966 musical, *Cabaret*, says angrily, "Sally, can't you see—if you're not against all this, you're for it—or you might as well be."[1] If there is a distinct ring of 1960s political confrontation in this line, it is duplicated throughout the text of *Cabaret* with its series of narrative and stylistic divisions that position characters, musical numbers, and staging devices in oppositional ways. Whereas the Sally Bowles of the 1950s adaptations may have been located somewhat ambiguously in relation to German fascism, in this play she is confronted with a much sharper political choice, which bears the imprint of a more radical ideological interrogation. If you're not antifascist, you're fascist, says the protagonist, and the either-or rhetoric glosses over a host of other contradictions, including a didactic political agenda that ends up being located in a vision of Home and America ironically at odds with the campy irreverence found throughout this version of Weimar cabaret.

Generally, the stage musical *Cabaret* is marked by contentions and splits that resemble or duplicate those that appear in Isherwood's Sally Bowles story and in the earlier stage and screen adaptations. Producer/director Hal Prince, concerned with producing "good heter stuff"—a hit stage musical—recognized the need to rework Herr Issyvoo into a more standard leading man for 1966 Broadway: "We gotta put balls on the guy," as Prince remarked.[2] Prince, like Isherwood, aimed at courting a mainstream audience, but Prince was also consciously aiming at delivering an uncomfortable 1960s political message as well. A further complication of this project was the fact that the collaborators of *Cabaret* recognized the campiness of their material and were able to address, more openly than the 1950s adaptations, Isherwood's gay subtext. They did this by employing a dubious new character, the emcee of the cabaret. Yet in masculin-

---

[1] Joe Masteroff, *Cabaret* (New York: Random House, 1967), 95. This is the complete, published libretto. All page numbers in the text refer to this edition.

[2] Frank Marcus, "Ich Bin Ein Berliner," *Plays and Players* (May 1968): 15.

izing and Americanizing Herr Issyvoo into Cliff Bradshaw so that he
can woo Sally Bowles, the play's creators ended up with a romantic
plot so clichéd and obvious that they agree these characters are far
less engaging than the characters of the subplot: boarding-house
landlady Fräulein Schneider and her Jewish fiancé, Herr Schultz.

Both romances, in fact, are far less interesting than Prince's innovative staging and framing, which include the use of metaphorical
stage space and onstage observers. Thus there is (again) a problem
having to do with whose story the play wants to tell—a problem literalized by these innovations. When the lights go up on one-half of
the stage, the audience sees the traditional three-walled space of nineteenth-century theater, Cliff's dingy boarding-house room or
Schultz's grocery. In this space, characters sing traditional musical-
theater ballads about love and even—ultimate musical cliché—fall in
love during their duets. But portions of these scenes are observed by
cabaret characters perched on a winding staircase off to one side of
the stage. And when the lights go up on the other side of the stage,
the audience is suddenly part of the garish Kit Kat Klub, its spaces
opened dizzily with a mirror against the back wall—a world of spectacle narrated by an emcee whose gender codings mock the tidy heterosexuality that is represented on the other side of the stage. At this
point, the emcee introduces us to a "real" cabaret, whereas in other
numbers he performs in what the makers of the show called a
"Limbo" space, a metaphorical positioning from which he can comment on the plot. That is, in a notable move away from the "realism"
of the traditional Broadway musical, Prince positions characters outside of ongoing scenes in a "limbo" that is clearly not part of the action and world of the play, even though a traditionally "realistic"
scene is being acted out.

Paralleling the multiple dichotomies and contradictions of narrative and theater codes already suggested here, the space outside the
theater was also split. Todd Gitlin, in his study *The Sixties*, uses an
instance from popular culture as indicative: the meteoric rise of
Barry McGuire's "Eve of Destruction" on the rock sales charts in 1965
immediately followed by a similarly "instant" hit by Staff Sergeant
Barry Sadler, "The Ballad of the Green Berets." Remarking on the
implication of this "battle of the Barrys," Gitlin says, "Plainly a new
constellation of moods was in the air."[3] The moods signaled confrontations between irreconcilable positions. Nineteen sixty-five saw the
first major demonstration against American troops in Vietnam—
25,000 students marching in April at the Capitol, as well as Martin

---

[3] Todd Gitlin, *The Sixties: Years of Hope, Days of Rage* (New York: Bantam, 1987), 197.

Luther King's Selma-to-Montgomery civil rights march the previous month. The confrontations were often violent; there was rioting and burning in Harlem and then in Watts during the summers of 1964 and 1965. In the popular vocabulary, "Black Power" was a new, often threatening term. Other new words giving evidence of what would eventually be called the counterculture included "kinky," and—in reference to the enormous impact of British rock music—"Mod." Within the space of Broadway, too, the conservatism of the theatrical musical was gradually being challenged by innovations that would result in a more experimental musical theater in the following two decades. So while the 1951 *I Am a Camera* had played opposite *Gigi* in a dichotomous paradigm concerning gender and narrative, the stage play *Cabaret* emerged in a mainstream theater in which multiple kinds of differences were becoming possible. The Broadway hits playing concurrently that year included *Fiddler on the Roof* and *Hello, Dolly*, traditional musicals in which characters burst into song to further the narrative. On the other hand, reflecting a new interest in Berthold Brecht, a revival of his *Caucasian Chalk Circle* made a successful run on Broadway just a few months prior to the opening of *Cabaret*. Even more significantly, when the new Hal Prince musical was enjoying its seventeenth month in performance, the hit that opened across town was the rock musical *Hair*; so while the leering emcee was making a suggestive *Willkommen* to the audience of the former show, the audience of the latter was hearing a far more plaintive ode to perversion in the rock ballad "Sodomy."

Prince's project, as he and his collaborators admitted later, was consciously concerned with an experimental theater and also consciously addressed to the larger political scene, in particular the issue of racism in America. Treating the Isherwood material as a study in the banality of evil, with the warning of It Can Happen Here, Prince even considered using film footage of the Little Rock riots at the end of the show.[4] So the Sally Bowles story becomes reinscribed in a wholly different politics as well as in another popular genre, and the Isherwood characters' 1930s problems once again enact anxieties circulating in a different era.

Within the issues and concerns of this study, probably the most re-

---

[4] Although this play was often termed "Brechtian," Hal Prince has made it clear in subsequent interviews that he himself is no fan of Brecht. His major influence, he contends, was the experimental staging he witnessed at the Taganka Theatre in Moscow in 1965. For these details and for Prince's account of his political agenda, see Carol Ilson, *Harold Prince: From "Pajama Game" to "Phantom of the Opera"* (Ann Arbor: University Microfilms, Inc. Research Press, 1989), 137–44.

markable thing about the Prince/Ebb/Kander/Masteroff *Cabaret*[5] is that the character Sally Bowles is not the center of the text or even the most privileged performer. Of all the adaptations, this is the only one in which her character and story are upstaged not just by other narrative concerns, but by stronger performances as well. Whereas Julie Harris and Liza Minnelli have come to be closely identified with the other texts, the stage play *Cabaret* is strongly identified with Joel Grey (who in the 1987 revival was billed as the star, even though in the original production he won his Tony as Best Supporting Actor). The emcee part was written specifically for Grey; likewise, by the time the collaborators had developed the Schultz and Schneider characters, they specifically had Jack Gilford and Lotte Lenya in mind.[6] The latter two longtime Broadway veterans were in fact the real stars of the Hal Prince production in that they were its most well-known and accomplished players. Lenya brought the show an additional kind of reputation; the widow of Brecht's most famous lyricist, Kurt Weill, she had also been Brecht's original Jenny in *The Threepenny Opera* in Berlin's Epic Theater and in the 1931 G. W. Pabst film. Her presence was intended to give the play an "authentic" Weimar touch, claim the collaborators. In contrast, the Sally and Christopher characters were more nebulously constructed. "I don't think we ever found exactly what we wanted for those parts," says Masteroff.[7] To a great extent, Sally Bowles in this play is only the tangential factor linking several other codes and discourses: the backstage-musical narrative, the narrative of the innocent American in Europe, the project of entertainment (producing the Big Show, which turns out to be Nazism), and finally, the cultural coding of camp. In the evolution of Sally Bowles, the text that features her least is nonetheless the one that irrevocably positions her as the true heiress of Lola Lola, as the latter herself has been established in camp discourse, as the cabaret singer in garters and feathers performing for the Nazis.

In the original Prince production, Jill Haworth as Sally received mixed reviews. At least one reviewer pointed out that her artless performance rings true for a character who is supposed to be "awk-

[5] Joe Masteroff is conventionally given credit as author of the "book" *Cabaret*, the published libretto for which he created most of the dialogue. However, most of the book consists of the lyrics of Fred Ebb's songs; the narrative, lyrics, and dialogue evolved gradually with the collaboration of Hal Prince and the music of John Kander. As Foster Hirsch reports, the collaborators agree that *Cabaret* was "written by a committee." See Hirsch's *Harold Prince and the American Musical Theatre* (Cambridge and New York: Cambridge University Press, 1989), 59.

[6] See the interview with Kander, Ebb, Masteroff, and Ronald Field in Otis L. Guernsey Jr., ed., *Broadway Song and Story* (New York: Dodd Mead, 1985), 144.

[7] Ibid.

ward," but others thought the thin characterization "damaging" to the show.[8] However, if Haworth made little impact as Sally, the blame has been wholly taken by Masteroff and Prince, who have made it clear in subsequent interviews that they were not interested in developing the Sally role as a star vehicle, or even as an important part. Masteroff claims that Prince, taking a position that is curiously opposite to the one taken by Van Druten in the previous decade, insisted "right from the beginning that he didn't want this to be a musical about Sally Bowles, whom he feels is the least interesting character in *The Berlin Stories*."[9] Even structurally the part created for her is minimal. Sally has two cabaret solos, shares one romantic duet with Cliff, and performs just three of the show's fifteen numbers. The Schneider-Schultz romance, on the other hand, is privileged with four songs and is additionally the occasion for the musical moment that is the turning point of the entire play, the "Tomorrow Belongs to Me" number at the end of act 1. Formally, Sally's main function is to personalize Cliff's involvement with the world of the Kit Kat Klub. As in the 1950s versions, she moves into Cliff's rooms, but unlike their chaste relationship in those versions, she and Cliff are lovers, and their relationship results in the pregnancy Sally eventually chooses to end. By 1966 this was not a particularly scandalous plot line, especially in comparison to what the play emphasizes as the more pressing (and more spectacularly produced) problem, the rise of Nazism. Masteroff remembers Hal Prince's insight concerning Sally that "the show was not going to live or die on how well her character registered. If, God forbid, she didn't work, the show would still succeed. In many ways, he turned out to be right."[10]

Far from constructing the show around Sally Bowles, Prince and his collaborators claim they began to shape the show around music, "the sound of Germany in that period . . . all the Kurt Weill music, all of the Lotte Lenya records . . . in the back of our heads that is how we wanted it to sound."[11] Polished and successful veterans of Broadway musical, they were primarily interested in the Isherwood and Van Druten material as an occasion for song and spectacle. Prince's musical successes included the hits *Pajama Game* (1954), *Damn Yankees* (1955), *West Side Story* (1957), and *Fiddler on the Roof* (1964). He had previously worked with the John Kander and Fred Ebb team on

[8] See Norman Nadel, " 'Cabaret' Fine New Musical," *World Journal Tribune* (21 Nov. 1966). See also Walter Kerr, "The Theater: 'Cabaret' Opens at the Broadhurst," *New York Times* (21 Nov. 1966).

[9] Foster Hirsch, *Harold Prince and the American Musical Theatre*, 59.

[10] Otis L. Guernsey, Jr., *Broadway Song and Story*, 145.

[11] Ibid., 135.

Flora, the Red Menace (1965), a political satire of the 1930s, which was far less successful, although Liza Minnelli won a Tony Award for her performance as Flora. Interestingly enough, considering Minnelli's award-winning display of her talents, she did not get the part of Prince's Sally Bowles, probably due to Prince's reluctance to make the show a star vehicle. From the start, then, Prince and the musical collaborators were less interested in creating a dynamic Sally and far more interested in the cabaret songs of the emcee and the "German-sounding" ballads they were fashioning for Lenya and Gilford. The show began to take shape, its makers report, once it was structured around the "little man in a night club," a character freely based on a dwarfish emcee whom Prince had seen fifteen years earlier in a club in Stuttgart.[12]

Given these specifically musical motivations and the centrality of the emcee character, it is clear that the Sally Bowles of this text needs to be positioned in the codings of musical theater, and also in relation to the character who has displaced her as focus of the play: the "little man" who eventually becomes Broadway's most famous master of ceremonies: ". . . *a bizarre little figure—much lipstick, much rouge, patent-leather hair parted in the middle,*" as Masteroff describes him in the book's stage directions (3). Certainly a major factor of displacement in this relationship is the centrality of the musical numbers and, in turn, the factor of performance. The emcee's performance of "*Will-kommen*" and his other songs (he performs six, twice the number of Sally) are simply better entertainment, more fascinating and memorable, due both to Grey's giftedness and the underwriting of Sally's character and talent. Whereas Joel Grey is a polished song-and-dance man, Jill Haworth's musical abilities are fairly limited (true to Isherwood's original conception of Sally as a performer). Prince was determined not to let the Sally character steal the show—which he intended to be "about" an era characterized by the emcee.[13] For the New York show, Haworth was coached to sing in a nervous soprano which contributes to a characterization that one irate theatergoer described as Betty Boop[14] and that in fact accurately describes the quality of her voice as it can be heard on Columbia's original Broadway cast recording.

But the larger issue here is the sexual displacement operating in the continuing history of Sally Bowles as transvestite. For the first

[12] Ibid., 137. See also Carol Ilson, *Harold Prince: From "Pajama Game" to "Phantom of the Opera,"* 140.

[13] Prince claims that the emcee is to represent first the Depression, then the Nazi mentality. See Foster Hirsch, *Harold Prince and the American Musical Theatre,* 60.

[14] Alan Rich, "The Triumph of the Cliché," *World Journal Tribune* (11 Dec. 1966): 30.

12. Broadway musical *Cabaret* (1966). The character Sally Bowles was played by a stan-
dardly "sexy," or voluptuous, actress, Jill Haworth, but was no longer the center of the
play.

time, Sally is played by an actress who is traditionally "sexy," the voluptuous young Jill Haworth, but the focus of sexual fascination shifts to the ambiguously gendered emcee. In the spectrum of androgyny, Joel Grey in a tuxedo with rouged cheeks and lipstick can be imagined as a more parodic version of the slightly built Julie Harris overdressed into vamphood. Harris onstage may have camped-up the feminine disguise while remaining within the codes of Broadway comedy, but Grey's character fifteen years later manifests the disguise overtly when, at the beginning of act 2, he appears in drag as one of the Kit Kat Klub chorus girls. The bolder play with difference is directly attributable to another cultural coding to which Prince and his associates could refer by 1966, and this, of course, is camp, which had gradually developed beyond the gay community into the avant-garde, and eventually into multiple sites of mainstream culture, so that Sontag in her 1964 essay was wholly prepared to identify as camp both a sensibility and a number of cultural artifacts: Visconti's *Salome*, Von Sternberg's Dietrich films, but also Tiffany lamps (imitations of which would eventually saturate restaurants and bars attempting camp ambiance). John Waters's 1965–66 films, *Roman Candles* and *Eat Your Make-up*, or Andy Warhol's 1966 *Chelsea Girls* may have had limited audiences, but the parodic, self-conscious style of camp was commercially mainstreamed by the mid-1960s in films such as *What Ever Happened to Baby Jane?* (1962) and television programs such as *Get Smart* and *Batman*, which began their runs in 1965 and 1966, respectively. Pop music furthered the trend, with the rise of effeminate male rock stars such as Mick Jagger and the popularity of the Beatles and other British groups arriving on the scene in granny glasses and old military uniforms.[15] Popular camp played to an increasing cultural sexual sophistication—and decreasing censorship in film and television—that could flirt with kinkiness as fashion, sexual aberration as avant-garde. Thus the political use of camp could remain ambiguous. If, as Andrew Ross suggests, everyone "knew" about Batman and Robin,[16] the effect was certainly no progressive stance against homophobia; "kinkiness" could be recontained all over again as a joke, displacing homophobia as a real issue altogether.

A great deal of the Kit Kat Klub portion of *Cabaret* is unabashedly camp in its artifice, theatricality, and humor, as seen in the use of feather boas and garter belts, the effeminacy of the emcee, and even the Betty Boop quality of Sally. The question is how camp works as

---

[15] Mark Booth outlines this popularization in *Camp*, 155–57. See also Andrew Ross, *No Respect: Intellectuals and Popular Culture* for an account of the mass marketing of camp and crossover effects from the counterculture in this era, 148–56.

[16] Ibid., 153.

13. Broadway musical *Cabaret* (1966). Sexual fascination in this musical shifts from Sally Bowles to the rouged and lipsticked emcee (Joel Grey).

part of the political agenda in this text, how it operates in relation to
an unabashedly didactic trajectory, manifest in the distinctly non-
camp melodramatic subplot of the middle-aged couple, Schneider
and Schultz, who are torn apart by Nazi anti-Semitism. Given this
didacticism, the fascination of camp humor and artifice—its success
as entertainment—seems to be located on the wrong side of this trajectory; as one critic put it, "*Cabaret* invites us to enjoy what it presumably aims to mock and denounce."[17] But this split perception is intrinsic to the camp sensibility of pleasure in the outrageous and in black
humor. Moreover, the most stereotyped images of German fascism as
they have evolved in popular culture are rich sites for camp parody:
the super-macho SS, the spectacular "show" at the Nuremberg rally,
the spastic fanatic with the Charlie Chaplin mustache, the discipline
and spectacle of parades. Twenty years after the war, this material
was being trivialized and parodied by the popular television comedy
Hogan's Heroes (1965) and later specifically camped-up by the recurring German soldier on *Laugh-In* (1968), who only had to say a simple
line in a fake German accent to get a laugh. That same year, Mel
Brooks would take Nazi spectacle to perhaps its campiest extreme
with the production number "Springtime for Hitler" in his film *The
Producers*. Likewise, Nazi macho, discipline, and penchant for parades is the campy joke material in *Cabaret* for the emcee's appearance in drag with the chorus girls; just as he identifies himself as one
of the dancers in stockings and garters, the music changes to a jazzy
version of "Tomorrow Belongs to Me" and the chorus line becomes a
line of goose-stepping soldiers. The move is a brilliant example of
camp's wicked humor which recognizes the "joke" at the heart of the
Third Reich's serious masculinism, the Fatherland's privileging of its
boys on parade.

The exaggerated artifice of camp, as well as the glittering, haunting
appeal of the emcee, are central to the show's project, which—as
Dana Polan says of the genre of film musical—is "the project of 'entertainment,' the world transformed into a good show." Polan points
out that this project is intrinsically ideological, in that spectacle itself
privileges immediacy and visual gratification over the distancing of
analysis and criticism.[18] This is a key consideration in *Cabaret*, with its

[17] Harold Clurman, review of *Cabaret, The Nation* (12 Dec. 1966): 652. Foster Hirsch
similarly comments on how Prince's split aims—"a good show" and a nightmarish les-
son in politics—run the "danger of making Fascism attractive," *Harold Prince and the
American Musical Theatre*, 65.

[18] Dana Polan, "Above All Else to Make You See: Cinema and the Ideology of Spectacle," *Boundary 2* 11 (1982/83): 130–31. Polan mentions Benjamin's description of fascism as "the aestheticization of politics" in this context, which is of particular relevance

heavily didactic anti-Nazi agenda tacked onto the conventions of the musical and the codes of camp. A clue to the operation of song-and-dance spectacle as substitute for analysis is present in the opening "*Willkommen*," in which the emcee cleverly uses three languages to welcome the diegetic and theater audiences: "*Willkommen, bienvenue,* welcome/*Fremde,* étranger, stranger" (3). The three languages are flattened, so to speak, into lyrics with a score so rhythmic and smooth that differences in nuance between the phrases ("*Je suis enchanté/* Happy to see you") are virtually effaced in the interest of song, music, performance. The theatrical conflation in fact matches the impact of Sally's character as originally drawn by Isherwood: the triumph of performance over meaning, theatrical effect over language. But in this text, those effects are much less subtly aligned with fascism. The cabaret eventually becomes the site of spectacle that can seamlessly encompass a variety of positions into the broad category of entertainment, so that toward the end of the play, when Cliff is being beaten up by two Nazis at the Kit Kat Klub, this too is appropriated as spectacle. The stage directions read, "*The EMCEE appears—laughing rather hysterically—as if the fight were part of the floor show*" (105).

The centralization and fascination of the emcee, who operates outside the narrative as a "metaphor" that is nevertheless pure spectacle, pure entertainment, is in turn a key factor in the ideology of spectacle in this play. His "Limbo" numbers make lewd commentaries on the central action, and he acts as the leering host in the background to each cabaret number—nodding his approval, for example, at the end of the first "Tomorrow Belongs to Me" performance. To a great extent, his exaggerated effeminacy and camped-up mannerisms are both exposure and celebration of the gay sensibility that has always been central to the Broadway musical. As Richard Dyer points out, gay men constitute one of the nonmainstream groups that has had enormous impact on the formation of American show business. Gerald Mast notes the particularly strong influence on the musical, with its propensity toward "masquerade of extravagent excess and outrageous frippery," given that many of the major American composers and lyricists for Broadway and film musicals in the first half of the century were gay.[19] However, given the generally conservative nature of the musical as characterized by many critics of the genre, the gay sensibility therein has been carefully recoded, most often into some

in the stage play *Cabaret* with its elaborate choreography of German fascism in the emcee's most entertaining numbers.

[19] Richard Dyer, "Entertainment and Utopia," in *Genre: The Musical,* ed. Rick Altman (London: Routledge, 1981), 184; Gerald Mast, *Can't Help Singin': The American Musical on Stage and Screen* (Woodstock, N.Y.: Overlook, 1987), 38.

version of the romance. Mast notes the gay subtext, for example, of Rodgers and Hammerstein's *The King and I* with its "glimpse at a forbidden and impossible love."[20] When the gay agenda is surfaced and foregrounded in *Cabaret*, what also surfaces is this troubling split between Broadway musical as "straight" entertainment and as vehicle for a gay sensibility. To some extent, the codings of camp can allow an audience to enjoy the emcee "safely," with camp sophistication about kinkiness as "fun." But the campy sexual spectacle is positioned through staging and narrative opposite a powerful set of norms involving conventions of theater space, character, plot, and music, ultimately suggesting a norm that is, not surprisingly, heterosexual and male.

The contradictions here entail the production of "good show biz stuff"—to paraphrase Isherwood's project—that is ideologically correct (heterosexual, antifascist) and the production of the "exotic" and "decadent" elements of the Weimar period embodied in the sexually ambiguous emcee—who is also innately "good show biz stuff." This contradiction is actually represented by the gap between the stage spaces and performances that structure the play: the spectacles of the Kit Kat Klub and the emcee's metaphorical numbers, on the one hand, and on the other, the two romances that take place in Schneider's boarding house—splits that reveal both the ideology of the spectacle and the (displaced) location of Sally Bowles between these two spaces.

Most contemporary critics regarded the split staging of *Cabaret* as brilliant, and Prince is still given credit for opening up the genre of the musical in a powerful way with this stage play. Reviewers were most often impressed by the unusual cabaret setting which extends into the theater seats. The arriving audience finds itself reflected on a giant mirror across the back of the stage; during the first cabaret act, the mirror tilts upward so that the performers onstage are doubled in an odd distortion. This opening convergence of audience and spectacle, which is then duplicated in the mirrored diegetic audience and performers of the cabaret, is an experimental strategy that is also aligned with camp's seamlessness between theater and "life." Yet this concept of spectatorship is alarmingly and explicitly aligned with German fascism by the end of the play. In the last scene, the swastika arm bands in the cabaret audience converge with the garish colors reflecting the entire cabaret crowd in the mirror. Fascism has been seamlessly encompassed into the spectacle of "the world transformed into a good show," and Sally Bowles is telling us in song that "life is a

---

[20] Ibid., 358n.

cabaret." In the political uneasiness of 1966, part of the effect here is surely didactic, illustrating the danger of passive spectatorship. The narrative on the other side of the stage reinforces this message by suggesting that "real" life is no crazy cabaret, but closer to middle-class melodrama, a story of courtships and broken hearts, which is the subject of the traditional Broadway musical.

Significantly, the cabaret performers themselves are distortions of what one traditionally finds in the Broadway musical. Masteroff remembers that many audience members walked out on the play's first run in Boston because "they expected it to be a normal kind of Broadway musical. Within ten minutes, they had seen these not-so-great-looking chorus girls, and the show seemed to be a little on the grim side."[21] Cecil Smith and Glenn Litton, in their history of musical theater, remember the "not-so-great-looking chorus girls" as embodying more than a reversal of expectations: "Patricia Zipprodt's costumes for the chorines and the all-woman band were out of a misogynist's fantasies, garish and clumsy and as hard and meretricious as the girls' makeup, blotches of rouge and mascara around hollow cheeks and eyes."[22] That is, the opening spectacle at the Kit Kat Klub is specifically the spectacle of grotesque sexuality, which in turn implies a positioning against some norm that is even more specific than middle-class melodrama, a norm designated in Masteroff's assumption of the ideal chorus girl, a concept and image that posit the norm of male spectatorship and female spectacle.

This use of camp as sexual grotesque—in the garish chorus girls and in the emcee—suggests the blur of sexual identity that the text positions in some places both as "entertainment" and as the specifically anti-Semitic evil of German fascism. This contradiction needs to be further unpacked, but in regard to the character Sally Bowles, the reassignment of the sexual fascination of the play to the emcee corroborates the theory that a powerful dynamic of disavowal is at work here in regard to female sexuality. Indeed, a traditionally attractive actress playing Sally has her sexuality undermined by her casting as a poor performer, by minimalizing her role, and by having her construction as "sexy chorus girl" mocked not only by the hideously painted Kit Kat girls but also by the heavily rouged emcee. Although the element of performance may have worked as subversive to the oedipal narrative for Julie Harris's earlier Broadway Sally, theatrical performance is a major factor in the trivialization of this musical

[21] Otis L. Guernsey, Jr., *Broadway Song and Story*, 143.
[22] Cecil Smith and Glenn Litton, *Musical Comedy in America* (New York: Theatre Arts, 1981), 286.

Sally. Even a ghost of Mummy is evoked in the war against Sally; the corrective or normative sign in opposition to her sexuality will be a saintly motherhood that is anticabaret and eventually even antifascist, yielding particular irony in regard to Nazism's own saintly mothers.

In the reduced scale of Sally's character, she can be summed up as the charming, ambitious young thing who is determined to be a star and thus does not understand the implications of swastikas in her audience. Predictably, her romantic lead will be the handsome young man who *does* perceptively grasp the political issues at hand. The Kit Kat Klub is doomed to become a kind of boundary between them, a literalization of an ideological split, and ultimately the terms of their estrangement. Whereas the opening number produces a breathless and immensely entertaining introduction to the world of spectacle, the following scene immediately specifies Cliff as someone who will not be a part of that world—in particular, according to the codes of the musical, someone whose songs will be more traditional "story" songs or plot songs. "There must be two worlds on that stage," Prince claimed, a "real" world as opposed to the Kit Kat Klub and the emcee's metaphorical space.[23] However, the two styles in the stage play are also functions of ideology, as is evident in the concept of "real" character and setting, positing a norm that, in Broadway musical, closely conforms to what we find in the narrative's hero. When the lights go down after the opening "*Willkommen*," they come up again on Cliff, American writer abroad, innocently riding into Germany and about to meet his first Nazi.

Cliff, ensconced quietly in his train compartment and on his way to Berlin/experience/the Kit Kat Klub, is a standard representation of the bourgeois norm by which the emcee is both freakish and campy. The mirror on the cabaret wall distorts the Kit Kat Klub into images that reviewers often compared to German Expressionism, and the "realist" motif in this next scene plus the physical appearance of Cliff operate as another, corrective mirror to the cabaret. According to the description of Cliff in the stage directions, "*He is in his late twenties, pleasant-looking, intelligent, reserved. His suitcase and portable typewriter are on the rack above his head*" (5). This is the Americanized "Christopher." Masteroff explains that he invented an entirely new character because the Chris of *Goodbye to Berlin* and *I Am a Camera* was "a cypher" and he himself was "more comfortable writing an American than an Englishman."[24] For the Broadway audience, moreover, the Americanization of Herr Issyvoo has obvious political appeal: the in-

[23] Foster Hirsch, *Harold Prince and the American Musical Theatre*, 61.
[24] Otis L. Guernsey, Jr., *Broadway Song and Story*, 138.

nocent young man from Harrisburg, Pennsylvania, witnesses decadence and the beginnings of Nazi Germany. Cliff Bradshaw would
also satisfy a sexual norm of musical theater. British reviewer Frank
Marcus "was told in New York that the producer of *Cabaret* banished
Herr Issyvoo with the remark, 'We gotta put balls on the guy. If he
shacks up with the girl, he's gotta sleep with her!' "[25] The result is the
only straight, actively heterosexual version of Isherwood's original
narrator among all the adaptations; even in the 1987 revival, Cliff
admits to bisexual inclinations and is followed around by someone
named Gottfried who has guessed his secret. But the 1966 version
retains not much of the original Christopher except the last name,
which is Isherwood's middle name and an echo of William Bradshaw,
the narrator of *The Last of Mr. Norris*. According to biographer Brian
Finney, this is also the only adaptation that Isherwood himself never
saw, advised against this "malformed offspring" by his friends.[26]

The brief narrative scene on the train also alludes to the opening
of the *Mr. Norris* novel and Bradshaw's meeting with Norris. Cliff is
joined by handsome young Ernst Ludwig who is engaged in some
smuggling between Paris and Berlin—some perfume and silk stockings, he tells Cliff. Though Ernst befriends Cliff and later even convinces him to make some money with a similar smuggling job, Ernst
is actually a full-fledged member of the Nazi party, and his smuggling
activity is directly related to this political "good cause," as he calls it.
Thus Cliff is inadvertently drawn into Nazi politics even before he
arrives in Berlin at Schneider's rooming house.

The play's second musical number takes place there in the next
scene, again confirming several norms of musical theater. The setting
is recognizable and coded as lower-class German: "*The furnishings are
ugly and ponderous: a bed, a table with two chairs, an armoire, and, behind
a curtain, a washstand*" (10). Whereas the opening scene had invited a
dizzying conflation of spectacle/spectator, this staging repositions the
spectator as located along the traditional "fourth wall" of the stage,
peering into a room where "real" characters appear—Schneider and
her boarders in "realistic" makeup as opposed to the garish makeup
and costuming of the denizens of the Kit Kat Klub. Schneider, the
Jewish grocer Schultz, and the less respectable Fräulein Kost, who
entertains sailors in her room to pay the rent, are the strictly noncabaret characters who never appear in the Kit Kat Klub staging at all.
Nevertheless, in the conventions of the musical, these characters

[25] Frank Marcus, "Ich Bin Ein Berliner," 15.

[26] Brian Finney, *Christopher Isherwood*, 268. Isherwood died on January 4, 1986; the
revival headed by Joel Grey opened on Broadway the following year.

spontaneously burst into song as a way of continuing the narrative. Addressing how this illusion of inevitable singing and dancing operates in the film musical, Jane Feuer describes the "myth of spontaneity" as a privileging characteristic; the ability to break spontaneously into song and dance codes characters as positive.[27] Following this code, for example, Fräulein Kost (who turns out to be a Nazi sympathizer) is never given one of these narrative songs but instead later sings as "entertainment" a song originally heard at the Kit Kat Klub. The larger point is that in conforming to this musical norm, the story and characters in the boarding-house portion of the play are further coded as the positive alternative to the spectacles at the Kit Kat Klub, in that they are identifiable as "real" characters. Even though the plot songs are purely artifice, they fall under the code of acceptable artificiality in musical theater as opposed to the more outrageous artifice of the Kit Kat numbers.

More importantly, the Schneider-Schultz subplot is articulated as the romance that is victimized by Kit Kat politics—specifically, by an effect of performance and spectacle at the end of act 1 that works to collapse the separate spaces of narrative and cabaret. But first, the romance is performed solely through story numbers. In this early scene, Schneider agrees to compromise on the cost of renting the room to Cliff as part of her solo "So What?" about the indifference that comes with age. But a sympathetic character who displays such indifference is bound to change, according to the codes of musical theater, traditionally by falling in love. Schneider eventually becomes romantically involved with her tenant Schultz, as is evidenced in their duet "It Couldn't Please Me More" in scene 7. When Kost discovers Schultz leaving Schneider's room one night several scenes later, Schultz honorably declares their intended marriage, an idea that actually surprises all three of them, but that Schultz and Schneider gradually talk themselves into during their musical number "Married." In spite of the cynicism evident in Schneider's first solo, she and Schultz are quickly coded as shy, lonely, middle-aged lovers through the sentimental music and lyrics of their duets.

The romance turns to melodrama, though, when the political threat latent in the cabaret portion of the play literally crashes their engagement party. During the party scene at the grocery, Ernst arrives wearing his swastika arm band, and the nature of the smuggling jobs to Paris is suddenly revealed to Cliff. After a slightly drunken

---

[27] Jane Feuer, "The Self-Reflexive Musical and the Myth of Entertainment," in *Genre: The Musical*, 164–65. This essay's insights into the film musical are also applicable, I believe, to the stage musical.

Schultz performs a song based on the Yiddish word *meeskite* (ugly), revealing that he is Jewish, Ernst angrily tells Schneider that "this marriage is not advisable" (82). Ernst is about to storm out, but Fräulein Kost convinces him that the party can become "amusing," and as a way of entertaining the crowd, she sings the melodious nationalistic anthem first heard sung by the waiters at the Kit Kat in a previous scene, "Tomorrow Belongs to Me." She is quickly joined by others at the party, and as the tempo increases, so does the intensity. The iconography of the scene specifies the meaning of the song as Ernst, proudly sporting his swastika, becomes the center of the group. The first act ends, then, with Ernst, Kost, and most of the party guests joining in the singing, *"their voices growing louder and louder, even rather frightening"* (83), while Schneider, Schultz, Cliff, and Sally look on.

"Tomorrow Belongs to Me" had originally been heard immediately following Schneider and Schultz's first romantic duet and it was performed piously, a cappella, by a group of waiters who, according to stage directions *"are handsome, well-scrubbed, idealistic"* (55). The first two stanzas portray a rather clichéd German romanticism and mysticism conjuring up the "sun on the meadow," "the stag in the forest," "the branch of the linden," and the Rhine, so that the refrain "Tomorrow belongs to me" could easily be the pledge of the lover/poet/mystic. The pointedly nationalistic last stanza converges easily with this romanticism when arranged and sung with the restraint and harmony of a church choir, as it is in this earlier scene:

> Oh, Fatherland, Fatherland, show us the sign
> Your children have waited to see.
> The morning will come when the world is mine,
> Tomorrow belongs to me (55).

George Mosse has pointed out how the rhetoric of German fascism often alluded to unique German mystical and romantic traditions in an effort to establish that the community of National Socialism was not an enforced political one but rather "natural" or "genuine."[28] But the threatening implications of these lyrics are literally underplayed through the means of performance until the song is sung more aggressively by Kost and Ernst at the party, and at this point the political signification of the cabaret is suddenly apparant. The Kit Kat musical spectacles may have seemed like mere decadent distraction, the scene suggests, but it takes only a change in key and tempo to reveal them as Nazi theme songs. What appeared to be a romantic ballad

---

[28] George Mosse, *Masses and Man: Nationalist and Fascist Perceptions of Reality* (New York: Fertig, 1980), 195.

becomes an anthem that turns an engagement party into a rally for National Socialism and explodes the Schneider-Schultz romance.

Significantly, this is the only musical number that loses all the traces of camp playfulness evident in other skits from the Klub. Instead, the staging and delivery at the end of act 1, when the song is sung by Ernst and the others, aims at shock, or an effect that is "rather frightening": a group of German partygoers instantly transformed into Nazis. What is odd about the scene is that its success as a "show biz" moment (complete with drama, contrast, rousing music) is as obvious as its reductive, even defensive concept of history—but this concept of history can in fact be supported by the show-biz style of the spectacles of German fascism. This sequence points to the understanding of German-fascism-as-show-biz that structures the text: politics is articulated as the phenomenon of spectators being willing to join in the show—a privileged moment in the American musical in which whoever else is in the scene (for example, the sailors behind Nellie Forbush in *South Pacific*, Maria's co-workers at the dress shop in *West Side Story*) suddenly become the chorus. Here, too, the choreography emerges as spontaneous performance, with the presence of Fräulein Kost's sailors conveniently supplying a sense of dance costumes. But this very let's-all-join-the-show technique is reversed in this text in order to make a political distinction. Not everyone joins this little show at the end of act 1, after all. The two romantic couples—who have been the points of "real" character identification in the narrative—stand to one side. The moment becomes an especially stagey, highly artificial one, which freezes into a tableau. The emcee enters to walk around and through it, nodding his approval. A strong appeal is being made here to locate the scene as a "picture," a recognizable iconography: the masses transformed. The sources of that iconography are surely the scenes and stills familiar to us from *Triumph of the Will*, in which the waving, cheering spectators indeed become part of the show, and in which the regiments of young white men seem to burst into spontaneous song and recital. The point is that this very choreography, even though a familiar move in musical spectacle, is posited here as Other, a mass phenomenon to which "good" narrative characters seem to be immune. What needs to be noted, too, is the particular sexuality of the split; the heterosexual couples stand to one side in disapproval, while the effeminate emcee enters to give his approval to the group surrounding Ernst.

This tableau signals that the "spectacle" numbers of the Kit Kat and the "Limbo" space are implicitly inimical to the traditional story lines taking place in the boarding house. Early in the next act, Schneider breaks off the engagement, explaining that she cannot afford to lose her rooming license. Confirming her fears, a rock flies through Schultz's grocery window, though he cannot believe this is an anti-Semitic gesture. His sad reprise of the song "Married" signals the end of the relationship, and Schneider's last solo a few scenes later, "What Would You Do?" defending her pragmatic choice, ends this segment of the narrative. This entire subplot, then, is securely bound to the space of the stage that operates "opposite" the cabaret. Within this space, sympathetic characters meet and fall in love, become victimized by unjust politics, and are forced to separate. Lotte Lenya claims that Hal Prince later regretted making the Schultz character so sympathetic that he emerged as more of a protagonist than Cliff.[29] Certainly he is centrally located in the play's political didacticism, which is in turn most sentimentally located in the middle-aged romance, even though Cliff's later political "heroism" contributes to this trajectory in a different way. Thomas Elsaesser points out that certain kinds of popular plot lines work to "contain" fascism by reworking a political problem as a family problem, as in the melodramatic television series *Holocaust*.[30] Similarly in *Cabaret*, the Holocaust is reduced to sentimental clichés of the Schultz-Schneider plot: love that melts cynicism; the second chance of middle-aged happiness interrupted by callous youth; the sympathetic victim who refuses to believe the worst is possible.

In act 2, the "Limbo" number "If You Could See Her," performed by the emcee and his partner in a gorilla suit and tutu, is an even more searing commentary on the anti-Semitism that has refocused the Schneider-Schultz plot. This number is positioned immediately after Schneider breaks off the engagement and the rock comes through the window. The emcee leads his gorilla partner around the stage, complaining in song how her many virtues seem not to be appreciated by the world: "What good's a first impression? / If you knew her like I do, / It would change your point of view" (92). But the joke quickly becomes a political and anti-Semitic one with the last lines: "But if you could see her through my eyes, / She wouldn't look Jewish at all." At least, this is the original Kander-Ebb lyric. As Ebb explains, ". . . the song could serve to show how anti-Semitism was creeping in. . . . It got an amazing reaction from the audience, because they did laugh, and then they kind of realized what they were laughing at, and they would stop laughing. There was sort of a polite hand. It

[29] Interview of Lotte Lenya by George Voskovec, 1972, videotape, Lincoln Center Library for the Performing Arts, Billy Rose Theatre Collection, New York Public Library.

[30] Thomas Elsaesser, "*Lili Marleen*: Fascism and the Film Industry," *October* 21 (1982): 132.

made them very nervous, which is exactly what Hal wanted."[31] The "nervous" reaction was also a sensitive one; Prince received so many protests and so much pressure from religious groups that the last line was changed to "She isn't a *meeskite* at all." The creators of the show were unanimously unhappy with the change to "*meeskite*" because the intent of the line was to shock the audience with their own prejudices, and they remained mystified about their "theatrical miscalculation."[32]

The "theatrical miscalculation" is probably related to the positioning of the audience in this Limbo portion of the play, in which the boundary between diegetic and theater audience has been made ambiguous. "If You Could See Her" is staged without the cabaret tables and patrons visible earlier in, for example, "The Telephone Song," so that the audience of *Cabaret*—an audience that would presumably be shocked by the anti-Semitic joke or shocked by "how easily you could fall into a trap of prejudice"—is also positioned as the Kit Kat Klub audience for whom the emcee can play with smug assurance that it will enjoy the performance and the joke. Although this continuum between diegetic and theater audiences was often praised as part of Prince's innovative staging, its dynamic is curiously conservative, or at least traditional; far from being alienated or positioned uncomfortably, the audience is in fact positioned like the watchers of traditional music hall or even nightclub entertainment. Although these performances are wholly successful as entertainment, "the world transformed into a good show" with choreography and intriguing melody, the text presses for a political disavowal of the spectacle even as it presses for the success of "good show biz."

The sources of this split are at least partially evident in the ambiguous positioning of the Kit Kat Klub as a "real" or historical allusion to Weimar Berlin, and its use within the ambitiously historical trajectory of this play. Like the film version of *I Am a Camera*, *Cabaret*'s opening scenes take place on New Year's Eve; during the scene in which Cliff first sees Sally perform at the Klub, the emcee makes a brief grotesque appearance as a drag Baby New Year, 1930. But in spite of this specific positioning in diegetic time, Kander and Ebb admit they did almost no historical research on that era beyond listening to recordings of German music, especially Kurt Weill's. Kander claims that the music received criticism for being "watered-down Kurt Weill," but that Lenya had assured him, "When I walk out on stage and sing those songs, it is *Berlin*."[33] In a 1972 interview, though,

---

[31] Otis L. Guernsey, Jr., *Broadway Song and Story*, 141.

[32] Ibid., 141–42.

[33] Ibid., 145–46.

Lenya claims that even though she "adored" Prince's version of Berlin cabaret, it had "very little to do with cabaret" as it had actually existed in Weimar. There, she says, it was far more "satirical" and "political."[34] Ebb admits that the actual history of musical theater in pre-Hitler Germany was difficult to track down, so that instead he listened to records that gave him "sort of a feeling" for the era. One of the most interesting recordings, he says, contained lyrics that produced "screams" from the audience, presumably because the songs "were impudent and irreverent and were often sexual," but he was unable to understand a word of it, though he does not specify if this was a problem with the German language or with the quality of the recording.[35]

Yet the misunderstanding about the implications of Berlin cabaret extends further than fuzzy understanding of recorded songs. Weill and Lenya had fled Berlin because the rise of National Socialism had meant the end of both the freewheeling cabarets and the bold experimentation of Weimar theater. The cabarets were banned precisely because they were impudent, irreverent, and sexually explicit, thus offensive to the official high morality of the Nazi platform to eradicate Weimar "excrescences." Cabaret humor was also often explicitly anti-Nazi; in that sense, the musical number of *Cabaret* that comes closest to the spirit of the theater remembered by Lenya is the dance number in which the chorus girls and the emcee in drag transform themselves into a mockery of goose-stepping soldiers. This third and campy use of the "Tomorrow" song, and its second performance at the Klub, explicitly suggests that the cabaret "knows" the political implications of the song that had been performed there so innocently and, beyond that, is willing to satirize that politics. But if anti-Semitic humor can also be represented within the space of the cabaret because it, too, "makes a good show," then the Kit Kat Klub within this play is constructed as space that simply "reflects," like the back mirror, everything that coexists in 1930s Berlin. As Martin Gottfried explains in a reading that showed up frequently in the play's reviews, "the garish cabaret reflects the Germany that spawned Nazism."[36]

Even such a reductive conception points to more complicated conventions and codes of the spectacle as used in this musical. "The Germany that spawned Nazism" is constructed not only as pure entertainment but also as the opposition to another kind of entertainment—the musical melodrama of Schultz and Schneider, which ends

---

[34] Lotte Lenya, interview with George Voskovec.

[35] Otis L. Guernsey, Jr., *Broadway Song and Story*, 146.

[36] Martin Gottfried, *Opening Nights: Theater Criticism of the Sixties* (New York: Putnam, 1969), 126.

up being victimized by the operations of the cabaret specifically because the "good" narrative musical characters do not seem to recognize that they are part of a larger, ongoing political spectacle. The
two issues emerging from this are directly related. First, in spite of
the originality of *Cabaret*'s staging, the play draws on multiple theatrical and historical preconditions and conventions that can permit the
Kit Kat Klub performances to operate as both "entertainment" and,
didactically, as a reprehensible, profascist world. Second, the play
makes use of the Sally Bowles character not only as a culturally recognizable prop in this world but also as the conflation of decadent
spectacle and passive spectatorship. Unlike all the other cabaret performers, she is the only one who also interacts in the traditional, narrative portion of the play, insisting to Cliff that "the Kit Kat Klub is
the most *un*political place in Berlin" (95) and then going on to sing
"Life is a cabaret" to a room full of swastika armbands. That is, Sally
Bowles in this play operates as a rhetorical strategy that extends the
fascist politics into the sexual politics of musical theater. The ultimate
dizzy chorus girl, she simply cannot comprehend the larger scenario
of the Big Show.

As part of the ongoing narrative in Schneider's boarding house,
Sally Bowles is a witness, like Cliff, to the Schneider-Schultz romance
and its unhappy ending. She witnesses the sudden demonstration of
Nazi sympathy at the engagement party and hears Schneider's explanation that she cannot afford Nazi retaliation should she marry
Schultz. However, Sally is more directly involved in the other romantic plot line, which is related to the political situation in a more
oblique way through a variation of that highly stylized theatrical cliché, the backstage musical. The narrative structure of the classic
backstage musical consists of song-and-dance numbers that reveal the
development of the show-within-the-show in alternation with behind-
the-scenes sequences that develop the romantic plot line. By revealing the goings-on backstage, as Jane Feuer has pointed out, this kind
of musical posits on one level a demystification of entertainment even
as it "remythicizes" on another level, since only the less-than-dazzling
musical numbers are actually exposed as illusion, while the illusions
of the entire entertainment project remain untouched.[37] This Hal
Prince musical exploits the expectations of the formula by reversing
it: the backstage romance of Sally Bowles which, traditionally, would
be resolved just as the Big Show is being resolved/played, instead un-

---

[37] Jane Feuer gives this description of the backstage film musical and the "remythi-
cization" effect in "The Self-Reflective Musical and the Myth of Entertainment," 160–
62.

ravels (and will not reconnect) as Sally is about to go on for her big number, "Cabaret." Rather than resolving conflicts about show business and romance, as in the classic backstage formula, the "Cabaret" number reveals that the Kit Kat Klub audience now includes Nazis and seems to exclude politically "good" characters such as Cliff, who is beaten up and dragged away just before Sally's stage appearance. The Sally-Cliff romance in fact begins and ends with Sally's cabaret songs—he first meets her after her performance there on New Year's Eve. Thus the scuffle with the Nazis which is the context of her last song suggests the political twist of the backstage-musical narrative in this play. Cliff develops from innocent spectator to victim of specifically political agendas within the Kit Kat Klub, and the Klub itself develops into the Big Show of German fascism. But as the convention demands, the Big Show has got to be a successful one; thus Sally's initially wobbly rendition of "Cabaret" gets better as it goes on, and it is eventually repeated more forcefully in a final "dream" sequence which incorporates it into an even bigger Big Show of the closure, complete with swastika arm bands.

The backstage musical narrative here is complicated, then, by the narrative of the innocent American abroad (among the Nazis), with the result not only that the romance will be an unsuccessful one, but also that the very experience of female sexuality will have to be disavowed in a number of ways. Cliff Bradshaw is coded as the naive young writer seeking European experience, supposedly so that he can write his second novel, and Sally Bowles is the stage floozy who will clearly give it to him. But as a specific kind of European stage floozy—the Weimar cabaret siren—she is also coded from the start as a threat that will have to be either domesticated or renounced. In her first number, which is the occasion of their meeting, she appears in a slinky gown, sparkling with sequins and rustling with feathers, sporting the inevitable stockings and garters. Her song, entitled "Don't Tell Mama," is an odd reference to Van Druten's Sally and Mummy, similarly asserting sexual freedom as a disavowal of maternal identity:

> Mama thinks I'm living in a convent,
> A secluded little convent
> In the southern part of France.
> Mama doesn't even have an inkling
> That I'm working in a nightclub
> In a pair of lacy pants (18).

The song pleads "Shush up, don't tell Mama, / Don't tell Mama whatever you do" (19) because the cabaret life is apparently the opposite

14. Broadway musical *Cabaret* (1966). In feathers and garters, chorus girl Sally Bowles (Jill Haworth) performs her song "Don't Tell Mama," positioning cabaret glitz and naughtiness against a pious motherhood at home.

of everything Mama signifies: "I'm breaking every promise that I gave her" (19). So the first appearance of Sally identifies her specifically in opposition to a certain kind of respectability that is gradually posited with the "good" narrative characters in the other stage space—and also identifies this contending force as a maternal wish to keep daughters away from the project of entertainment, where they will inevitably exhibit themselves as female spectacle. As the choreographed bump and grind of the number continues, Sally is joined onstage by the Kit Kat chorus girls who imitate her exaggerated gestures of coy pleading and sexual assertion. In the meantime, the song offers more information about the singularity of "Mama" as the enemy of this sexuality, and also the enemy of the cabaret and the project of entertainment. Specifically, the lyrics identify other "family" members as conspirators in the entertainment: "You can tell my papa, that's all right, / 'Cause he comes in here every night, / But don't tell Mama what you saw!" (19). The father figure who had been a co-conspirator against Mummy in *I Am a Camera* is now co-conspirator (the necessary male viewer) in female spectacle; the admonition not to tell "what you saw" specifically locates the father as voyeur. Other family members are conjured up as similarly okay to "tell" because they, too, are part of the world that privileges "putting on the show" above respectability. This includes an uncle who is her "agent," and even a grandmother who is part of the chorus line: "You can tell my grandma, suits me fine, / Just yesterday she joined the line." However, the song concludes, "If you see my mummy, mum's the word!" (21).

This contention between sexual daughter and virtuous mother will be repeated in the narrative as her eventual pregnancy in conflict with her career at the cabaret, and this early song foretells the conclusion and also the repeated split agenda of this musical: the triumph of putting-on-a-good-show over the relative drabness of motherhood, but also the positing of the maternal as a pious alternative to the "spectacle" of an ugly politics—a nexus that is particularly ironic in light of Nazi policy concerning motherhood.

More specifically, this song foretells the conclusion of the Sally-Cliff story, and it indicates how the premises of the backstage musical narrative (in which Sally will become a success) will be contradicted by ideological pressures. Since the cabaret is the space that excludes Mama, it is certainly no place for the clean-cut young man from Harrisburg. Cliff is predictably the privileged spectator during this performance, positioned nearly at her feet so that the theater audience is aware of him as viewer, and the two characters strike up a conversation when she appears at the tables after her song. Cliff tells Sally he came to Berlin because he is looking for "something to write about" (25), and Sally asserts herself as good material by trying to shock him with a reference to "Max": "He's just the man I'm living with (CLIFF *looks a little surprised*)—this week. (*She studies his face*) I say—am I shocking you—talking like this?" (26). When Cliff indicates he knows her game here, he wins Sally's respect, so much so that the next day she appears at his door with all her baggage, explaining that there was a problem with Max and she now has nowhere to go.

Because Cliff, worried about writing his novel, is reluctant to have her move in, Sally persuades him—again predictably—with a song, the number "Perfectly Marvelous," which is significant in that this is Sally's "plot song," establishing her as the character that the narrative will follow "backstage" and also establishing her within the representational world outside the cabaret, a part of the "real" world that is witnessing the impact of Nazism through the Schneider-Schultz subplot. In addition to these codings, the song is notable for its witty use of the exaggerated language that has marked all the Sally Bowles characterizations. The song in fact emphasizes the quality of her language as in-quotation-marks because it cleverly has her imagining what someone else—Cliff—is saying about her. The lyrics instruct Cliff that if someone should question their living arrangements, he should say:

(*SALLY sings*)
I met this perfectly marvelous girl
In this perfectly wonderful place
As I lifted a glass to the start of a marvelous year.
Before you knew it she called on the phone, inviting.
Next moment I was no longer alone,
But sat reciting some perfectly beautiful verse
In my charming American style (38).

When Cliff interrupts to say that she will be a distraction to his writing, she sings about how she will in fact become its subject, so that the song is a rather significant Sally Bowles theme song:

Distracting? No, inspiring! (*She sings*)
She tells me perfectly marvelous tales
Of her thrillingly scandalous life
Which I'll probably use as a chapter or two in my book.
And since my stay in Berlin was to force
Creation,
What luck to fall on a fabulous source
Of stimulation (38–39).

As some of the fanciful rhymes ("creation/stimulation") indicate, Sally's language fits comfortably with the style of the breezy Broadway ballad, illustrating how the campiness inherent in the Broadway musical/comedy easily accommodates her character. If, of all the adaptations, the stage-play *Cabaret* Sally is the most scantily developed, this may be partially a function of what happens when Sally's frivolous language is put to music and when she interacts in the Broadway discourse of "frippery" and excess. Pushed in the direction of caricature, she turns into Betty Boop.

Cliff joins this song, and its cutesy melody splits into harmonious duet, signaling the backstage musical convention that during the course of a song, the boy and the girl grow increasingly attracted to each other, or even manage to fall in love. At the end of "Perfectly Marvelous," in a more advanced stage of musical romance, Cliff has been persuaded to let Sally share the room and, implicitly, also his bed: "(*They are in each other's arms as the lights fade*)" (40). In some ways, this song is a follow-up of her first one in that she demonstrates a cheerful promiscuity that prompts her to move into Cliff's room so casually. But in a text in which characters' songs are also their major speeches, the two songs mark the extent of her character development, which is not much. Almost everything we know about the character is summed up in this number, which defines her mainly as "perfectly wonderful" material for Cliff's writing, just as her first song had defined her as perfectly opposite whatever Mama is. By the end of the play, after Sally has made important decisions to leave Cliff and have an abortion, her only explanation is that she is "a rather strange and extraordinary person" (110). In contrast, Fräulein Schneider had introduced herself with the complex and ironic ballad "So What?" and her later difficult decision to end her engagement is given an entire song of explanation ("What Would You Do?").

All this suggests that Sally functions more as prop than as center of the stage musical because she operates as part of several cultural and theatrical clichés. She is the love interest of the backstage-musical narrative, the link between the two stage spaces, and also the archetypal dizzy chorus girl, a characterization that puts a specific spin on the Isherwood dynamic of earnest young writer versus the demimondaine. But an additional extratextual pressure operates in this Broadway musical, which involves the positioning of dizzy chorus girl in relation to the larger spectacle of Nazism. This relationship, too, is clearly established in this scene, when Sally picks up a book in Cliff's room: "This is your novel! (*She opens it*) It's in German! (*She looks at the cover*) *Mein Kampf*?" Cliff assures her that it is not his book—with the instant establishment of political difference based on authorship, for the audience knows what the play coyly pretends not to know at this moment: that the young writer from Harrisburg is the "good" writer/authority who will shortly be at war with the "bad" writer/authority for whom he has been mistaken. Cliff explains, "I thought I should know *something* about German politics" (37). Thus the Sally-Chris / Herr Issyvoo relationship continues as in all the Sally Bowles texts, but the joke on Sally's political ignorance is much more sharply played up in the stage musical version. The *"something"* she is supposed to know is represented clearly in this text, as opposed to its vaguer hints in the 1950s adaptations. The 1966 text presupposes a knowledge not just of Nazi political agendas—as had been true of the Isherwood text—but beyond that, a knowledge of the entire history of the war, including the Holocaust.

Fred Ebb recalls that it was this knowledge that made the last line of "If You Could See Her" objectionable: ". . . we started to get letters. One was from a rabbi who said that the graves of six million Jews were pleading for us not to do it [use the line]."[38] Public awareness of the Holocaust in the United States was just gaining momentum following almost two decades of muted response. The silence on the subject during the 1950s was largely the silence of both recovery and trauma on the part of survivors, who were first subject to a postwar draining of energy in attempting to reestablish themselves, and who later suffered the aftereffects of severe crisis. Elie Wiesel, whose concentration-camp memoir *Night* remains one of the most important chronicles in Holocaust literature, recalls that its original French publication in 1958 received some acclaim in Europe, but very little attention after its translation and publication in the United States the next year.[39] American public awareness increased substantially with the 1960 publication of William Shirer's *The Rise and Fall of the Third Reich*, and the considerable press attention accorded to the trial of Adolf Eichmann in Jerusalem the following year. Hannah Arendt's controversial book *The Origins of Totalitarianism*—"the banality of evil" thesis—was serialized in *The New Yorker* in 1963. The first serious Holocaust history in English, Raul Hilberg's *The Destruction of the European Jews*, appeared in 1961, but most scholars agree that the book that made the most impact on American response to the Holocaust was Richard L. Rubenstein's best-selling *After Auschwitz* in 1966. As

[38] Otis L. Guernsey, Jr., *Broadway Song and Story*, 141.

[39] Samuel G. Freedman, "Bearing Witness: The Life and Work of Elie Wiesel," *New York Times Magazine* (23 Oct. 1983): 66. See also Martin S. Bergmann and Milton E. Jucavy, eds., *Generations of the Holocaust* (New York: Basic Books, 1982) for an account of the collective trauma of the survivors which impeded immediate public accounts of their experience (5–6).

for public representation through film, the topic of Jewish persecution during the war had generally been avoided by Hollywood and was only gradually appearing in major American films by the end of the 1950s: *The Diary of Anne Frank* (1959), *Exodus* (1960), and *Judgement at Nuremberg* (1961). Sidney Lumet's successful 1965 film *The Pawnbroker* not only called attention to the horrendous history but effectively made the point, with its New York City setting, that survivors were still attempting to come to grips with it.[40]

That is, the twenty years' distance from the war that had allowed the Third Reich to become the topic of campy humor also allowed the victims to begin an identification process that would culminate not just in Holocaust studies in the 1970s but also in institutions such as the Simon Weisenthal Center in New York and the Holocaust Centers in St. Louis and Pittsburgh. Obviously, this intersection of camp and consciousness in the 1960s is significant, raising the question of cultural disavowal in the former as a means of dealing with the latter. A major problem in the two *Cabaret* texts, the 1966 stage musical and 1972 film, is the use of both these cultural codings in tandem. On the one hand, knowledge of the Holocaust makes the number "If You Could See Her as I Do" the most didactic and politically effective moment in the play. Its ability to lure a 1960s audience into both laughter and embarrassment at an anti-Semitic joke illustrates the relevance of Hal Prince's agenda to make the play a parable about how It Can Happen Here. On the other hand, this sobering parable is crossed with a campy performance-interpretation of "the Germany that spawned Nazism" as a site so kinky and outrageous that we can both "know" it as camp but also safely gain distance from it, since the "bizarre little figure" who emcees us into this world is clearly Other and monstrous.

The Sally Bowles character is located at a crucial intersection of these two codings since she is both the performer of campy Kit Kat entertainment (a part of the mechanism of disavowal) and also part of the serious narrative (unlike the purely camp/performance creation, the emcee). Her "comic" line about *Mein Kampf*, a joke that is surely meant to convey a kind of innocence, is positioned less comfortably in a text that both specifically refutes that innocence and locates her as part of the pervading camp humor about Nazism. The grounding of that humor is, after all, specifically sexual, the joke that the macho SS on the march is secretly the gay chorus boys on parade. But the stage play *Cabaret* suggests a particular cultural use of that

[40] See Annette Insdorf, *Indelible Shadows: Film and the Holocaust* (New York: Random House, 1983), 3–10.

comedy and code. Through the gender reversals (which can be used in a variety of ways in camp), Nazism can be disavowed for its secret female sexuality manifest in a grotesque way in the emcee, and manifest in a more ambiguous way through Sally Bowles, who is still aligned with the "good" narrative characters and one of the romances.

Predictably, the Kit Kat/Limbo numbers perform two cynical commentaries on the Cliff-Sally narrative. Immediately after the "Perfectly Marvelous" scene in which Sally has become Cliff's "roommate," the emcee and two chorus girls appear on the Kit Kat stage in direct address to the theater audience. "Everybody in Berlin has a perfectly marvelous roommate," the emcee announces. "Some people have two people!" (41). Thus begins the "Two Ladies" number, in which the three singers entwine themselves in suggestive poses and sing about the joys of sharing, which seems to include lesbian as well as heterosexual possibilities. By echoing Sally's language in his introduction to the song, the emcee suggests that her own casual promiscuity is part of the larger continuum of Weimar "decadence" evident in the kinkier arrangement represented by the emcee's lewd prancings with his own two "ladies."

The two "histories" of Sally and Weimar are progressively linked until the inevitable moment when Cliff forces Sally to choose between himself and cabaret life, enacting another cliché of the backstage musical except that this one is laced with disavowals of and alignments with fascism. In a scene that apparently takes place a few months after they have become roommates, Cliff admits that he has neglected his writing because he has been partying with Sally. The scene turns on rather strained audience knowledge of history. "It's so tacky and terrible—and everyone's having such a great time," says Cliff. "If this were a movie, you know what would happen? A volcano would erupt—or there'd be a tidal wave . . ."(56–57). As Elsaesser points out, such tactics of irony in narrative move the story of German fascism in the direction of melodrama "since the reader-viewer knows in advance 'how it ended.' "[41] The scene also appeals to cultural knowledge of the history of Sally Bowles, and "how it ended:"

SALLY: There must be *something* to write about?
CLIFF: Or someone? Sally Bowles? Who would ever believe it?
SALLY: You're right—I'm much too strange and extraordinary! (57)

As it turns out, Sally is the "*something* to write about" which is also the *something* Cliff needs to know and disavow about German politics,

[41] Thomas Elsaesser, "*Lili Marleen*: Fascism and the Film Industry," 132.

eventually conflated into issues surrounding her sexuality: fidelity, maternity, and female spectacle. In the meantime, in the scene describing his writing crisis, motherhood again surfaces as the contending or threatening Other that was originally suggested in the song "Don't Tell Mama." Borrowing from the Van Druten play, Masteroff has Cliff admit he has been writing "lies" to his mother in Harrisburg about how well his writing is progressing; in return, his mother is sending him money. The Harrisburg Mama, like Sally's Mama, is thus positioned in a dichotomy pitting a host of traditional values (hard work, honesty, trust) against wild partying, performances, and show business in Weimar Berlin. As the play's supposed protagonist, Cliff will have no choice eventually except to go home (to noncabaret / Mama). In the present scene, though, Cliff breaks into a love song, "Why Should I Wake Up?" positing that life with Sally is better than "real" life.

But motherhood takes a more specifically threatening turn at this point. First, Sally gets a letter from a girlfriend who has "come to a bad end. . . . She met this absolutely dreary boy and fell hopelessly in love with him and married him and now they have two children. (*She indicates the letter*) Probably another one on the way" (59). Moreover, Sally suddenly reveals that she, too, has "one on the way," about which she feels rather ambiguous, mostly in deference to Cliff: "It does seem—a bad idea. Good heavens, if you find *me* distracting—can you imagine a baby!" (60). But Cliff, apparently because he is "in love with the world's craziest girl," as he puts it (60), is willing to extend the romance into the romance of the family: "Who says I'd be a terrible father?" (60). He decides, in fact, that this will be the motivation for serious writing on his part, translating the pregnancy entirely into paternal terms without questioning whether Sally would be a terrible mother—a likelihood for which the narrative sets her up while at the same time valorizing Cliff's idealistic fatherhood.

Sally's suggestion that she, too, will help with money, by her work at the Klub, is shut out with a quick protest from Cliff. But a better opportunity for money conveniently arrives at the door through Ernst, who appears with an offer to have Cliff do a smuggling job for "a very good cause" with a payoff of seventy-five marks. "Seventy-five marks!" Sally exclaims. "Cliff—it's a gift from heaven!" (62). Cliff and Sally do not realize the "gift" is actually from the Nazis, as they discover later at the engagement party, although Sally had mentioned to Cliff in an earlier scene that Ernst is involved with "some political party" (36) which should make the audience suspicious, especially when Cliff now protests that he does not want to know about the source. When the lights go down on this happy moment, with the toast—"*Prosit!*"—they come up again on the emcee's cynical introduction to his "Money" song: "*Prosit!* You see? There's more than one way to make money!" (64).

The "Money" number, distinctly different from the one later developed by Kander and Ebb for the Fosse film, is a campy send-up not only of the new financial complication in the narrative but also of female spectacle as a kind of prostitution. The emcee's lyrics frankly extoll the financial security of the pimp business. He explains that in these bad times, he is "sitting pretty" with a lot of money even though everyone else in his family is desparate enough to sell one another:

> I know my little cousin Eric
> Has his creditors hysterical,
> And also Cousin Herman
> Had to pawn his mother's ermine,
> And my sister and my brother
> Took to hocking one another, too (65).

As for the emcee, "I've got all the money I need," his song boasts. The emcee stops to explain: "You wonder where I get my money? I have something to sell! Love! For all tastes! From all over! Meet Olga, my Russian ruble!" (65). With that, the emcee introduces a series of scantily and exotically costumed women who each represent a foreign currency. They wear erotic costume-toys which the emcee plays with and fondles: the "Japanese girl" has a yen pinned to each breast, the "American girl" sports two military half-drums around her breasts, and finally "Brünnhilde, my German mark," is lifted through the air with a golden gong between her thighs—which the emcee strikes on the way down.

Although commenting cynically on Cliff's unwitting prostitution of himself to Nazism, this number is in addition a brilliant camping-up of a musical cliché from the 1930s, the "big number" that, as Richard Dyer has pointed out, produces an abundance of choreographed female bodies as an "answer" to the poverty that is represented in the narrative portion of the text.[42] The Broadway *Cabaret*

---

[42] This is Richard Dyer's theory of how this works in the film musical *Gold Diggers of 1933*, in which capitalist "solutions" are offered in the musical numbers (abundance instead of poverty) and then undercut by the patently nonrealistic presentation of these numbers. But Dyer claims this paradigm is complicated beyond such a dichotomy because the representational elements of the numbers (women's bodies exposed onstage) also suggest certain "truths" deriving from the "realism" of the narrative—for example, "that women's only capital is their bodies as objects," the continuum of gold digging and prostitution, and the fact that their bodies are clearly subservient to the larger system: in this case, the overall design of the choreography. See "Entertainment and Utopia" in *Genre: The Musical*, 186.

"Money" number with its refrain, "I'm sitting pretty," is perhaps a direct allusion to the Busby Berkeley number "We're in the Money" in Mervyn LeRoy's *Gold Diggers of 1933* (1933) in which show girls are dressed like giant, glittering coins. But *Cabaret's* "Money" blatantly foregrounds the relationship between prostitution and female spectacle by the emcee's boastful self-description as a pimp who controls that spectacle, which includes, in addition to the "currency" women, the cabaret chorus girls (in stockings and garters) who join the dance and at one point lie on their backs close to the edge of the stage, legs stretched upward in the classic Busby Berkeley V-spread framing the rest of the choreography.

Because these are not in fact Busby Berkeley chorus girls but rather grotesque imitations of them, the effect is rather shocking. Yet as campy send-up of Berkeley, this number is also enormously successful as the project of entertainment. By the time the emcee is surrounded by his "currency" and framed by the spread, stockinged legs in the song's finale, their gestures attuned to the jazzy melody of the "Money" song, it would be difficult to locate a point of distance or irony from which the number could be anything but "successful" Broadway spectacle. The camp irony that anchors the terms of the send-up has been contained by the camp elements of excess and "frippery" which are inherent elements of "good show business." With the rouged emcee in charge of this spectacle, and with the addition of a number of effeminate Kit Kat waiters who also join this number at the end, the "exposure" this number makes—that much of Broadway musical's inclination toward the excessive "big number" derives from a gay, camp sensibility—does not detract from its impact as entertainment. Likewise, the fetishization of female sexuality in the excessive costumes and in the choreography ends up being celebrated as camp rather than positioned as subject to critique. This also applies to the positioning of Sally Bowles in her own two cabaret numbers; the peek a boo effect of the feathers, garters, and lacy pants constitutes a fairly classic mechanism of fetishization and disavowal even as it is part of the ongoing campy "joke" about Weimar decadence.

Indeed, particular ideological positionings of fascism within popular culture make possible *Cabaret's* project of the Big Show, seamlessly positioned within an anti-Nazi trajectory even as it utilizes a sense of spectacle that is shamelessly aligned with the Big Show in *Triumph of the Will*. The cabaret and "Limbo" numbers are gradually aligned with concepts of decadence (sexual promiscuity and lesbianism in "Two Ladies," prostitution in "Money"), and then more specifically with fascist politics (the reprise of "Tomorrow Belongs to Me" as an anthem for National Socialism, the anti-Semitism of "If You Could See Her"). An entire complex politics can be made to seem comprehensible—that is, immediate and inevitable—through song and dance: the economic problems of Weimar can be replayed as gold digging à la Busby Berkeley: impoverished Germans will do anything to survive, sell anything—including one another—and by implication will also eventually "buy" anything that seems to work (National Socialism). Moreover, National Socialism has itself become popularized, through camp, as the look and sound of a spectacle that works in a neat continuum with the campiness of Broadway musical. Chorus girls can instantly move from a high kick into a goose step because both steps share an artificiality that makes good show business; the drag/chorus girl number deliberately foregrounds this continuum between *Triumph of the Will* and Busby Berkeley. One of Adolf Hitler's favorite film scenes, according to Gerald Mast, was Berkeley's "By a Waterfall" number from Lloyd Bacon's *Footlight Parade* (1933), supposedly because it so much resembles the Nazi aesthetic of the human figure abstracted into a huge design.[43]

In foregrounding this continuum, *Cabaret* works on a more sophisticated premise than simply inviting us to enjoy what we denounce. The denouncable has already been articulated in popular culture through the embrace of Nazi style by camp, which recognizes Nazi self-representations as show-biz excess, and in extension makes it accessible as theater and as spectacle specifically related to a gay sensibility. When the emcee appears in drag as the cabaret girl, the chain of signification extends not just to Dietrich's Lola but also to a camp recognition of the excesses of Lola as material for a joke about gender—which can be surfaced in drag performance. Once again, then, Sally Bowles as a particular sign makes meaning in relation to a gay subtext or reference.[44] In this text, the relationship is suggested through the narrative in which Sally's final choice is between a wholly bourgeois heterosexuality and the "other" sexuality of the Kit Kat Klub.

A rigorous hierarchy of gender and sex operates in this narrative

[43] Gerald Mast makes this point about Hitler in *Can't Help Singin': The American Musical on Stage and Screen*, 134.

[44] In Mark Booth's introductory pages to *Camp*, three large photos illustrate the inheritance from Dietrich: the famous upraised-leg still from *The Blue Angel*, a still of Helmut Berger doing Dietrich in drag in Visconti's *The Damned*, and finally a shot of Liza Minnelli in the Fosse film: "a further remove from Lola," says Booth, "though the references are unmistakable" (12). In Fosse's later film version, this inheritance through transvestism is much more blatantly developed with shots that play up specific physical resemblances between Sally and the emcee.

location of heterosexuality in regard to Cliff. As the Kit Kat numbers display progressively more "decadent" positions regarding sexuality, Cliff grows progressively more inclined toward family, fatherhood, and "home" (site of the invisible but wholly good and anticabaret Mama). As such, his relationship with Sally grows predictably argumentative, articulated as cabaret/political evil versus patriarchal righteousness. In act 2, following the disastrous engagement party, Sally is unable to understand why Cliff refuses to allow her to go back to her job at the Kit Kat, and why he himself refuses to take on any more of Ernst's smuggling jobs which would pay so well—"the very easiest way in the world to make money," she says, unwittingly aligning it with prostitution. Cliff is aghast at her political indifference, and as the following exchange illustrates, his moralistic antifascism is easily conflated with his authority as traditional father:

> CLIFF: . . . Someday I've simply got to sit you down and read you a newspaper. You'll be amazed at what's going on.
> SALLY: You mean—politics? But what has *that* to do with us?
> CLIFF: You're right. *Nothing* has anything to do with us. Sally, can't you see—if you're not against all this, you're for it—or you might as well be.
> SALLY: At any rate, the Kit Kat Klub is the most *un*political place in Berlin. Even *you've* got to admit *that*.
> CLIFF: Sally—do me a favor? Let *me* earn the money for this family (95).

Later in the scene, Cliff announces that he intends to take Sally "home" to America with him immediately. Shocked, Sally protests, "But we love it here!" This allows Cliff to reveal that his all-American political purity has triumphed over his capacity for decadent partying. The conflict here between the protagonist's prescient wisdom and Sally's political indifference stretches the ironic into the corny as Cliff's full-blown alarm (The Nazis are coming!) makes Sally a rather predictable fool of history: "Sally—wake up! The party in Berlin is *over*! . . . And it's going to get a lot worse" (100).

Significantly, with Sally's show-biz objection to this, the narrative crisis of backstage-musical converges with the crisis of history at the point of her sexuality. The conflict is signified literally as erotic showgirl-for-the-Fatherland versus an asexual motherhood in the land of the free. "But what about *me*?" Sally demands. "My career?" Cliff replies, "You've got a new career" (100–101). Thus the prurient motherhood first evoked in "Don't Tell Mama" has returned to ground one side of an increasingly polarized opposition between cabaret life/Berlin/fascism and motherhood/America/antifascism. Yet the "motherhood" evoked here is certainly no less a patriarchal construction than the construction of Sally with feathers and garters as cabaret show girl. "Motherhood" acts as a signifier directly in relation to Cliff as father who makes the money, makes decisions, and demands monogamy as a kind of inevitable alternative to show business: "And the only way you'll get a job in New York or Paris or London is by sleeping with someone else! But you're sleeping with *me* these days!" he tells her angrily in the next scene (103). Cliff is the Law of the Father, too, in that he is literally the authority and knowledge that will write history—as he does in the last scene of the play, pulling out his writing pad as the train crosses the border: "There was a cabaret and there was a master of ceremonies and there was a city called Berlin in a country called Germany," he says aloud as he writes, "—and it was the end of the world and I was dancing with Sally Bowles—and we were both fast asleep" (112–13). Of all the narrative characters, Cliff is the only one to "wake up," as he had urged Sally to do in a previous scene, so that he is located not only as the language/authority of "the story of 1931 Berlin" but also literally as the play's consciousness as well as its conscience. In this oedipal scheme, his guilt of sleeping with the mother (partying/sleeping with Sally in wild Weimar Berlin) can be expunged by having the maternal entirely recontained within the terms of the symbolic—which in this case is politically specific: the patriarchal family at Home, in America, entirely removed from the sexual and political decadence of Germany.

As this dynamic illustrates, Sally's metonymic function as an extension of this sexual-political evil is much more privileged than it had been in the two 1950s adaptations, just as the sexual-political evil "mirrored" in the Kit Kat Klub is more didactically articulated. In the key scene, immediately following Cliff's demand that she return home with him, he finds her at the cabaret where she runs backstage before he can persuade her otherwise. Cliff is then quickly approached by Ernst, who offers another smuggling job on behalf of National Socialism. Cliff responds by socking Ernst in the jaw, thereby repeating the one gesture and episode each adaptation lovingly retains: the protagonist gets an opportunity to punch a Nazi. After Cliff is dragged off by two more men wearing swastika arm bands—a spectacle that the emcee enjoys *as if the fight were part of the floor show*," as the stage directions specify—Sally appears onstage to sing "Cabaret," its lyrics confirming what the play's larger structure has been emphasizing—that life is indeed a cabaret. What appears as entertainment at the Kit Kat is "life" and in fact history, and Sally performs it (and in fact "is" it, in that she is a manifestation of threatening sexuality) but does not understand it.

History outside the theater in 1966 worked to prove Sally an additional kind of fool or more seriously implicated in what was happening around her. The convergence of history, theater, and spectacle would be gradually developed throughout the decade as street theater or "happenings," but already the phenomenon of the mass demonstration was highly evident in both the civil rights movement and in protest over American involvement in Vietnam. The lyrics of Sally's song, "What good is sitting alone in your room?"—worked with double irony at a moment in which young people were increasingly interested in political activism and were denouncing passivity as dangerous or even immoral. Television news coverage regularly provided footage of the sit-in, the demonstration, the march—the spectacle that became history. These street tactics were often laced with violence. Both the 1963 demonstration in Birmingham and the police attacks with dogs and cattle prods were caught on camera, as was the burning of Watts in 1965. Sally Bowles's determined indifference— "You mean—politics? But what has *that* to do with us?"—is more suspect than innocent in the double positioning of 1966 commentary on 1931 Berlin and the growing prevalence of Cliff's discourse: "If you're not against all this, you're for it." The reference to National Socialism in this context has its own historical hooks. Todd Gitlin recalls how, following the years in which knowledge and memory of the Holocaust were suppressed, the "guilt" of American survivors worked itself out in the issues of the 1960s: ". . . to me and people I knew, it was American bombs which were the closest thing to an immoral equivalent of Auschwitz in our lifetimes. . . . atrocities committed by innocent America rang the old alarms—even if the parallels were drawn too easily, overdrawn, with crucial differences obscured. . . . We were going to be active where our parents' generation had been passive. . . . Then we could tell our parents: We learned when we were children that massacres really happen and the private life is not enough."[45] Especially in contrast to Sally's defensiveness about her "private life" during the rise of the Reich, Cliff's disavowal of Berlin and his ability to write about it constitute a certain kind of heroism for him in the 1960s. In turn, the lyrics of Sally's "Cabaret" song are especially alarming in the double perspective of 1930 and 1966: "No use permitting some prophet of doom / To wipe every smile away. / Life is a cabaret, old chum, / Come to the cabaret" (105). By the time the play was in its third year on Broadway, concurrently with *Hair*, Sally must have been read as a particularly suspect young woman, Betty Boop in the Age of Aquarius.

In her final appearance of the narrative, Sally appears in Cliff's room the morning after her "Cabaret" song, pours herself a gin, and

[45] Todd Gitlin, *The Sixties: Years of Hope, Days of Rage*, 25–26.

makes a toast: "*Hals and Beinbruch*. It means neck and leg break. It's supposed to stop it from happening—though I doubt it does. I doubt you can stop *anything* happening" (109–10). This could be read merely as a fatalistic interpretation of history, but it resonates as moralistic irony in the context of Cliff's idealistic decision to take action (by fighting with the Nazis in the cabaret and by returning to America). It has even more peculiar resonance in the context of Sally's own decision revealed in this scene, her announcement that in fact she could stop something from "happening." She has just come back from a doctor who, in exchange for her fur coat, performed an abortion. Significantly, when she tells this to Cliff, he slaps her, just as he had struck Ernst. The political positioning of the abortion is reinforced with the brief, heavily portentous appearance of Herr Schultz in this scene, who has come to say good-bye (but surely, as a Jew in Hitler's Germany, also the Big Good-bye). He has barely closed the door and walked off to his doom when Sally makes her announcement and—almost as a stand-in for the Nazi Ernst—is struck by Cliff. This use of abortion as signifier of Sally's political alignment is especially ironic in light of the actual politics of National Socialism in regard to motherhood: the fanaticism of the Mother's Day campaign and the nationalistic basis of the Third Reich's staunch antiabortion policies.[46]

Sally then explains her decision in virtually the same terms that Van Druten's Sally had used in refusing to go "home" with the protagonist at the end of *I Am a Camera*. "I'd spoil it, Cliff," the *Cabaret* Sally says. "I'd run away with the first exciting thing that came along. I guess I really am a rather strange and extraordinary person" (110). But whereas the refusal of Mummy and England in the earlier play had suggested a freedom from the wider 1950s narrative of women's stories, Sally's freedom in the latter play is aligned with the entire cabaret and Berlin scene that Cliff must renounce. Unlike the previous adaptations, this play ends with Sally not in a moment of triumph, but on a note of distinct regret; the stage directions specify that she "wipes her eyes" while she forces herself to smile farewell. "Goodby, Cliff. Dedicate your book to me!" she calls as he walks out. He literally leaves her to darkness: "*Her smile fades. She turns to the door as the lights dim very slowly*" (111).

---

[46] Claudia Koonz documents how the Reich's antiabortion policy was based on the proposition that procreation was the business not just of the state but the race: "Nazi policy rested on the axiom 'Your body does not belong to you' " but rather belongs to " 'your blood brethren (*Sippe*) and . . . your *Volk*' " (267). Carrying out this policy, she reports that "arrests and convictions of people performing or aiding in abortion doubled, and punishments became more severe" (186).

As a variation of the backstage musical, *Cabaret* engineers a shocking reversal in that the world of performance and entertainment becomes what the hero must denounce to maintain his integrity. Although the classic backstage musical most often uses the theater world (or film world) as backdrop for the all-American success story, this all-American character can be a success only by distancing himself from it. At the same time, the "success story" of Cliff's writing career, which is also the story of his political heroism, works as a signifier only in relation to the other and more ambiguous career story in the narrative, which is Sally's. She has rejected the option of domesticity and made the decision to go on with the show, the latter being exactly what the heroine of the backstage musical is supposed to do.[47] But Sally is clearly not pointed to success in show business, and she can attain heroism in the dynamics of this text only by denouncing Berlin and joining Cliff for life in Harrisburg, with the abortion as her final alignment away from this option.

With these reversals of the formula stage-success story, the Sally Bowles character thus concedes the point of identification in the backstage-musical narrative to Cliff, just as she concedes the fascination of sexuality to the emcee. Neither as exciting as the master of spectacle nor as virtuous as the putative hero, Sally becomes in this text another kind of vanishing lady—more specifically, a vanquished one, whose disavowal is politically imperative. Even in the "final story" as written by Cliff at the end, she is not as important as the emcee: "There was a cabaret and there was a master of ceremonies and there was a city called Berlin . . ." (112). Perverse, smooth, haunting, the emcee in charge of the Big Show—the Kit Kat and Nazism— wins back Sally, so to speak, in the suggested rivalry with the Forces of Good. In the logic of the backstage musical, this will be Sally's mate and dancing partner, though it will be another six years before Bob Fosse actually has them mate and dance together as part of the cabaret.

It could be argued that the relatively unsympathetic treatment of Sally in relation to the political/narrative hero had some uncomfortable correlations in the sexual politics of the real political activists of the 1960s. Todd Gitlin recalls from his own experience in the SDS that the "sexual intensity" matched the political intensity, but in an

---

[47] See Richard Hasbany, "The Musical Goes Ironic: The Evolution of Genres," *Journal of American Culture* 1 (1978): 120–37. Hasbany makes the argument that the show-business world usually functions as a microcosm of American society, enabling the all-American success story in the narrative. He claims that Sally Bowles's decision to "go on with the show" can be positioned in relation to typical American backstage musical heroines who make similar decisions.

atmosphere of "homoerotic bonding" which the men would not have admitted: "The movement hangs together on the head of a penis," one of his colleagues told him "half-ironically." "The vulgar way to say it," Gitlin admits, "was that the clan was consolidated through the exchange of women."[48] In *Cabaret*, Cliff's political heroism operates in a similar exchange; what gets "consolidated" is his opposition to fascism and anti-Semitism, and what has to be embraced and disavowed is Sally as sexual experience and as "play," mere performance as opposed to political action.

So far, this trajectory sorts itself out into an oedipal constellation that seems duplicated in contemporary history, a political/narrative heroism that hangs together on the head of a penis. But it is not Cliff who has the last word in this text, no matter how piously he begins to write the story on the train. The final word belongs to the emcee, of course, who "gets" Sally in the exchange by which Cliff wins political/ moral heroism. In the final "dream" sequence composed supposedly of Cliff's memories of Berlin, the stage turns into a cabaret again, with the emcee triumphantly announcing the success of the performance: "Where are your troubles now?" he asks in direct address to the theater audience. "Forgotten? I told you so!" (113). Gradually the orchestra, waiters, and tables appear, too, but the stage directions specify that *"this time the picture and the mood are much different. The girls are not as pretty, German uniforms and swastika arm bands are apparent; it is not as bright, a dreamlike quality prevails"* (113). Sally also reappears to sing a stanza from "Cabaret," and eventually everything disappears into darkness except the emcee, who lingers to wish the audience good-bye in German and French. This sequence as positioned in the text is literally Cliff's daydream, his last indulgence in the fantasy of the Kit Kat before he goes off to do his serious work of writing about it. In a more general way, the Kit Kat performances operate as the fantasy of the narrative, like the tilted mirror, distorting the story into its most garish but also most entertaining moments. Whereas the oedipal story encourages the hero to get on with his serious politics and work, Sally's song beckons him back to the world of play and music.[49]

[48] Todd Gitlin, *The Sixties: Years of Hope, Days of Rage*, 108–9.

[49] Describing a similar moment in the film *The Bandwagon*, Dana Polan argues that the musical number "works in another direction to acknowledge the claims of a pleasure principle against a performance principle. . . . If the Oedipal trajectory insists on the need to go beyond primary attachments, to cast off incest for the sake of 'respectability,' the musical is a world which refuses this trajectory (even when the story doesn't)." The hero of *Bandwagon* finally manages to negotiate a romance that is turned into (and displaced by) musical spectacle and the assurance of an eternal "big show," so that, Polan claims, "Oedipus has been left behind with a world of responsibility, a world where people face the social Other." See "It Could be Oedipus Rex: Denial and

But the stage play *Cabaret* wants to have it both ways: to validate the righteousness of the good oedipal hero who will renounce romance and fascism (the giant social Other looming here) and also to validate the insistence—and pleasure—of the fantasy in which the show goes on forever.

Little wonder that the show brought Joel Grey not only stardom but also strong identification and recognition as an archetypal master of ceremonies of the fantasy world where languages and genders are blurred. Within that world, German fascism as history can be represented as the shocking, evil past but also virtually disavowed because it is positioned as entertainment. Whereas the overt political boundaries of this text are clearly articulated—the National Socialists of the 1930s, the implied racism of the 1960s—the boundaries evoked most often in the Kit Kat performances are those of gender, and the transgressions of those boundaries are quickly recontained. That is, the very mechanisms of a disavowal of history—the campy performances, costumes, and hints of transvestism that provide such powerful entertainment—comprise a discourse that denies the oedipal world of responsibility only to rearticulate it as a final positing of political and sexual boundary. By challenging the ordered heterosexuality of the two romances in the narrative, the Kit Kat fantasies of "Two Ladies" or the emcee in drag evoke the possibility of the blur of differences, polymorphous pleasure. But among all the assorted colors and genders of the Kit Kat Klub, one sign works to stop the play of difference abruptly and with particular force. This is the swastika worn first by Ernst, then by other customers on the cabaret side of the stage. You could say that the antioedipal fantasy stops here, not so much with the didactic narratives providing the corrective mirror in the other staging as with the Kit Kat wall mirror embracing the signification of final, irrevocable difference. In relation to that sign, the entire discourse of camp entertainment operates as utopian ("Where are your troubles now? Forgotten?") in a particularly ingenious way. The pleasure of the entertainment consists of a disavowal of German fascism, itself made instantly uncomplicated, direct and vivid. Nazism is represented as perversion, but it is a perversion that can be enjoyed as black humor, a sense of the outrageous, a "secret" knowledge of sexual aberration. Thus any rational analysis of fascism is cut off by the fascination of the spectacle itself, in a specifically sexual aestheticization of politics.

Difference in *The Bandwagon* or, The American Musical as American Gothic," *Ciné-Tracts* 14 (1981): 18, 25.

Chapter Six

"DOESN'T MY BODY DRIVE YOU WILD
WITH DESIRE?"

FOSSE'S CABARET

WITHOUT DOUBT, the most prescient reviewer of the
stage musical *Cabaret* was Roger Dettmer of *Chicago's American*, who complained that Hal Prince's project amounted
to "a watered-down *Sweet Charity* with swastikas."[1] The *Sweet Charity*
to which he refers is the musical that opened on Broadway the same
year as the Hal Prince production. The brilliant choreographer of
Charity was Bob Fosse, a song-and-dance man who had been a child
performer of a vaudeville family and whose choreography on Broadway had included the immensely successful *Pajama Game* (1954), followed by hits such as *Damn Yankees* (1955) and *How to Succeed in Business Without Really Trying* (1961). The success of *Sweet Charity* on stage
led to Fosse's being given his first director's chair for the far less successful 1969 film version with Shirley MacLaine. Nevertheless, the
following year, producer Cy Feuer, who had worked with Fosse on
two earlier Broadway projects, chose him as director for the film adaptation of *Cabaret*, cofinanced by Allied Artists and the American
Broadcasting Company.

In one sense, then, Dettmer's irate observation unwittingly pointed
to *Cabaret*'s future in Hollywood, where Nazism would be choreographed by a master of show business for the much wider audience
of mainstream film. Dettmer's observation is also a prediction of the
fate of Sally Bowles at the hands of the master choreographer who is
accustomed to working with first-class women performers such as
Gwen Verdon and MacLaine. Isherwood's demimondaine makes a
dazzling comeback after her doubtful singing career in all her previous texts, and like MacLaine's dancing prostitute, Charity, is clearly
the dazzling star and center of the film. With the swastikas already in
place, the musical starring Liza Minnelli was bound to be a *Sweet Sally
Bowles*, a major film breakthrough for Minnelli, who won an Acad-

[1] Roger Dettmer, " 'Cabaret' Diluted 'Sweet Charity,' " *Chicago's American* (28 Nov.
1968).

emy Award for her performance and whose image in boots and garters would become the new film iconography of wild Weimar Berlin.

In an interview shortly after the release of the film, Christopher Isherwood himself pointed out the historical and narrative contradictions that emerge with the casting of a genuinely big-star Sally Bowles: "You have this little girl saying, 'Oh, I'll never make it. I haven't really any talent.' Then she comes on the stage and you realize that she's every inch Judy Garland's daughter. . . . The truth is that this cabaret would have attracted half of Europe. You wouldn't have been able to get in for months on end."[2] Director Fosse's approach to historical research was entirely visual; interestingly enough, in trying to capture the "look" of Weimar, his primary source was apparently the grotesquely stylized cartoons of George Grosz.[3] But Fosse admits he was not interested in history per se, and in one interview he shows some confusion about what exactly a cabaret in that era had been, and how it differed from Weimar nightclubs. Yet his remarks also hint at the inevitable historical hooks of his project in film history as well as in Weimar history: "I was not out to make a factual film, a documentary," says Fosse. ". . . I was not trying to do *The Damned*. I was not trying to do a documentary on that period. I wanted to tell a love story, about human relationships."[4] The defensiveness of his statement no doubt can be traced to the comments of the many reviewers who were quick to mention Visconti's 1969 *The Damned* (as well as Von Sternberg's *The Blue Angel*) as precedents for the new Sally Bowles story, which is at once "a love story" like its immediate stage predecessor, but also a dynamic song-and-dance vehicle for Minnelli.

Isherwood's complaint about inconsistencies of history and narrative also points to the larger problem of a Sally Bowles whose construction is split between Fosse's aim to create a powerful, mainstream musical (high-quality performance and a centralized romance) and the film precedents that had articulated Weimar cabaret decadence as a more sexually marginal phenomenon. Fosse's Sally Bowles, in taking up the familiar positioning of the cabaret siren à la Dietrich, is appearing, after all, in the wake of *The Damned*'s famous Dietrich drag scene performed by Helmut Berger, supposedly during the burning of the Reichstag. Although he denies having any concern for history, Fosse nevertheless borrows extensively from this film

[2] David J. Geherin, "An Interview with Christopher Isherwood," *Journal of Narrative Technique* 2 (1972): 147.

[3] See the account of on-location filming in Kevin Boyd Grubb, *Razzle Dazzle: The Life and Work of Bob Fosse* (New York: St. Martin's, 1989), 145–51.

[4] Lil Picard, "Interview with Bob Fosse," *Inter/View* (Mar. 1972): 8.

history in Sally's construction. The Sally Bowles who appears in high-heeled boots singing a relentless good-bye to *"Mein lieber Herr"* is not entirely his own invention, or entirely a quotation from Hal Prince's stage version, but works as a cultural reference to Dietrich's theme song about fatal attraction from *The Blue Angel*: "Men cluster around me / Like moths around a flame / And if their wings burn / I know I'm not to blame." As Mark Booth puts it, lining up Minnelli with both Dietrich and the drag version in *The Damned*, Minnelli "brings cheerleader enthusiasm" to the role[5]—Sally as the American cheer-leader Lola.

The Americanization of Sally Bowles was not Fosse's idea but orig-inates in Jay Presson Allen's 1970 screenplay, which sketches out most of the major narrative moves that eventually came to the screen. The Christopher character is reincarnated as British Brian Roberts, and his relationship with Sally is once again centralized. Early in the narrative, Brian confesses that he "doesn't sleep with girls," but Sally seems to reverse this condition—at least temporarily—and their friendship develops into a love affair. The Fritz-Natalia romance from the *I Am a Camera* adaptations returns again as the subplot, and the wealthy American Clive from the 1950s versions is replaced by an equally wealthy German baron who seduces both Sally and Brian. Sal-ly's pregnancy results from this ménage-à-trois, so that she does not know which is the father, but she takes up Brian's courageous offer of marriage. As in the musical version, this plan ends when she de-cides to have an abortion, which also ends her relationship with Brian and precipitates his departure from Berlin. Allen's screenplay bor-rows extensively from all three previous adaptations, then, but is the first to bring forward the submerged gay identification of Brian/Christopher.

Curiously enough, rather than resurrecting Mummy from Van Druten, Allen introduces Daddy, giving Sally a major father complex as a motivation for her ambition and promiscuity. In her original screenplay, Mr. Bowles appears in two key scenes to confirm Sally as his little-girl-with-silly-ambitions and later to disavow her entirely when she appears as sexual spectacle in front of his colleagues. Later, the character Mr. Bowles was eliminated from the film altogether ex-cept as the offscreen reference that remains as Sally's rather heavily Freudian motivation and as the opportunity for Brian to comfort Sally and suddenly gain his virility: Sally "cures" Brian's failed het-erosexuality at the moment when she has taken off her garish makeup and is crying because Daddy doesn't love her. In Allen's

[5] Mark Booth, *Camp*, 12.

screenplay, Sally also retains the careless anti-Semitic language that had marked her character in Isherwood's original story, and this, too, was eventually eliminated, no doubt in order to make the character more attractive. Liza Minnelli understood her role to be fairly sympathetic, if immature: "Most people like Sally. She very much represents her era. She tries desperately to be original, and enjoys shocking people. She's also selfish and childish. . . ."[6] In fact, Sally's childlike behavior often operates in a dynamic that parallels Van Druten's concern to "neutralize" her sexual threat, in this case also making her more palatable as Big Star of a musical.

Although ABC studios thought Allen's screenplay was "great," Fosse reports, he himself thought "it needed a great deal of work," and he eventually convinced the producers to bring in Hugh Wheeler to do extensive revisions. The screenplay dispute was apparently the first skirmish in Fosse's long battle for control of the film project. Even though Cy Feuer admired Fosse's work, this directorship was a major risk for the studio because Fosse's first film, *Sweet Charity*, had been a box-office bomb. According to Fosse, Feuer and the studio consistently attempted interference with techniques and elements that later won considerable praise, such as the heavy use of lens filters to produce the colors and tones of the smoky cabaret. The struggle with Feuer became heated, but sources agree that Fosse won the major skirmishes and the final product was his own.[7] Generally, the final text bears the imprint less of Allen's talky screenplay than of the visual style that has become synonymous with Fosse: dynamic editing, dazzlingly original and sexy musical performances, the use of suggestive and unusual lighting, and a camera that, during musical numbers, is almost as mobile as the performers.

In terms of the evolution of Sally Bowles, it is precisely this unique and overwhelming visual style that brings to the forefront of this text many of the issues that had been present as subtexts in all her other versions. This includes the play of concealment and revelation as sexual identity and crisis; ambiguous physical representation of gender boundary; and the dynamics of spectacle and spectatorship as representative of German fascism. These issues are immediately evident in the film's remarkable opening sequence which, like the stage play, positions the audience so that it is confronted with a representation of itself in an opening shot of a mirror reflecting the crowd at the

---

[6] "Liza Minnelli 'Cabaret' Role a Character Study," *Entertainment Today* (31 Mar. 1972): 2.

[7] A detailed account of the struggle with ABC from Fosse's point of view can be found in Robert Alan Authur's "Hanging Out," *Esquire* (Aug. 1973): 6ff. Also see Kevin Boyd Grubb, *Razzle Dazzle*, 153.

cabaret. However, this mirror is a textured, distorting one that transforms human figures into barely recognizable shapes; in the center, a bright, hard shape that might be a strand of pearls bears a distinct resemblance to a set of open teeth. The distortion itself suggests that the film audience is both represented by and displaced by the diegetic audience, the latter sharing its positioning as an ugly version of the former.

The emcee enters the shot as one of the figures in the mirror, but he turns to address the camera directly as he begins his opening song, "*Willkommen.*" In this brief backward-tracking shot which includes his turn to the camera, the frame is split between the representational emcee—gaudy, leering, but recognizable as a certain kind of campy performer—and his reflection as a colorful abstraction in the mirror that includes the cabaret audience. Directly addressed by his performance, the film audience is also positioned with the reflected crowd in that shot, creating an uneasy relationship between the two audiences which the text both courts and attempts to occlude. That is, like the stage play, the Fosse film often wants to have it both ways, with a film audience shocked by the spectacle, disengaged from the diegetic spectators, and a film audience wholly caught up in the project of entertainment. Although this split spectatorship was also present in the Hal Prince production, it is greatly exploited in the film version with the camera's powerful ability to enunciate and interpolate the spectator in processes of identification and disavowal. This first close-up gives us, moreover, not a privileging shot of a sympathetic narrative character who can suture us into the text, but a garishly painted face that is at once disconcerting and also recognizable by 1972 in the highly publicized theatrics of "gender-fuck" and camp. Unlike Cliff in the stage version, no character in Fosse's film uses the discourse of confrontation to say "If you're not against all this, you're for it." Instead, the framing and editing that conflates us with and distances us from the diegetic cabaret audience and its freaky performers make more subtle cultural distinctions concerning sexual spectacle and the politics of looking.

Although Liza Minnelli's performance in many ways dominates the film, it is the spectacle of the emcee that brings us into the text and glosses over Minnelli in an introduction that is a significant departure from the formulized opening of classic narrative films using the establishment shot and cut-in to "the star." Instead, Minnelli is introduced en masse with an assortment of transvestites, overweight chorus girls, acrobats, and a dwarf ventroloquist on the stage of the Kit Kat Klub. The camera first catches a glimpse of her as it sweeps past to focus on a contortionist who has tucked her head between her

15. *Cabaret* (1972). In a marked departure from mainstream film tradition, star Liza Minnelli as Sally Bowles is introduced en masse with an assortment of garishly costumed cabaret performers.

black-stockinged legs and bends over to smile from behind. The emcee's later introduction of "Fräulein Sally Bowles" is also undermined, framed so that she is almost wholly obscured by a heavy chorus girl bent over toward the diegetic audience. Toward the end of
the performance, a brief shot finally singles out Minnelli, framed medium length and shot with a filter that suggests the smokiness of the
cabaret but that also keeps her slightly out of focus. Even more disturbingly, it is graphically matched two shots later by a focused close-
up of the dwarf and his gaudily painted wooden doll, suggesting that
this clearer and sharper shot could be the privileging of an important
character. Sally Bowles takes her first bow, then, in a performance
that immediately raises questions about her status as spectacle among
the freaks and about the specifically sexual freakiness of her Kit Kat
costars.

By 1972, questions of spectacle and spectatorship, as well as questions about gender identity, had been virulently mainstreamed in
American culture. One of the most startling images of the explosion
of spectacle in that era comes from William Styron's essay on the August 1968 Democratic convention in Chicago, which itself functioned
as the spectacle that further split the country's divided politics. The
essay concludes with a startling scene suggesting there was no position of safe spectatorship anywhere near the convention. During one
of the moments that was most intensely covered by television cameras, the riot erupting in front of the Hilton Hotel, with the street
people shouting "the whole world is watching!" Styron retreated to
the Haymarket Lounge inside, where the scene could be watched as
if on a giant television set: the "sound-resistant plate-glass windows
offered me the dumbshow of cops clubbing people to the concrete,
swirling squadrons of people in Panavision blue and polystyrene vi-
sors hurling back the crowds." Suddenly, as if the giant television
screen had erupted, the riot crashed through the window and into
the supposedly secure space of the spectators: ". . . an explosion of
glass at the rear of the bar announced the arrival of half a dozen
bystanders who, hurled inward by the crush outside, had shattered
the huge window and now sprawled cut and bleeding all over the
floor of the place while others, chased by a wedge of cops, fled
screaming into the adjacent lobby."[8] Styron's report is part of the
larger movement of New Journalism, the shunning of cool objectivity
in light of Tom Wolfe and Norman Mailer. Yet the power of this particular description resides in the image of the exploding glass win-

[8] William Styron, "Chicago 1968," in *The Quiet Dust and Other Writings* (New York:
Random House, 1982), 240.

dow, the spectacle tumbling inward to include those who thought they were safely looking on.

That week in August quickly became an emblem of the breakdown of politics, law, and order at the peak of the movement against the Vietnam War. "Mass repression . . . could turn whole areas of the country into Lincoln Park," warned writer/witness John Schultz.[9] "Convention Week" also became an emblem of the breakdown between bystanders and provocateurs, reporters and participants, with the understanding that to have been present was to have been part of the spectacle, part of history. *The Walker Report*, summarizing the events for the National Commission on the Causes and Prevention of Violence, totals at least forty-nine incidents of newsmen struck, maced, or arrested by Chicago police. Even television spectatorship led to a political positioning; Gallup polls of the television audiences who had watched the police battle the protesters showed that over half of the viewers sided with the police.[10] In short, the politics of looking had been forefronted in American culture in a violent way, signaling the specularization of what popular discourse was calling social conscience or consciousness. Activism meant being visible, being on the street, getting television coverage. Moreover, in the confrontational tactics of protest that continued throughout the American involvement in Vietnam, the discourse of accusation was frequently specific to German fascism. It was not simply that "fascist pig" was the most common epithet for a cop, but also that demonstrators used swastikas and references to Auschwitz and "Gestapo tactics" in struggles against police and other authorities. Andrew Sarris reminds us that in cultural reformulations of the Holocaust during that time, "radical journalists chose to describe the late Hubert Humphrey as a war criminal on a Hitlerian level." The discourse permeated popular culture; journalist Nora Sayre remembers "the first activist comic books" in which, in one encounter between heroes, the Green Lantern protests he must do his job and the Green Arrow retorts, "Seems to me I've heard that line before . . . at the Nazi war trials!"[11] By the time the film version of *Cabaret* was being planned,

[9] John Schultz, *No One Was Killed: Documentation and Meditation, Convention Week, Chicago, August, 1968* (Chicago: Big Table, 1969), 297.

[10] Daniel Walker, *Rights in Conflict: Convention Week in Chicago, August 25–29, 1968* (New York: Dutton, 1968), 330; see also Todd Gitlin, *The Sixties: Years of Hope, Days of Rage*, 471n.

[11] Andrew Sarris, *Politics and Cinema* (New York: Columbia University Press, 1978), 112; Nora Sayre, *Sixties Going on Seventies* (New York: Arbor House, 1973), 14. Todd Gitlin also documents the allusions to German fascism in *The Sixties: Years of Hope, Days of Rage*, 308, 317, 334–35. He points out that the allusions to Nazism were often pure sensationalism.

written, and shot, between 1970 and 1972, American culture not only had had a new experience of spectacle—often violent spectacle—as politics, but had also heard German fascism rehashed as part of the divisive discourse in fierce struggles that often represented the forces of good and evil in terms as absolute as any comic-book plot: the flower children versus the fascist pigs.

My argument here is that *Cabaret* very much bears the imprint of this dramatic era of confrontation and politics as spectacle, as well as the didactic use of German fascism as a referent that is more emotional and theatrical than analytical or even historical. It is not that *Cabaret*'s political narrative works as a correlative to the political narrative of the late 1960s; rather, its continual play with spectatorship and performance as a continuum of politics reworks a constellation of anxieties that had been latent in the ongoing historical confrontations of that era: the "guilt" of passivity (spectatorship) as a motivation for activism, the conflation of spectator/spectacle, the radical positionings that quickly cast figures of authority on the side of the "fascist pigs." When the persecution of the Jewish Landauers is parallel-edited as part of a frantic Kit Kat performance toward the end of the film, the evils of passive spectatorship seem obvious. ("We were going to be active where our parents' generation had been passive," Todd Gitlin reminds us.[12])

Yet the "guilty" spectator is drawn into a world that is highly erotic and visually pleasurable, if morally reprehensible. The specific impact of this confrontational/fascist discourse on the construction of Sally Bowles is that in the years since her 1966 Broadway incarnation, her context of fascinating fascism has become an almost radically split sign. On the one hand, the less fascinating aspects of fascism had become a signifier of conservative authority; on the other hand, German fascism in particular had emerged as a campy cultural signifier of militant marginality—sadomasochism, especially associated with gay sexual practices. These contradictory articulations of Otherness—sexual and political—converge with the representation of fascism as both virulently brutal and ugly *and* irresistibly fascinating, though in a particularly sexually aberrant way. This had been true of the stage play as well, but the difference is that the new focus on a dynamic Sally Bowles, a performer who is "every inch Judy Garland's daughter," much more closely recreates the sexual dynamic of Cornelius's *I Am a Camera* or Von Sternberg's *The Blue Angel*: a dominating female presence/spectacle becomes the locus upon which narrative conflicts or cultural contradictions are projected. In addition,

---

[12] Todd Gitlin, *The Sixties: Years of Hope, Days of Rage*, 26.

Sally in this film must sustain the conflicting claims of identity implicit in playing the American cheerleader Lola, both femme fatale and childlike—or as Brian puts it an one point, "as *fatale* as an after-dinner mint."

The centralization of Sally Bowles in this configuration is best illustrated in an early scene in which the film's first shocking representation of Nazi violence is introduced literally through a scream of pleasure initiated by Sally. In this scene, Sally shares with Brian her secret of standing under the railroad trestle and screaming when the train roars overhead because, she says, "You feel terrific afterwards." The scene operates as Brian's introduction, through Sally, into a world of dropped inhibition and sexual expression. As they open their mouths to scream, there is a cut to a shot of the nightclub owner being beaten by Nazi toughs, a scene that in turn is parallel-edited with a Kit Kat version of a Bavarian folk dance that is heavy on slapping of partners' thighs and buttocks. The violence outside is choreographed seamlessly as the underside of the stage performance, as if the distinctly German folk dance were the acceptable public enactment of unconscious cultural violence and intolerance. Likewise, the violence is situated as Sally's unconscious, the underside of her thrill, a particularly sadomasochistic pleasure. Ostensibly, the screams could be the reaction of horror at the beating, but Sally's positioning in this scene negates such a reading. She is clearly titillated by it in a sexual way: "You feel terrific afterward."

This scene encapsulizes Sally as the conduit through which Brian experiences Berlin as violent and erotic, thrilling and corrupting, but most of all as a sexual/political Other that must eventually be disavowed. However, her relationship to the ensuing violence and spectacle in this scene also reveals the film's curious epistemology. Three levels of knowledge are articulated here: Sally's kinky or sexual knowledge of a specific thrill; the Kit Kat performance that suggests a sly knowledge of cultural violence; and the image of the back-street beating which, with glimpses of Brownshirts and swastikas, makes claim to historical truth. But the Kit Kat number, with its privileging close-ups of the emcee's wicked leer, is surely the anchoring authority here, acting out the cultural unconscious of titillating violence which seems to be Sally's unconscious, too.

The point is that despite Sally's centralization in this text, her position as Brian's entry into sexual and political experience, she is actually positioned suspiciously as what feminist film theory terms the pseudo-center of the film. Narrative authority belongs not to her, and not even to Brian, but rather to the Kit Kat musical numbers, which repeatedly know what the characters themselves do not—in this case, the beating of the nightclub owner. Likewise, in the performance of "Money," she and the emcee enact a mating dance that reveals they are much more similarly matched than she and Brian; in "Two Ladies," the song points to the switching of sexual partners that the narrative reveals much later; and both the persecution of the Jewish Landauers (the killing of Natalia's dog) and Sally's abortion are represented as rapidly edited, feverish Kit Kat performances.

In addition, this center of textual authority "knows" Sally as body and spectacle—that is, as the performance whereby female sexual "unknowability," to use Mary Ann Doane's term (its diffuseness, as opposed to phallic specificity) can be contained through the fetishizing techniques that are Fosse's signature. In this aesthetic, body parts are often fragmented and used as framing; the human figure is obscured by or delineated by lighting or filters; and performances are rapidly reframed through editing. On the other hand, the problem of knowability is made more complex in this film in that Sally Bowles is virtually the only Kit Kat performer whose gender is readily identifiable. The crisis of knowability is epitomized by the stage performances that confound or question gender identity altogether, literalizing the question with Fosse's repeated crotch shots. Female sexuality undergoes multiple displacements, beginning with the casting of Liza Minnelli as female sexual authority in the text—as Natalia calls her, a woman "giving her body frequently to men."

Much more than the slightly built Julie Harris, Minnelli's attractiveness verges on masculine handsomeness. In an early scene with Brian, Sally has him do an inventory of her bodily shape with his hand, emphasizing that she is much flatter and longer than the traditionally curvacious show girl. Once again, as in the 1950s adaptations, Sally is not sexy but "sexy." Even more than that, this is "every inch Judy Garland's daughter." Minnelli's facial resemblance to her mother is a powerful extratextual coding in this film that points to another kind of sexuality. Judy Garland was a "gay institution" in this country, according to Michael Bronski's history of gay culture, at whose death "many New York City gay bars draped themselves with black crepe in mourning."[13] When Minnelli, minus the clownish makeup she wears in most of the film, sobs and breathlessly stammers out her frustrations to Brian in her Daddy scene, it is difficult not to hear Garland's voice from her backstage breakdown in *A Star Is Born* (1954). Similarly, in Minnelli's performance of the "Cabaret" song, extolling her friend who died from "too much pills and liquor," the

---

[13] Michael Bronski, *Culture Clash: The Making of a Gay Sensibility* (Boston: South End, 1984), 103.

reference to and conflation with her mother is more than subtly suggested. In short, the casting of Minnelli as an Americanized Lola already suggests a gay subtext in the film; Garland as much as Dietrich is a favorite subject of cross-dressing performances. This is not, after all, simply *Sweet Charity* with swastikas but *Sweet Charity* in drag.

In relation to this gay subtext, the film reveals disturbing gaps in the connection between marginalized sexuality and political oppression. Nazi oppression is specified as anti-Semitic but never as homophobic; it is represented with sadomasochistic iconography and signified as a monstrous, secret femaleness that is immediately evident in the emcee's effeminate mannerisms, but also in Sally's scream of pleasure introducing the scenario of pain. The film specifically reworks a major cultural anxiety that was additionally present in political spectacles such as Convention Week in Chicago in the very iconography of the long-haired freaks against the macho cops. This is the challenge to traditional gender identification, certainly visible in the celebrations of androgynous dress in the counterculture, but also in the more radical movements of both women's liberation and gay liberation, that had crystallized as of 1969 and that emerges as a key historical condition of this text.

1960s radical feminists were often women who had participated in the male-dominated antiwar and civil rights movements, and who broke off in pursuit of their own goals after 1968. Much of the anger and energy of the early days of this feminist movement was violent backlash against the sexism of other leftist groups, frequently represented by Stokely Carmichael's famous remark concerning the ideal position of women in the movement as "prone." Feminist rhetoric, especially in these early years of organization, was often furious. Robin Morgan, in her introduction to the anthology of key essays and position papers, *Sisterhood is Powerful*, describes her disbelief at how angry she could become—"something like a five-thousand-year-buried anger." While Betty Friedan's organization of NOW in 1966 represented a less alienating middle-class spectrum of positions, the most colorful rhetoric and images of the movement emerged from more radical groups such as SCUM (Society for Cutting Up Men) and WITCH, self-described in the Morgan anthology as "theater, revolution, magic, terror, joy, garlic flowers, spells."[14] What roughly characterized both middle-class and radical feminism was a concern with "sexual politics," itself a new term in the culture, meticulously defined and illustrated by Kate Millett's ground-breaking 1969 book of the

[14] Robin Morgan, ed., *Sisterhood is Powerful: An Anthology of Writings from the Women's Liberation Movement* (New York: Random House, 1970), xv, 539.

same name, which was also an early study of Nazi sexual politics as a variation of "acceptable" Western ideology.[15] Like leftist rhetoric against American interference in Vietnam, the rhetoric of sexual politics was divisive and confrontational: "know your enemy," "the male oppressor," "the hand that cradles the rock." And like the earlier movement, the challenge to gender identity in the late 1960s and early 1970s was often staged as dramatically as opposition to the war. Women burned bras for national television as men had burned draft cards, and August 26, 1970, was proclaimed a national women's strike day to protest confinement to traditional roles and duties. Although the Sally Bowles character is obviously not thus inclined toward spectacles of feminism, it is nevertheless interesting that during this time Jean Ross was besieged by "bright young journalists" who wanted to know if the "real" Sally Bowles had in fact been "a sort of forerunner of the emancipated woman."[16]

In light of this specularized cultural attack on traditional gender roles and the proliferation of "buddy films" at this time which, as Molly Haskell has suggested, indicates a distinctly misogynist Hollywood response, the casting of Liza Minnelli as a dynamic, centrally located Sally Bowles immediately raises questions about the kind of sexual threat she actually represents. It seems to me that the threat of female sexuality in *Cabaret* is conflated with the threat of the sexual otherness manifest most obviously in the emcee and in the distinctly grotesque Kit Kat transvestites, but also in the secret femaleness of Brian and Max. That is, both female sexuality and gay sexuality function as the same term of difference. As Teresa de Lauretis comments in her use of Jurig M. Lotman's analysis of myth, the result is a paradigm positing "the human being as man and everything else as, not even 'woman,' but non-man."[17]

Cabaret's imprint of the recent cultural acknowledgement of (and anxieties about) a gay sensibility is fairly obvious, both in the narrative and in the representation of transvestism. Socially, the representation of a gay sensibility as spectacle had taken a dramatic turn since 1966. Though gay activism had begun on the West Coast in the previous decade with Harry Hay's Mattachine Society, it had remained a Southern California phenomenon until the late 1960s. The turning point was the Stonewall riots in June 1969, a three-day confrontation protesting New York City police harassment at the Stonewall Inn, a Greenwich Village gay bar. The Stonewall riots brought extensive

---

[15] Kate Millett, *Sexual Politics* (New York: Avon, 1969), 157–68.

[16] Sarah Caudwell, "Reply to Berlin," 28.

[17] Teresa de Lauretis, *Alice Doesn't: Feminism, Semiotics, Cinema* (Bloomington and Indianapolis: Indiana University Press, 1984), 121.

media coverage and became a rallying point for the cause. In the ensuing struggles for organization and identification, the gay liberation movement was specifically linked to theater because of the theater as a traditional haven for gays. The more marginal Off-Off Broadway gay productions from 1958 to the late 1960s eventually made their way to mainstream theater by the 1970s. Theatricality was a key element in gay politics, particularly in the phenomenon of "radical drag"—a politicalization of camp—which became a highly publicized and powerful enactment of "coming out of the closet," itself a term suggesting a politics of exhibiting and looking, an emergence from darkness and a coming-into-view. Radical drag went beyond that into making the self a spectacle, as in the case of the Cockettes, the most famous troupe of radical drag performers, whose theater of excess was particularly carnivalesque. The theatrical spectacle was part of a larger enactment of "gender-fuck," as could be seen in San Francisco's annual Gay Pride celebration, for example, so that whereas the Cockettes performed as theater, other enactments broke down the performer/spectator distinction altogether in a more genuine kind of carnivalesque celebration.[18]

The impact of the growing gay liberation movement on the film project *Cabaret* is predictably contradictory, enabling a certain kind of narrative but also positioning it in hostile ways. Public discourse by 1970 allowed the topic of gay relationships to be spoken of and to be encompassed by mainstream stage and film. Although the stage musical *Cabaret*, typical of Broadway of the first part of the decade, reveals cautiousness about the topic (Lotte Lenya specifically recalls that the Cliff character could not have been anything but straight[19]), the second half of the decade saw the success of Mart Crowley's play *Boys in the Band* (1968) followed by William Friedkin's film version in 1970. The film *Cabaret* could likewise utilize the issue as part of the narrative in a way that had been impossible just six years earlier. As reviewer Stanley Kauffman remarked cynically, the story "trades on the New Liberation of film,"[20] evident in the commercial success of *Midnight Cowboy* (1969) despite its X-rating, and also in such films as the British *Sunday, Bloody Sunday* (1971) and the Canadian *Fortune and Men's Eyes* (1971). The bisexuality of Brian Roberts in fact is central to the narrative and gives this Sally's story an additional twist. She has

---

[18] For details of this use of spectacle and theater in the gay liberation movement, and in particular the Cockettes, see Mark Thompson, *Gay Spirit: Myth and Meaning* (New York: St. Martin's, 1987), 52–57, 65–66. Michael Bronski discusses the mainstreaming of gay political theater in *Culture Clash*, 128–30.

[19] Lotte Lenya, interview with George Voskovec, 1972.

[20] Stanley Kauffman, review of *Cabaret, New Republic* (4 Mar 1972): 22.

an affair with a young man who claims that he usually "doesn't sleep with girls," and he betrays her not with another woman but with another man. Isherwood, who had himself become active in the gay liberation movement by then, disapproved of what he called the " 'off-again, on-again role that was assigned to Michael York," finding it "fundamentally anti-gay in attitude."[21]

But the dubious, even reactionary positioning of homosexuality in this film extends far beyond the vicissitudes of Brian's sexual preferences, and is part of the text's problematic representation of sexuality in relation to German fascism. In this chain of signification, Sally Bowles is much more directly aligned with the emcee and his ambiguous gender than she had been in the stage version, and the emcee in turn more centrally anchors the varieties of sexuality that appear at the Kit Kat Klub—including Brian's. In the opening scene, the *"Willkommen"* performance is cut by shots of Brian's arrival in Berlin, his clean-shaven face and angelic good looks an obvious contrast to the garishly painted emcee. Yet the narrative eventually suggests that the two characters may be similar in their sexual ambiguity. In spite of his coding as "romantic leading man," Brian's "secret" is extracted from him by Sally in a later scene when she attempts to seduce him. The parallel editing in this opening scene thus points to a sinister joke about a distorted, mirroring relationship between the emcee and Brian. In one shot, Brian's reflection is caught in a passing bus window, so that he is inscribed (and distorted) onto the city scene in the same way that the emcee is inscribed onto the cabaret mirror; the matched shots suggest a rhyming relationship here, just as the introductory shot of Sally is matched by the shot of the dwarf and his grotesque doll.

This opening constitutes a significant variation of the parallel-shot structure that is typical of the film musical and that usually signifies heterosexual duality, as Rick Altman describes it in his formal analysis of the genre. Altman argues that the film musical is likely to work on a principle of parallelism, with alternating shots of the male and female lead, especially at the beginning of the film, establishing a series of differences between them, which the narrative eventually aims to resolve. The sexual contrasts are additionally constructed as matching differences in setting and performance style of musical numbers, but also include details of casting such as coloring, costume, background, national origin.[22] This is certainly true of the Sally-Brian

<hr />

[21] Norma McLain Stoop, "Christopher Isherwood: A Meeting by Another River," 62.

[22] Rick Altman, *The American Film Musical* (Bloomington and Indianapolis: Indiana University Press, 1987), 33. Altman illustrates how these paired opposites often point to a contrast between the world of entertainment versus everyday reality; the narrative

pairing in *Cabaret*; his British reserve, physical slightness, and light coloring operate as the sexual opposition for her American brashness, big body, and dark coloring/cosmetics. Yet the first set of contrasts and sexual tension occurs in the parallel shots linking Brian to the world he will encounter in the Kit Kat Klub, paralleling him not to his eventual female romantic lead but to another kind of sexuality that is not just gay or transvestite, but that is particularly grotesque and sinister. Crisp daylight shots show Brian as the genial, smiling tourist in his conservative trenchcoat and fedora, navigating the city's trains and buses and doing the kind of polite, interested looking suitable to the city visitor. In contrast, we see dark, filtered shots of the tawdry colors inside the Kit Kat where the emcee is fondling garishly made-up chorus girls and prancing for the delightedly shocked audience. Much more is suggested here than simply the world of entertainment versus the more prosaic world outside the theater. Brian will in fact be "attracted" to the cabaret, but as this opening suggests, the parallel editing blatantly posits a sexual and cultural normality in opposition to a sexuality and culture that is gaudy, fascinating, freakish. The editing thus duplicates the function of the split staging in the Broadway production with its suggestion of an identifiable norm, but as Altman points out, this editing technique is explicitly coded in the film musical as one that indicates an inevitable "coupling" of the two persons privileged in the shots.

This opening "coupling" of Brian and the emcee actually addresses a gap that is later evident in the heterosexual coupling and uncoupling of Brian and Sally. While the formula of the ideal musical leads to a marriage based on both parties' abilities to change or compromise, a resolution in *Cabaret* is possible only through a virulent rejection of the female romantic lead. However, since the Sally Bowles character shares many of the traits coded as admirable for musical leading ladies—her vivacity, her spontaneity, her musical ability— what Brian "really" renounces, the text suggests, is a particular erotic milieu, to which he had been temporarily mated. The opening parallels with the emcee, then, suggest an inevitable sexual Other for the hero according to a code familiar to the audience of the musical, but with the pointed suggestion of a gay subtext not very subtly contained within the later heterosexual romance.

The opening sequence also points to Sally's construction in this text as part of a signifying chain consisting of variations of male sexuality. Whereas the emcee's resemblance to Brian works as a distorted mir-

will eventually move toward a merger of these opposite traits, ending in a literal marriage which is also the marriage/merger of values or life-styles, 48–51.

ror image, the resemblance between the emcee and Sally is suggested much more openly with the similarity in their stage makeup—their similarly painted red lips, thick false eyelashes, and heavy eyeliner. In the scene in which they sing "Money" together, one shot catches them in profile, nose to nose, so that they appear as literal mirror images of each other. Whereas the garish makeup tends to emphasize the heaviness and masculinity of Minnelli's features, Grey's features in comparison seem more girlish, so that in this profile he is surprisingly "prettier" than she.

I would argue that this relationship and its context—the emcee as anchor to a grotesque spectacle later conflated with Nazism—considerably limit the androgynous appeal of Liza Minnelli in this film. The lesbian appeal of Sally Bowles's predecessor Lola is to a great extent based on Dietrich's power and authority in the Von Sternberg film; in contrast, the sexual authority of Minnelli's Sally is not only undermined in several ways but also linked more directly to male rather than female sexuality. As I pointed out in my previous discussion of camp, drag versions of female sexuality as grotesque have very different stakes for women than for men. In Fosse's *Cabaret*, the grotesquery of Sally's sexiness is doubly inscribed with her juxtaposition to the film's representation of female "beauty," Marisa Berenson as Natalia. Sally's heavy, clownish makeup and outrageous costumes take on meaning—as a joke, as a drag version of femininity—in relation to Natalia's clear, luminous face and ladylike dresses, a culturally approved model of the feminine, as opposed to Sally's alignment with the garishly femme emcee.

In turn, the emcee's hints of femininity are physically mirrored in the male stars, too, who tend to be equally lovely; York's boyishness is more than a little androgynous, while the Baron Maximilian Van Heune (Helmut Griem) and the fortune-hunting Fritz Wendel (Fritz Wepper) have provokingly feminine features. At least one reviewer complained that Griem and Wepper "resemble each other so closely that there's confusion."[23] The resemblances are intertextual, as well: Griem played the smooth, sinister SS officer who helps to take over the Essenbeck family in Visconti's *The Damned*, giving corrupt, smooth-talking Germans a homogeneous appearance in these two films.

The Max character as played by Griem in *Cabaret* raises political questions that are eventually resolved with sexual answers. Sally's fling with a German aristocrat is, after all, a significant turn of the screw from the American Clive character in Isherwood and the 1950s

---

[23] Stanley Kauffman, review of *Cabaret*, 33.

16. *Cabaret* (1972). The performance of the song "Money" enacts the mating dance of Sally (Liza Minnelli) and the emcee (Joel Grey), who are similarly made up with heavy eyeliner, false eyelashes, and rouge.

adaptations. Max seems to be a handsomer, wealthier, more successful version of Brian: "He's everything you're not," Sally taunts Brian.
This comparison and taunting also occurred in relation to Clive in
Cornelius's *I Am a Camera*. But Max is also the protofascist in this text,
an identification made both obliquely (history proves him "guilty")
and more directly with visual cues; after he drops off Brian in his
limousine following their final rendezvous, for example, he also
drops his veneer of Continental civilization with an impatient snarl of
orders to the driver, suggesting that Max is actually the secret brute-
authoritarian. The problem posed by this suggestion is the one articulated by Alvin H. Rosenfeld in his analysis of Western postwar
fascination with Nazism; in documentary footage of the masses adu-
lating Hitler, we find "familiar faces in the crowd, the look of neighborly, even family, resemblance."[24] In *Cabaret* the question is how
someone so dignified, Western, cultured, and capitalist (so much like
the ideal male norm/spectator) could eventually succumb to the Nazis. But the answer is a sexually reassuring one: his mark of difference is his secret gay identity. The turning point of his seduction of
Brian, in fact, occurs just as they are about to watch the performance
of the blond *Hitlerjunge* in the beer-garden scene. The lovely, Aryan
Nazi youth shares the pretty facial features of Max, continuing the
series of resemblances linking the characters to the secret femininity
of the emcee.

Whereas questions of sexual identity had operated as various subtexts of the other Sally Bowles adaptations, they are forefronted here
not only in the narrative—Brian's "cure" by Sally and his later seduction by Max—but also in the general *mise-en-scène* and in specific visual gags. The musical number "Two Ladies," for example, operating
very differently than in the stage play, parodies the narrative's mé-
nage à trois. During a shot of Brian, Sally, and Max riding in the
backseat of Max's limousine, the emcee's voice-over introduces this
number with his pronouncement that "Berlin makes strange bedfel-
lows these days." The musical number reverses the genders of the
narrative situation (two men and a woman), thus commenting cynically on the masculinity and femininity of the narrative characters.
Emphasizing this confusion even more, the "two ladies" in the musical number are made up so heavily that it is difficult to tell whether
or not these are two of the cabaret transvestites, who on another occasion are men playing women playing men (in the number in which
the performers turn around their show-girl hats and become goose-
stepping soldiers).

[24] Alvin H. Rosenfeld, *Imagining Hitler*, 16.

The challenge to sexual identity is surely epitomized in the scene in which a relatively inexperienced Brian, on his first night at the Kit Kat, goes to the men's room and is joined at the urinals by the beautiful stage performer Elke. In his great shock, he is unable to resist a peek at his/her genitals. The film audience is located as looking at his looking—which is the film's major trajectory: the audience gaze is aligned with the gaze of the boyish young man from England whose arrival and departure from the world of the Kit Kat Klub frames his initiation into sexuality, corruption, and moral prostitution. Altman explains that the sexual dichotomy that usually structures the film musical is part of an overlying secondary or thematical dichotomy, often a cultural contradiction, which the film resolves as it resolves the sexual dichotomy through marriage.[25] In *Cabaret*, however, the secondary dichotomy is a divisive political one that can only be resolved by having Brian renounce what he has enjoyed—sexuality, spectacle, and the cabaret world—because it has coincided with his experience of the beginnings of the Third Reich. What Altman points to as the cultural contradiction usually embedded and resolved in the musical genre is here perhaps the contradiction of fascinating fascism itself: how can such a grotesque spectacle be so irresistible, and how could so many ordinary, middle-class spectators (glimpsed in the first scene as the Kit Kat audience, but also as the Germans whom Brian sees on the street) have fallen for it?

This is the question posed in the stage play as well, but that text's answer (sexual decadence) creates new problems in the film. Unlike the stage-play Cliff, Brian is wholly seduced in a variety of ways by the Berlin scene, even though his distinguishing characteristic continues to be his opposition to Nazism, and like all the other Christopher characters, he is required to renounce and leave the politics, morality, and sexuality of Berlin. But as the scene at the urinal suggests in a comic way, and as the text generally suggests with the scenes of spectatorship and spectacle, Brian is posited as the spectator in the text who supposedly represents the sexual and political norm, the witness to the political ugliness that is represented as sexual aberration. The problem is that his own sexual ambiguity fails the narrative demand for an either-or political positioning, a clear distinction between (secretly female) monstrous fascism and clean-cut (heterosexual) antifascism. The possibility of such a clear distinction is articulated in the plan he devises toward the end of the film: he and Sally will marry, she will give up show business, they will return to Cambridge, and become the happy nuclear family safely removed from Berlin poli-

---

[25] Rick Altman, *The American Film Musical*, 50–58.

tics. What is interesting in the various adaptations is that this particular vision of "heroism" always fails, but with varying effects. For Cliff in the stage play, a qualified kind of heroism is still possible because he at least can claim narrative authority, writing up the tale on the train, and because he is clearly posited as the heterosexual norm. Narrative closure for Brian, on the other hand, is much less effective; he simply disappears at the train station while Sally Bowles goes on to perform a terrific show which is itself authoritative in its power and success as musical number. As the text's enemy of the project of entertainment, Brian is the character who is least sympathetic in the codings of the musical. But even as sexual norm, he falls short; in a text so homophobic, his dubious masculinity seriously undermines his heroism.

The scene at the urinal, moreoever, which identifies Brian as the spectator in the text for the film audience, indicates that Brian as the moral ("normal") witness to Nazism is also the representation of another kind of spectatorship that is specifically motivated by fear and fascination with genital space. The many ambiguities of gender in this film can be read as an almost parodic scenario of an obsessive castration complex: Brian's curious gaze at Elke is duplicated dozens of times in the text with the camera's repeated crotch shots during the musical numbers, and in a more general way, with the dubious genders of the characters—the emcee's femininity, the Kit Kat performers who may or may not be transvestites—and with the gender confusions of the main characters, the range of resemblances among Sally, the emcee, and the male stars. As Altman points out, the crotch shot, often associated with Busby Berkeley's signature tracking shot between the legs of a hundred chorus girls, is actually the signature of the entire genre, the musical's "semantic unit" of voyeurism.[26] But in *Cabaret* these shots often serve to literalize the anxiety that the crotch-shot fetishization supposedly serves to diminish: what really *is* or is not there between the legs of these males/females onstage? While the emcee is giving his opening spiel, a brief shot shows Elke placing on his/her head a voluptuously curled blond wig, so when the camera focuses on the crotch area of the chorus girls in their first high-kick sequence, the effect is more unsettling than alluring. As if to confirm the joke, the emcee bursts into their line immediately following a tracking shot that zooms forward just below their upraised legs. What works as an obvious gesture of disavowal, the displacement of female genital space by the male figure, is a more literal joke about what might or might not be present among those lifted thighs.

[26] Ibid., 223.

In this opening number, various kinds of crotch shots are frequently set up as lurid jokes. The contortionist's head appears between her legs when she is introduced alongside Sally Bowles. When the emcee reaches out to shake the hand of an audience member, the arm of one of the other performers instead shoots out between his legs to complete the handshake, so that it appears he has sprouted a gigantic phallus. And while the Berkeley crotch shots feature series of legs that are well shaped according to cultural specifications, Fosse's camera lingers on what is designated as female-grotesque. In one shot, the emcee crouches down to be framed by the legs of a performer who is standing close to the camera, with heavy legs spread wide apart, clothed in baggy, lumpy stockings; using his walking stick, the emcee points directly to his/her genitals as he begins his introduction of "the cabaret girls." During the following sequence of shots in which the camera pans over these performers, the raised legs of others are positioned so closely to the camera that a mask effect is created, as if the camera were positioned directly inside the darkness of genital space.

The camera's repeated positioning between the legs of the heavy or garishly made-up Kit Kat dancers may work on one level as campy parody of Berkeley and traditional musicals, but the ongoing sexual/political dynamic suggests multiple and ultimately hostile agendas here. Certainly the representation of campy sexuality as a specifically female grotesquery points to the uncomfortable relationship of woman to the carnivalesque hag as described by Mary Russo. But beyond that, the anxious gaze between the legs enacts as sexual anxiety the dilemma of visibility that is central to this narrative, the trajectory of concealment and revelation as described by psychoanalyst Stephen Bauer: "Maximillian's heterosexuality conceals his homosexuality; Brian's homosexuality conceals his heterosexuality; Fritz, the gentle imposter, conceals his Jewishness; the prim and proper Natalia conceals her passionate sexuality."[27] That is, a range of difference is reinscribed as the biological one, with the suggestion that a "natural" biological order (the phallus is there or is not) is being evoked as the norm. The reduction of sexuality and identity to "having one" or "not having one," repeated visually in the text, occurs later as a verbal joke as well. To get rid of an older male customer at the Kit Kat, Sally tells him she has syphilis and passes him on to Elke. "Wait till he gets a load of what little old Elke's got," Sally says. In a more romantic moment, Brian's newfound potency/heterosexuality in the Daddy scene is suggested with a tentative camera movement toward his

---

[27] Stephen Bauer, "Cultural History and the Film *Cabaret*," 193–94.

crotch; he and Sally find that his consoling hugs and kisses begin to be genuinely arousing, and the camera, briefly following Sally's gaze downward to confirm what she suspects, teases the viewer with the possibility of showing what cannot of course be seen in mainstream film.[28]

This obsession with visibility, the camera's peer between the legs, may enact the general oedipal trajectory of mainstream film, but the anxieties reinscribed as questions of visibility are also specifically political. As I have suggested, the "invisible" homosexual inclination of Max links him to the "prettiness" of the *Hitlerjunge* singer and to the supposedly concealed fascist tendencies of Germany. In the film's final shot, Fosse's brilliant visual maneuvers make fascism itself an element in the play of spectatorial revelation when the swastikas appear in the cabaret mirror, the space that had contained Sally's performance. As Bauer's previous summary suggests, the question of difference and visibility includes not only female unknowability (Natalia's secretly passionate nature) but also the question concerning Fritz's "invisible" Jewishness. In chapter one, I had suggested that the privileging of the visible in German fascism, the exaggeration of difference, can be read as an anxiety concerning racial purity in regard to Jewishness, which is not a trait that is visibly obvious, unlike black/white or male/female distinctions. But the paradigm of visibility as a specifically genital anxiety in *Cabaret* reminds us that this was in fact an element of "visible" proof during the Third Reich: circumcision was often used to identify men as Jewish, a male definition that is specifically at odds with how Jewishness is actually determined, as the maternal inheritance. "The Nazis viewed circumcision as a Jewish mutilation of the penis," reports historian Frank Rector. "In every corner of Nazi domination, the circumcision criterion was applied to males of all ages during roundups of Jews for liquidation. A circumcised penis . . . could spell death for that person and everyone related to him regardless of whether or not they were in fact Jews."[29]

The fact that this dynamic—visibility and the positing of a "natural" biological order—in the film *Cabaret* parallels the actual politics of the Third Reich is not very surprising in light of what I have emphasized in past chapters concerning the intersections of German fascism and mainstream film: the heightening of sexual difference, the

---

[28] This is surely an instance of censorship as a continuum of the dynamics of male spectatorship: this verification of masculinity would threaten the relationship of voyeur to spectacle with the possibility of reversing it into male exhibitionism; moreover, it would expose the film project as one in which male arousal is at stake.

[29] Frank Rector, *The Nazi Extermination of Homosexuals* (New York: Stein and Day, 1981), 132.

triumph of image over verbal text, the excessively choreographed Big Show. Thomas Elsaesser suggests that the fascination of fascism may have resided, for ordinary citizens, directly in the specularization that is central to cinema: "Might not the pleasure of fascism, its fascination have been less the sadism and brutality of SS officers than the pleasure of being seen, of placing oneself in view of the all-seeing eye of the State?"[30] Elsaesser's analysis is part of his discussion of Fassbinder that aims to historicize the operations of spectatorship which have often been analyzed as functions of the cinematic apparatus. Thus he locates the problems of spectator positioning and identity in Fassbinder as historical consequences rather than exclusively as consequences of the Lacanian split subject duplicated in the structures of cinematic visualization. Likewise, my concern here has been to unpack several kinds of historical contexts—the politics of spectacle, challenges to gender identity, and the film history that produces Sally as a reference to Dietrich's Lola—in which the question of visibility—as anxiety, disavowal, or affirmation—emerges.

Elsaesser is further instructional here in his warning about applying a certain model of reading to any director who problematizes spectatorship. He argues that Fassbinder privileges voyeurism more than narrative or character, with the result of making "the act of seeing itself the center of the narrative."[31] Elsaesser cautions us that we read this not with the models of modernist or deconstructive film in mind, but rather with careful attention to the historical context and inscriptions particular to Germany's experience of fascism as seeing and being seen. Although Fosse is working much more within mainstream film guidelines ("I wanted to tell a love story . . ."), he has also created in *Cabaret* a film that makes "the act of seeing itself the center of the narrative," and the film has likewise been read as modernist or Brechtian.[32] Such a reading seems to me similarly to impose a modernist model inappropriately, even though Fosse's complex and multiple positionings of spectatorship invite such an analysis. Whereas Fassbinder's history is haunted by Germany's fascist past—and whereas his personal history is complicated by his gay identity—Fosse emerges from a lifetime of mainstream show business: a family in vaudeville, his own dance act by the time he was thirteen, show-busi-

---

[30] Thomas Elsaesser, "Primary Identification and the Historical Subject," in *Narrative, Apparatus, Ideology: A Film Theory Reader*, ed. Philip Rosen (New York: Columbia University Press, 1986), 545.

[31] Ibid., 540.

[32] Gerald Mast reads this film as modernist cinema in *Can't Help Singin': The American Musical on Stage and Screen*, 324; Stanley Solomon gives it a Brechtian reading in *Beyond Formula: American Film Genres* (New York: Harcourt Brace, 1976), 106–110.

ness marriages, ambitious film and Broadway projects. Since my analysis has already suggested several ways in which *Cabaret* utilizes sexual dynamics that presume a male spectator—the various disavowals of female sexuality, as well as the underlying homophobia—it seems more valid to argue, not that Fosse has suddenly shifted into a more marginal kind of filmmaking, but rather that the very intricacy of the visual structure of this text, and its duplication in the narrative structure's centering of spectacle and spectatorship, visibility and voyeurism, considerably complicate spectatorship and *nearly* undermine the male, moral spectator-in-the-text.

Whereas Bauer reads this text's obsession with concealment and revelation as straight oedipal narrative, I have already suggested visual and narrative elements that would problematize such a reading: the hero's ambiguous sexuality, the "coupling" effect of the editing that relates him to the emcee, the various gay subtexts that undermine the heterosexuality of the oedipal family romance. The problem of the male gaze here in some respects duplicates Isherwood's in the original Sally Bowles story. In Sally's would-be seduction scene, the dynamic of failed desire is literalized: "Doesn't my body drive you wild with desire?" Sally asks Brian as she parades herself in front of his polite gaze. Unlike the 1950s adaptations, the Christopher character in this film is finally able to admit that no, it does not, but he does not then identify himself as the "confirmed bachelor" whom the text must rescue into marriage. Instead, he claims to be a rather terminally confirmed bachelor, someone who "does not sleep with girls," with the implication that although he does not sleep with boys, either—"My sex life is nil—plenty of nothin' "—he is probably struggling with a gay identity, since his sexual attempts with girls have been "disasters." In spite of this sexual frankness in the narrative, the heterosexual norm of mainstream film suggests that, like the confirmed bachelor of 1950s cinema, his "problem" will be "cured" by Sally Bowles, as in fact happens.

This resolution—which is a variation of the resolution of the Cornelius film—should end the film in the traditional formula, with everyone safely aligned into heterosexuality, just as Laurence Harvey is led pseudo-reluctantly away into offscreen romance by Julie Harris in the last shot of the Cornelius version. But the astonishing turn in the *Cabaret* narrative is that Brian achieves successful sexual experience with a man just after his first sexual success with a woman, and that another set of desiring gazes is at work around Sally Bowles while the narrative seems to be telling the classic story of the oedipal triangle. If the camera gaze aligns us to Brian's sexual and political experience and works to construct the desire for Sally Bowles, it also

FOSSE'S *CABARET* 225

acknowledges the desiring gaze of Max—whose portrayal by Helmut Griem represents a character much more traditionally attractive by Hollywood standards than Liza Minnelli. It would seem, then, that the male viewer of this film is presented with the problems of spectatorship usually attributed to the female viewer: identification with the controlling gaze necessitates opting for bisexual shifts.

Yet such a model of spectatorship is ultimately reductive in a film that complicates that model from the very first shot with the distortingly mirrored audience. My argument is that "the controlling male gaze" operates in this film more as a sexual anxiety throughout the trajectory, and that—at least until the closure—the visual and scopophilic gaze tends instead to be multiple, diffuse, and refracted, as suggested by the rapid editing of the musical numbers which makes it impossible to locate a singular position of spectatorship, thus undermining the show-girl effect as described by Mulvey.

It is true that Fosse's theatrical instinct for the project of entertainment seems at times to confirm the more traditional spectator relations of the musical. There often occurs in this film, for example, a positioning of the spectator purely as audience for the performance, as in Sally's last dazzling musical number, in which Brian is not present and in which the diegetic audience—made up of men in swastika arm bands, as the last shot reveals—is repressed. The effect is not Sally Bowles playing for the Nazis but Liza Minnelli exhibiting her considerable talent for the camera. But at other times, the traditional construction of the show-girl is radically reframed. Even in Sally's torch song, "Maybe This Time," the happy heterosexual ideal illustrated in the flashbacks to cozy sexual and domestic scenes with Brian is contradicted by the diegetic gazes present during her performance. The camera tracks back to show that the Kit Kat Klub is nearly empty, and four close-ups reveal that she is performing for two middle-aged businessmen alone at tables, the disgusted-looking tuba player from the all-girl (or transvestite) orchestra, and the emcee, who watches from backstage. Offering herself as spectacle, the show-girl is traditionally sutured into the text through the shot-countershot with the admiring diegetic viewer, securing the gaze into the trajectory of desire. Instead, the four close-ups register boredom, distraction, or—in the case of the emcee—a much more questionable kind of interest, since his sexual desire and inclinations are never specified. So the pleasurable gaze of the film viewer, whom Sally seems to be addressing directly in the first part of her song, is undermined rather than confirmed by the diegesis. Indeed, Sally's key line, the summary of the exhibitionist-voyeurist dynamic of the show-girl—"Doesn't my body drive you wild with desire?"—is continually being subverted, not only by the rejection it originally receives, but also by reversals in the diegetic audience, by her juxtaposition with the Kit Kat transvestites—including the beautiful drag queen Elke—and even by Brian's repetition of the line (showing off a rather androgynously slender body) in the flashback during "Maybe This Time."

Although these ambiguous positionings of Sally hint at the breakdown of a traditional trajectory of heterosexual desire, the shot that most openly suggests this breakdown is the one that focuses in on the drunken dance shared by Sally, Brian, and Max during the party at the baron's country estate. What had begun as an exhibitionist performance by Sally turns into the slower, more romantic dance with Max, but Max brings Brian into the dance/embrace, and the camera lingers on a close-up of their circling faces and the circle of their desiring gazes at each other. For a moment, the camera centers and focuses on Brian between them, with Sally and Max claiming equal space on either side of the frame, acknowledging a split desire. But the impact of this split is so unsettling that the next two shots work to resolve the conflict and to reimpose a heterosexual trajectory: Brian passes out so that Sally and Max must take control of the gaze, putting him to bed like the infant who has witnessed the primal scene. Exchanging a meaningful glance, they go off supposedly to the sexual encounter the "child" has both fantasized and seen.

What all this suggests, I propose, is that the narrative and the visual relations of the text that construct a male norm of spectatorship and an oedipal, heterosexual fantasy—the camera's obsessive gaze between the legs, the classic rivalry situation created by Max—are interrupted by other desires and positions that are not as rigidly constructed along gender lines. The opening sequence alone points to this, with the parallel editing "coupling" Brian with the emcee rather than with his romantic lead. As Gaylyn Studlar describes the diffusion of desire in the Von Sternberg films, the multiple points of identification can permit more polymorphous pleasures. In applying Studlar's theory to Cornelius's *I Am a Camera* in chapter 4, I emphasized that in order to account fully for the sexual politics of the film, the psychoanalytic dynamic had to be qualified or reframed by cultural practices and other contexts that pointed to much more hostile and misogynist agendas than can be tracked down in the pleasurable "heterocosm" Studlar describes. Likewise, I find Studlar's theory both particularly relevant to the Fosse film, but also in need of reframing by the cultural anxieties that permeate the text: the homophobia and signification of Nazism as a secret femaleness; the radical political confrontation with and positing of German fascism as an absolute, and absolutely Other evil; and the anxiety of gender identity by which Sally as threatening female sexuality is disavowed and renounced as part of a signifying chain linking her to Nazism, Max, and the emcee.[33] The trajectory's route is a circuitous one, but it nevertheless strains for the recovery of a gaze in which the confirming "natural" biological order is recovered.

The major advantage of an analysis of *Cabaret* as a preoedipal text is that it restores to Sally Bowles the authority that an oedipal analysis otherwise cedes to the much less effective and less dynamic Brian Roberts. There is no hint that Brian could possibly be the male sexual authority of the classic Hollywood text, whereas Sally's authority is openly named twice by Natalia, who on two different occasions seeks out Sally as a woman of "many sexual experiences." Sally maliciously uses this authority against Brian in the text's most obvious humiliation scenario; interrupting his little "party" with Fritz and Natalia, she deliberately launches into a conversation about syphilis to embarrass him in front of his pupils, a conversation climaxed with her ability to remember all too accurately the German word for "screwing." Wearing a huge, floppy hat in this scene and sporting her green fingernails, deliberately performing for Brian and his friends as sexual spectacle, Sally enacts in a different way here the sexual power and domination evident in her Kit Kat numbers. Brian, in turn, is revealed as the ideal helpless child/spectator to the powerful, all-engulfing mother/spectacle.

In the sequence showing Brian's first visit to the Kit Kat Klub, the iconography of Sally's stage performance vividly suggests painful pleasures. The camera frames her through the arms, legs, and bent-over torsos of the grim-faced transvestite chorus who translate Sally's sexual signals into robotlike, military maneuvers of submission or stylized writhings of pain. The lyrics of her song "Mein Herr," a ruthless good-bye to the abandoned lover, suggest the control she has already demonstrated over Brian by talking him into taking the room at Schneider's and insisting he can use her own room to give his English lessons. Later, when her seduction attempt fails, she is the one who articulates the new terms of the friendship, just as she later decides, against Brian's will, to include Max—as a "friend"—in their relationship. "You do what Sally says, and you end up, I think, in the prison cell," Fritz warns Brian.

Nevertheless, both men essentially do what Sally says, with the result that they both suffer in different ways, as surely as the victims in

---

[33] This chapter on Fosse's *Cabaret* constitutes this reframing of my essay, "Women, Monsters, and the Masochistic Aesthetic in *Cabaret*," *Journal of Film and Video* 39 (1987): 5–17.

17. *Cabaret* (1972). The sadomasochistic *mise-en-scène* of Sally's (Liza Minnelli's) performance of "Mein Herr" validates her position as controlling sexual authority.

the pornographic book that (again, at Sally's insistence) Brian translates for Herr Ludwig: *"Cleo the Whip Lady."* Doing what Sally says, Fritz takes her advice, "pounces" on Natalia, and wins her heart; but he also unexpectedly falls in love with her and must admit his Jewishness in order to marry her. As Fritz is well aware, to be Jewish in Berlin at this time is to suffer. The shot of the emcee's anti-Semitic last line of his love song to the gorilla is cut to a shot of Fritz approaching the Landauer doorway to announce he is Jewish, a match of an earlier cut from a cabaret performance to a shot of Nazi thugs approaching the doorway with Natalia's dead dog. Fritz and Natalia are obviously victims of history, and Sally's relationship to that history had been suggested earlier in the railroad-trestle scene, in which doing what Sally says becomes the introductory gesture into the scene of social and cultural violence.

Of all the Christopher characters of the adaptations, Brian is perhaps the most passive in relation to Sally. He lacks the comic resistance of the confirmed bachelor in the Cornelius film, and he does not have the writing ambition of all his predecessors. Even his newly potent heterosexuality occurs as an accident, and his attempts to pose as a seriously masculine lover are set up as jokes. Finding Sally at the Kit Kat with a customer in one scene, he pretends to growl in a fake American accent, "Tell him your gangster lover from Chicago is here." Sally doesn't even use his line—she uses the syphilis excuse instead and has Elke replace her with the customer—so that the more subtle joke about Brian's not-very-serious masculinity is deflected onto the genital joke about Elke. But when Max arrives on the scene and a more serious rivalry situation ensues, Brian can likewise do nothing more than make a feeble joke; he stands behind a potted plant at Max's estate to claim himself "King of the Jungle" while he watches his lover being wooed by another man. The narrative gives Brian only two moves that show him taking positive action, and both lead inevitably to pain: he provokes the street-corner Brownshirts and is promptly beaten up; and he decides to marry Sally after she discovers she is pregnant by either him or Max—provoking a different kind of suffering, his realization that it is a mistake, but a mistake that only Sally can "correct" with her decision to have an abortion—about which he also grieves.

Suffering at the hands of Sally affords Brian a specific kind of innocence, in spite of his "guilt" at acting out the fantasy of desiring and obtaining the authoritative mother. In the ideal masochistic male fantasy, desire for punishment leads him to take on traits of submissiveness, passivity, and even gender masquerade culturally ascribed to women. *Cabaret* goes much further in this cross-gendering by making Brian truly bisexual; he acts out the fantasy not just with the mother, but with the father as well, by eventually sleeping with Max. Brian's "punishment" at the hands of the Nazis is clearly positioned as the result of this effeminacy that Sally seemed to have "solved" but that Max sees in him and revives. Yet although Brian takes the punishment, he is not the guilty party. Guilt for the masochist is deflected onto the father, whose phallic resemblance in the son is disavowed.

Brian's disavowal of the father's guilt works especially well in his ambiguous status as "father" in the later part of the film. Sally is unable to verify who has actually fathered the child she is carrying, so Brian's offer to marry her seems especially heroic. But in the masochistic dynamic, it would threaten to displace the pleasure-punishment fantasy altogether by assigning him full phallic identity and real guilt. Instead, his ambiguous fatherhood serves to reinforce the ambiguous nature of his sexuality. The drunken engagement/baby-celebration scene in Sally's room literalizes this flimsy "masquerade," emphasizing Brian's essential boyishness: wearing a necktie on his bare chest and sporting an oversize fedora, pretending to smoke a cigar (the traditional sign of masculinity and fatherhood), he looks ridiculous—the child dressing in his father's clothes.

Yet as Kaja Silverman warns in her recent work on male masochism, the very disavowal of phallic power in the masochistic dynamic points to its importance in the wider scheme.[34] In Fosse's *Cabaret*, the clue is the political one. Brian's phallic guiltlessness is his political innocence; while Sally and Max will remain in Hitler's Fatherland, Brian will understand its corruption and will renounce it. But the guilt of the Fatherland, its particular corruption, is its secret femininity. This feminine "likeness" is what Brian has to have beaten out of him in his fistfight with the Nazis, achieving a literal disfigurement of his pretty-boy features which linked him both to Max and to the lovely *Hitlerjunge* singer, to whom they listened just after they made their first sexual connection with a gaze of complicity. The most direct inference of this sexual secret of the Fatherland occurs earlier in a Kit Kat performance. In the frantic chorus-girl sequence, which is parallel-edited with the attack on the Landauers, the emcee appears bare chested but otherwise in drag, suggesting a breastless woman, just after he and the chorus have turned around their caps to become goose-stepping soldiers.

My argument here is that the disavowal of phallic power only occurs as the acknowledgment that the Fatherland is a masquerade of the concealed feminine, and as a positioning of this concealed femi-

---

[34] Kaja Silverman, "Masochism and Male Subjectivity," 57.

nine as monstrous and corruptive. It is not surprising, then, that the dynamic that gives Sally sexual authority in relation to Brian's passivity, and that posits her fascination and power as the loving inflictor of punishment, is constantly being recontained by other textual strategies. In fact, because of Brian's submissiveness and lack of phallic authority, the text works hard to resist the trajectory of pleasurable suffering at the hands of Sally. Matching Brian's masquerade as father, for example, is the exposure of Sally's sexuality as masquerade as well, which is turned around into a joke on her, an undermining of the sexual authority of the worldly femme fatale. "You're about as *fatale* as an after-dinner mint," Brian tells her furiously. This line occurs just before he reveals to her that her grand delusions about "controlling Max" have backfired. They both "screw Max," the dialogue reveals, a move that points the narrative suspiciously in the direction of what Molly Haskell calls the era's "buddy movies," in which, as Laura Mulvey points out, the inconsequential position of the woman is overtly acknowledged so that the erotic bonding of the male pair can continue uninterrupted.[35]

The exposure of Sally's sexuality as fake *fatale* is reinforced by other reductions of her adult sexuality, a tactic that Van Druten had brought to the 1951 character with the teddy bear and kitten picture. In Fosse's *Cabaret*, Sally's childishness is positioned as part of her charm and spontaneity, the qualities that code her as musical star despite the dubious milieu of the Kit Kat Klub. The pressure of the text to produce such a star who is on some level sympathetic thus must undermine her own introduction of herself to Brian as an "international woman of mystery," a woman of "ancient instincts," as she says in their first scene together. So she is eventually repositioned as a little girl playing with adult high heels and whip—Daddy's little girl, in fact, who fails to guess the international mystery of Brian and Max. When the latter two are alone for a chat, they speak of her with condescending fondness. "Sally is an endearing child," says Max, "but I must admit I find it peaceful when she's taking her nap." In turn, Brian's first successful arousal by her occurs only when she puts the sophisticate pose aside in the scene in which she is stood up by her father. She has taken off her stagey makeup and is crying because Daddy doesn't love her. This disavowal of adult female sexuality permits the heterosexual romance to take place, but also allows the gay male relationship to develop, as a joke revealing Sally's naïveté—and also hinting at her failure to "cure" something in Brian's sexual nature, thereby suggesting a failure of her own femininity.

[35] Laura Mulvey, "Visual Pleasure and Narrative Cinema," 11.

Such a repudiation can also deny Sally's motherhood, the factor that in each adaptation becomes progressively more critical as the test of Sally as pure surface or as something with an "inside," a space that is verifiably female—in this case, in contradistinction to the construction of genital space as unknowable and possibly male. So the abortion in this text serves as a particularly powerful disavowal in that it works as the narrative complement to the anxiety that has been represented visually with the abundance of transvestites and crotch shots. The scene in which Sally tells Brian about the abortion is a visual and narrative match of the earlier Daddy scene, and in both scenes Sally is reduced to childish outbursts, so that the relationship's beginning and ending are made possible by disavowals of Sally's adult sexuality. Pouting in response to Brian's questions, Sally blurts out that the abortion was perhaps one of her "whims." Both scenes take place in the same kind of predawn lighting in the same corner of the bedroom, Sally without her clown makeup, crying, stammering about her stage ambitions—her "infantile fantasy," she tells Brian in this scene, to "amount to something as an actress." Since her resemblance in face and voice to Judy Garland is again remarkable in this scene, the allusion here suggests bad motherhood, or a motherhood sacrificed to stage ambition. Thus the issue of symbiotic merger, the blur of distinction in the maternal relationship, is oddly literalized with this extratextual reference.

The film soon indulges this "infantile fantasy"—and the fantasy of the maternal heterocosm as well—in Sally's superb final performance, her "Cabaret" number, which intensifies the reference to her mother with its lyrics about the roommate Elsie, who died from "too much pills and liquor," while the production and performance confirm that this is indeed "every inch Judy Garland's daughter." As in the stage play, the text strains here for the refusal of the world of Oedipus and responsibility and posits instead a heterocosm that seems distinctly preoedipal. Both diegetic and film audiences are positioned passively in relationship to the powerful female figure who specifically promises the pleasurable immersion into life as opposed to the isolation of the individual "alone in your room." Unlike the stage-play version of this number, "Cabaret" is performed after Brian has been entirely eliminated from the narrative, so that the oedipal story seems entirely disposed of, and Sally's authority entirely confirmed. Moreover, with the various underminings of Brian throughout the text, it could be argued that there is no actual representation of the phallic male norm anywhere, so that the pleasure of Sally's performance, which itself is haunted by a mother-daughter blur of distinction, resides in the pleasurable blur of boundary described by

Gaylyn Studlar as the bliss of maternal merger, in spite of the narrative's deliberate denial of Sally as mother. The striking male-female attractiveness of Liza Minnelli additionally blurs gender identification here (which, along with the Judy Garland reference, makes this number a drag-performance favorite in gay culture).

Yet this particular pleasure in performance is qualified not just by the previous narrative move of the abortion and disavowal of adult female sexuality, but also by the more overtly grotesque versions of that sexuality that are immediately presented in the space of Sally's performance. The curtain closes on Sally; the screen is dark for a moment, followed by a close-up of the emcee reflected in the distorting mirror. "Here life is beautiful," he says with a sneer, reiterating the standard utopian project of the film musical. His statement is deliberately undercut by a series of shots showing audience members as painfully distorted figures in Expressionist art—a result of Fosse's effort to visualize the era. One shot of a thin, masculinized woman at a table is a tableau duplication of Otto Dix's 1926 oil painting of Sylvia van Harden. From distorted figures in the audience, the camera moves to the various distortions onstage, culminating in a montage of shots from previous Kit Kat performances that amounts to a nightmare of female spectacle: a fragmented leg in black stockings framing the torso of one of the "girls" bent over a chair from the "Mein Herr" performance; a shot of Sally from the same performance, her head flung back and wildly tossing from side to side suggesting hysteria or lack of control; a close-up of the emcee's garishly lipsticked mouth; a shot of the female mud wrestler; the emcee in drag; and finally, a tracking crotch shot of the transvestite chorus during a high kick. The startling appearance of the mud wrestler most clearly evokes the monstrous in this montage, just as the final shot locates the monstrosity as hidden female space—or the space that is unknowable. (Are these transvestites or not?) In a sharp reversal from the glamorized production of Sally's last number, female spectacle is revealed as explicitly threatening precisely because—as the appearance of the transvestites suggests—it is "non-man." If the "Cabaret" number had evoked a fantasy of female plenitude and the pleasure of submission to merger with the powerful maternal sexuality, this pleasure is deliberately negated with the imposition of unmistakable horror at the violation of gender boundary, which here is the horror of the female grotesque.

The next shot suggests that this crossing of gender boundary in the montage is a misogynist nightmare with specifically historical hooks. A slow pan moves from the emcee's departure behind the curtains to the wall-mirror on which the diegetic audience is revealed as the Kit

Kat's ultimate spectacle, the spectators who include the men in Nazi uniforms and swastika arm bands, "mirroring" the previous spectacles of transvestism and sexual ambiguity. The reimposition of the oedipal world could not be more clear. Even without Brian as a representative phallic norm, that norm is nevertheless evoked in this paranoid vision of a Fatherland in drag, a dread of female sexuality or blurred sexual boundary. At the same time, the text has confirmed the nature of the distortion by which the diegetic audience is not identical with the film spectator. That identification had been teasingly suggested in the opening sequence, and had the frame become a true mirror, the spectacle would have threateningly extended its space in a virtual conflation with its spectators, like the imploding scene described by Styron in the Chicago Haymarket Lounge. Instead, the distortion, the space reflected in the mirror, can safely distance spectatorship because the space has been explicitly defined as Other: a monstrous kind of female sexuality—the grotesque emcee, the hideously made-up transvestites, but also Sally Bowles.

Unlike the other performers at the Kit Kat, Fosse's Sally cannot be reflected in this wall-mirror except by this signifying chain because she is so much identified as mainstream musical talent and star. Instead, the emcee as distorted image (literally, the face that appears in the mirror directly after her performance) can take on the negative signification that cannot be too openly ascribed to Minnelli as star: a borderline grotesquery, like the borderline masculine/feminine attractiveness of the both of them in this film. To further distance star-Minnelli from grotesque-Sally, her "Cabaret" song is framed and lit so that the Kit Kat is almost entirely eliminated as diegetic space. During most of this sequence, the background behind her is entirely black or, toward the end of the song, is exploding into lights and colors with special effects that, as Isherwood suggested, would be highly unlikely if the Kit Kat were actually a third-rate Berlin cabaret.

While this split representation of Sally most obviously points to the split nature of Fosse's project—the truly entertaining Big Show and the truly horrifying spectacle of Nazism—it also continues this character's ambiguous construction beginning with Isherwood. The Sally Bowles who in this text is situated precariously between show-business fascination and misogynist hostility oddly duplicates the inscription of Jean Ross in the memoirs of Isherwood and his friends, and in the later fictionalization in *Goodbye to Berlin*. When Sally refuses to answer Brian's questions about the abortion, and then blurts out that it was one of her "whims," it is not difficult to think of the mixture of awe and contempt with which Ross is described in those memoirs, and Isherwood's description of the Sally character as "a silly little capricious bitch."

Divinely decadent, flashing technicolor green fingernail polish, Minnelli's Sally Bowles is similarly split between a mainstream and a marginal desire, performing as "good heter stuff" but also as a campy joke in gay culture. Yet the homophobic subtext that I have traced in the film version of *Cabaret* is a reminder of the more disturbing route by which Isherwood's project has come full circle here. Sally was originally the "good heter stuff" for a literature that was compulsorily heterosexual, and the story was framed in the political anxieties of a forthcoming regime that enforced heterosexuality by rounding up gay men for concentration camps. In the razzle-dazzle of Fosse's dynamic entertainment, on the other hand, the sexual politics of the Third Reich is conveniently glossed over for the sake of "good heter" effect, an assurance that Nazism can be distanced by its identification with "perverse" sexuality—its "decadence." Sally Bowles's "decadence" may reside in the blurring of boundary, the play on ambivalence which, through its humor and excesses, challenges traditional gender categorization; but Sally's "decadence" also makes meaning as an ongoing cultural fascination with a masterful politics in which one knows one's place and acknowledges a "natural" hierarchy of both gender and race. Whereas the homophobic inflections of the latter adaptations work in cruel irony in relation to the original Isherwood text, it is this latter, cumulative identification of the decadent and the perverse as "female" that extends the problematics of the Sally Bowles figure into the multiple political agendas across which this fictional character has been played.

EPILOGUE

ALTHOUGH THE CULTURAL repetitions of the Sally Bowles story may give it the status of contemporary myth, another kind of mythologizing about a "real" Sally Bowles occurs in the context of Fosse's *Cabaret*. Jean Ross, Isherwood's model for the character, had gone home to England following her eighteen months in Berlin and had never returned; she devoted the rest of her life to her daughter and to a variety of liberal political causes and died in 1973 without having seen any of the film or stage versions of her own fictionalized Berlin days. But in the Fosse biography *Razzle Dazzle*, Kevin Boyd Grubb reports that during the filming on location in Germany, the crew learned that "the real Sally, an expatriate American then in her sixties, was still living in Berlin." Grubb speculates that since the project had been well publicized, "It seems unlikely she would not have heard about the film, though she never showed up at the Bavaria studio."[1]

If this is true, then the film crew's illusion serves as one more example of the fuzzy kind of "history" invoked in this entire project—in the Fosse film, but in the other adaptations as well. Especially in the latter texts, with the visual prominence of swastikas and Brownshirts, the Sally Bowles story seems straining to say something historically authentic about German fascism. Fosse denied that he was interested in the politics or the history of Weimar: "You know, the political aspect of it is being over-emphasized. The most important part of it is the love story."[2] Yet the surprising detail of the Otto Dix painting used in the opening and closing montage sequences reveals a concern at some level with meticulous authenticity; and few reviews of the film refrained from mentioning the "Tomorrow Belongs to Me" scene as one of the film's most powerful moments, the only non–Kit Kat number and the number that most clearly extends the site of the cabaret into "history." Fosse himself claimed the film shows "that what was going on in the cabaret was a reflection of what was to come in Germany."[3] What I have argued here is that history is imprinted in these texts not as "reflections" of what actually happened in Germany but as traces of many other discourses and interpretations of history from other eras. Fascism itself emerges as a variety of questions and tensions testing how the "nightmare" of the ultimate Fa-

[1] Kevin Boyd Grubb, *Razzle Dazzle*, 146.
[2] Lil Picard, "Interview with Bob Fosse," 8.
[3] Ibid.

therland can be understood and disavowed within other patriarchal cultural moments. In such a story of fathers and sons, fascism as the ultimate patriarchal fantasy must be exposed as secretly female, and thus not identical with male authority.

Yet I am reluctant to close my own history of these texts by suggesting that the psychoanalytic explanation is the final or master code in regard to German fascism, or to subsequent fascinations with that era, or to Sally Bowles as a rhetorical device. A single, all-inclusive theory fails to account for how these three elements interact in each text. Like her failed appearance at the Bavarian studio, Sally Bowles never shows up, as it were, as one single problem or strategy. Although this character seems particularly overdetermined in literary and film history—as spectacle, as updated Dolly Mickleham, as failed motherhood, as campy parody, as a version of Lola Lola, as passive witness to fascism—the Sally Bowles figure also illustrates the wider and more common problem of how we use historical and psychoanalytical tools in feminist criticism. After struggling to talk about both text and context, the social and the psychic, in these chapters, I feel great hesitation in ascribing to anything like a "historicized psychoanalysis" or "psychoanalytic materialism." I feel instead the need to keep these two theories in process, with and against each other, by constantly shifting frameworks of knowledge and their accompanying metaphors in order to describe different problems and contradictions.

Since this book is concerned with the sexual politics of German fascism and its relationships to mainstream cultural and cinematic concepts, I was of course aware that I had begun my manuscript and project at the end of the decade often jokingly termed the era of "Reagan's friendly fascism." Considering the show-business background implicit in Reaganism—with its star of the classic text—it is no surprise that the sexual politics of the Reagan legacy aimed to duplicate the traditional sexual dynamics of classic cinema: for example, the contradictory status of motherhood as both revered and disavowed (so that a pious discourse of Momism could coexist with lack of support for prenatal care). In spite of the modernist tendencies of the Prince stage play, the Sally Bowles texts are all predominantly from the classic tradition, and thus loaded down with the sexual ideology that can both idealize and castigate female sexuality and motherhood, as happens throughout these texts.

Perhaps only a radically different kind of text can attempt to deal with the paranoia and anxieties of postwar evaluations of German fascism. I like to think of Michael Verhoeven's 1991 film *The Nasty Girl* (*Das schreckliche Mädchen*), for instance, as a kind of anti-Sally

Bowles story, a postmodern text that in a very different way focuses on the identity, sexuality, and motherhood of a young woman in order to question the relationship between fascism and Western culture, or as Theweleit puts its, the question "Is there a true boundary separating 'fascists' from 'nonfascist' men?"[4] Rather than making that boundary a sexual one, as the Sally Bowles texts do by shifting authority to the disavowing male, *The Nasty Girl* gives narrative authority fully to its protagonist, Sonya Rosenberger Wegmus, the questioner and historian in the film, whose identity within the family, church, and state is the foundation of her ability to shake the mythologized and euphemistic history of her Bavarian town during the Third Reich. What Sonya discovers is both her town's complicity with the Nazis and the legal, institutionalized means of denying this complicity.

The town skinheads are the most obvious enemy to Sonya's project, and they make brief, threatening appearances with acts of terrorism and violence linking them directly to their fascist predecessors. But the shocking revelation is that they are only the radical front guard to the town's less obvious prejudices and authoritarianism which have remained respectably mainstreamed. The film carefully points out how, within that mainstream tradition, female sexuality has been consistently degraded and fetishized. In one of its more outrageous sequences, Sonya recalls how one of the respected town fathers once contrived a way to fold a German mark and hold it up to a mirror to get an image of female genitalia; having gone to great trouble to create the image himself, he then demands that the bill be withdrawn from the currency because of its obscenity. In another early episode, Sonya's mother is hanging up her laundry in her yard to dry, when she realizes that this commonplace household activity has become the voyeuristic object of the schoolboys next door who are staring at the laundered underwear and down her own blouse. Considering how the fetishization of women's underwear operates in the Sally Bowles cycle, it is especially refreshing to find that in this story of the town's "dirty laundry" coming to light, it is the underwear belonging to some town fathers that is at stake: an anti-Semitic story told by two clergymen about a Jewish merchant selling them 100 pairs of underpants had led to the Jew's denunciation and eventual death.

In breaking down the boundaries of "fascist" and "nonfascist," *The Nasty Girl* must break down a number of cinematic conventions, not only clichés about the relationship between female sexuality and fascism (Sonya is healthily unrepressed both sexually and intellectually)

---

[4] Klaus Theweleit, *Male Fantasies*, vol. 1, 27.

but also basic concepts of narrative, history, character, and *mise-en-scène*. Interior scenes are often filmed against the rear projection of city streets and monuments, dissolving dualities of the personal and the public, the intimate and the historical. The film's final explosion of narrative authority saves what might otherwise be too neat a classic closure in Sonya's gradual acceptance by the town's authorities, who want to place a statue of her in city hall. Refusing any history that closes down questions, Sonya erupts into a rage that literally stops the filming of what had become the "documentary" film *The Nasty Girl*. She thus escapes both the narrative and the town's new role for her of "heroic historian." Such a role, the film implies, is too convenient, too safe. Unlike the Sally Bowles figure who was destined to be projected over and over again as the key icon in a safe and convenient history, Sonya can break out of such containment because of the film's interrogative structure and its refusal to cast her sexuality in traditional cinematic terms.

Yet the popularity of the other, simpler, "decadent Weimar" mythology continues. The revival of the stage musical *Cabaret* appeared on Broadway and then as a road show while I was writing my first draft of this manuscript. It again received good reviews and interested audiences, though in a profoundly different context and in relation to a very different political climate. While the stage musical had originally appeared at a time when voices of protest and outrage against racism and sexism were gaining national attention, the revival occurs after the twenty-year lapse in which fascism had become fashionable again—beyond Reagan's fuzzy paternalism—as teenage fad, as skinhead fashion, or even more seriously, as neo-Nazi discourses on the political fringe, as propaganda claiming that the Holocaust was a hoax, as racist and anti-Semitic "jokes" that have become popular and casual on college campuses. The didacticism of Prince's original project—"It can happen here!"—resounds against both the disturbances of history and its own disturbing distancing devices which so much duplicate the homey platitudes of Reaganism: the wish for a simpler time when women were women and men were men, as opposed to the garish and kinky confusions of the cabaret.

Responding perhaps to contemporary realizations of a much more complicated sexuality, the Cliff of this revival is not as wholesomely straight as his 1960s counterpart; a young German named Gottfried follows him around and apparently has had some prior encouragement from him, though Cliff again manages to renounce all temptations, along with Sally, and to be aligned finally with the traditional "good" stage characters rather than the sinister Kit Kat performers. The decadence of the cabaret, meanwhile, takes on especially disquieting overtones considering the late 1980s emotional political battles concerning AIDS and the homophobic discourses that have become as epidemic as the disease itself.

Indeed, the issues of camp and homophobia have been the most troubling aspects of my exploration of the Sally Bowles texts and the most difficult to write about. The evolution of the Sally strategy from Isherwood's "good heter stuff" to Fosse's "divine decadence" can be described, without too much oversimplification, as a forty-year history of gay male discourse. The sexuality that could not be openly acknowledged in *Goodbye to Berlin* is recoded by Van Druten in the 1950s, represented as camp by Hal Prince in 1966, and then openly discussed in the 1972 film, when the protagonist can finally reply to Sally's frustrated exclamation—"Maybe you just don't like girls," with the answer that this is in fact the case. Over and over in these texts, I found the representation of a wild and attractive female sexuality at odds with a male indifference to it—an indifference that frequently erupts into resentment or hostility. The relationship of the Sally character to the gay male sensibility suggests the larger problem of relationships between feminism and camp, the problem of women who are sympathetic to the comic deconstruction of sexual stereotypes but who often find in those comic representations an indifference or outright animosity toward female sexuality—a casualty of a sensibility that simply does not "like girls." For these same reasons, I have argued, the Sally character as played by Julie Harris and Liza Minnelli lacks the lesbian appeal of Sally's predecessor Lola Lola as played by Dietrich, whose fascinating sexuality is never a joke at her own expense.

The relationship of Isherwood and Jean Ross, who provided the original material for his "good heter stuff," typifies the tension between sympathy for a liberated gay sexuality and the personal stakes of the woman-become-joke. Ross and Isherwood remained friends and never actually quarreled about it, but Ross's daughter Sarah Caudwell claims that her mother was "hurt" by the fictionalization in *Goodbye to Berlin*, and thus never cared to see any of the adaptations.[5] After Ross's death, Isherwood's last inscription of her in his 1976 memoir *Christopher and His Kind* continues the history of the fictional character in a series of texts in which she is progressively more aligned with crises of visibility and spectacle. When Ross got a job in Max Reinhardt's production of *Tales of Hoffmann*, says Isherwood, she appeared in a palace scene in which several pairs of lovers recline on litters as background to the central ballet: "But Christopher

[5] Interview with the author, 4 May 1991, New York.

watched one pair of lovers intently, through opera glasses, until the end of the scene. Even so, he couldn't be sure if what Jean had told him was true—that she had sex with her partner in full view of the audience at every single performance."[6] In Sarah Caudwell's article about her mother, she dismisses the story as "a rather schoolboyish speculation of Isherwood's."[7] Yet the very "schoolboyish" nature of the memory/fantasy points to the voyeuristic operations that have continued to construct the Sally Bowles character as spectacle and locus of male anxieties concerning the identity of female genital space and the threat of merger with a sexual or political Other. The image of Isherwood with his opera glasses, peering at Jean Ross to see what he could see, is in many ways an iconographic summary of the Sally Bowles character's history on stage and screen; indeed, since Isherwood is not interested in Ross in a sexual way, the gaze is more exclusively voyeuristic.

Later in the memoir, Isherwood gives Ross a speaking part, relating a telephone call from her in which she set him up for his first screenwriting job with Berthold Viertel. Since he has "no verbatim record of what she said," Isherwood explains, he gives us her conversation "in the style of Sally Bowles," complete with Sally's breathless exaggerations: " 'Chris darling, I've just met this absolutely marvelous man. . . .' "[8] Certainly part of my project is to ascertain that Sally's fluffy language is not the last record and last word of Jean Ross, who in fact never rewrote her own inscription in Isherwood's story. Caudwell remembers that her mother "did from time to time settle down conscientiously to write a letter, intending to explain to Isherwood the ways in which she thought he had misunderstood her," but the letter "was interrupted, no doubt, by more urgent things: meetings about Vietnam, petitions against nuclear weapons, making my supper, hearing my French verbs."[9] More generally, motherhood had seriously interrupted all Ross's writing, says Caudwell, "for the usual maternal reasons but also because my father left her almost immediately afterwards and this had, I think, a very damaging effect on her confidence in her abilities as a writer."[10] So a closure by Jean Ross comes here secondhand, through the memory of Caudwell, but at least accords Ross a place in a reading that has deliberately emphasized how this adaptation series returns to issues of motherhood—Ross and Caudwell, Garland and Minnelli, with a fictional Mummy

[6] Christopher Isherwood, *Christopher and His Kind*, 88–89.
[7] Sarah Caudwell, "Reply to Berlin," 28.
[8] Christopher Isherwood, *Christopher and His Kind*, 149.
[9] Caudwell, "Reply to Berlin," 28.
[10] Letter to the author, 2 Jan. 1989.

buried in between. Moreover, Ross's comments, as remembered by Caudwell, ironically illustrate the problem of representations of history in regard to female sexuality. When reporters came to the house to look for the "real Sally Bowles," Caudwell says, "the journalists always wanted to talk about sex and my mother always wanted to talk about politics." Ross would complain to her daughter: " 'They say they want to know about Berlin in the Thirties. But they don't want to know about the unemployment or the poverty or the Nazis marching through the streets—all they want to know is how many men I went to bed with. Really, darling, how on earth can anyone be interested in that?' "[11]

[11] Caudwell, "Reply to Berlin," 28.

BIBLIOGRAPHY

Adair, Gilbert. "Isherwood in Hollywood." *Sight and Sound* 46 (1976): 25.

Adorno, T. W., et al. *The Authoritarian Personality*. New York: Harper, 1950.

Allen, Jay Presson. *Cabaret*. Hollywood: Script City, 1970.

Altman, Rick. *The American Film Musical*. Bloomington and Indianapolis: Indiana University Press, 1987.

————, ed. *Genre: The Musical*. London: Routledge, 1981.

Appignanesi, Lisa. *The Cabaret*. New York: Universe, 1976.

Aurthur, Robert Alan. "Hanging Out." *Esquire* August 1973, 6ff.

Babuscio, Jack. "Camp and the Gay Sensibility." *Gays and Film*. Ed. Richard Dyer. Rev. ed. New York: Zoetrope, 1984, 40–57.

Bakhtin, M. M. *The Dialogic Imagination: Four Essays*. Ed. Michael Holquist. Austin: University of Texas Press, 1981.

————. *Rabelais and His World*. Trans. Helene Iswolsky. Cambridge, Mass., and London: MIT Press, 1968.

Baudry, Jean-Louis. "Ideological Effects of the Basic Cinematographic Apparatus." *Film Quarterly* 28 (1974–75): 39–47.

Bauer, Stephen F. "Cultural History and the Film *Cabaret*." *The Psychoanalytic Study of Society* 12 (1988): 171–98.

Baxter, Peter. "On the Naked Thighs of Miss Dietrich." *Wide Angle* 2 (1977): 18–25.

Bell, Arthur. "Christopher Isherwood: No Parades." *New York Times Book Review* 25 (Mar. 1973): 10–14.

Benjamin, Walter. "On Some Motifs in Baudelaire." *Illuminations*. Ed. Hannah Arendt, trans. Harry Zohn. New York: Schocken, 1969, 155–200.

————. "Theories of German Fascism." Trans. Jerolf Wikoff. *New German Critique* 17 (1979): 120–28.

————. "The Work of Art in the Age of Mechanical Reproduction." *Illuminations*, 217–51.

Bennett, Tony, and Janet Woollacott. *Bond and Beyond: The Political Career of a Popular Hero*. Hampshire, England: Macmillan Educ., 1987.

Berger, John. *Ways of Seeing*. London: Penguin, 1978.

Bergmann, Martin S., and Milton E. Jucavy, eds. *Generations of the Holocaust*. New York: Basic Books, 1982.

Bergonzi, Bernard. *Reading the Thirties: Texts and Contexts*. Pittsburgh: University of Pittsburgh Press, 1978.

Berman, Russell. *Modern Culture and Critical Theory*. Madison and London: University of Wisconsin Press, 1989.

————. *The Rise of the Modern German Novel: Crisis and Charisma*. Cambridge, Mass., and London: Harvard University Press, 1986.

Bersani, Leo. "Is the Rectum a Grave?" *October* 43 (1987): 197–222.

Blades, Joe. "The Evolution of *Cabaret*." *Literature/Film Quarterly* 1 (1973): 226–38.

Bluel, Hans Peter. *Sex and Society in Nazi Germany.* Trans. J. Maxwell Brownjohn. Philadelphia: J.B. Lippincott, 1973.

Booth, Mark. *Camp.* London: Quartet, 1983.

Bow!by, John. *Child Care and the Growth of Love.* 1953. Harmondsworth, U.K.: Penguin, 1959.

Bowles, Paul. *Without Stopping.* New York: Peter Owen, 1972.

Breen, Joseph I. Letter to Joseph Sistrom, 18 May 1953. MPPDA Files, Herrick Museum, Los Angeles.

Bridenthal, Renate, et al., eds. *When Biology Became Destiny: Women in Weimar and Nazi Germany.* New York: Monthly Review, 1984.

Bronski, Michael. *Culture Clash: The Making of a Gay Sensibility.* Boston: South End, 1984.

Brookes, Barbara L. *Abortion in England, 1919–1939: Legal Theory and Social Practice.* Ph.D. dissertation, Bryn Mawr, 1982.

Califia, Pat. "Feminism and Sadomasochism." *Heresies* 3 (1981): 30–34.

Caudwell, Sarah. Letter to the author, 2 Jan. 1989.

———. "Reply to Berlin." *The New Statesman,* 3 October 1986, 28–29.

Chapman, John, ed. *The Best Plays of 1951–52.* New York: Dodd, Mead, 1952.

———. "In 'I Am a Camera' the Characters Just Drift Along; So Does the Play." *Daily News,* 29 Nov. 1951. *New York Theatre Critics' Reviews* 12 (1951): 156.

Chodorow, Nancy. *The Reproduction of Mothering: Psychoanalysis and the Sociology of Gender.* Berkeley and London: University of California Press, 1978.

Churchill, Caryl. *Cloud Nine.* New York: Methuen, 1984.

Clurman, Harold. Review of *Cabaret* by Joe Masteroff. *The Nation,* 12 December 1966, 651–52.

———. Review of *I Am a Camera,* by John Van Druten. *The New Republic,* 24 December 1951, 22.

"Code Denies Seal to 'I Am a Camera;' DCA May Balk at Cuts Demanded." *Variety Daily,* 27 July 1955, 1.

Coleman, Robert. " 'I Am a Camera' Offers A Moving Experience." *Daily Mirror,* 29 November 1951. *New York Theatre Critics' Reviews* 12 (1951): 159.

Cook, Alton. "Van Druten's Latest Play Has Premiere." *New York World-Telegram,* 9 December 1943. *New York Theatre Critics' Reviews* 4 (1943): 201.

Costello, John. *Virtue Under Fire: How World War II Changed Our Social and Sexual Habits.* New York: Fromm, 1987.

Crowther, Bosley. "The Anomaly of a Code." *New York Times,* 14 August 1955, sec. 2:7.

———. Review of *I Am a Camera* by Henry Cornelius. *New York Times,* 9 August 1955, 29.

Curtin, Kaier. *"We Can Always Call Them Bulgarians": The Emergence of Lesbians and Gay Men on the American Stage.* Boston: Alyson, 1987.

"DCA Prez Fred Schwartz Asks Major Prexies Overrule Code, Help Him Get 'Camera' Seal." *Variety Daily,* 11 August 1955, 1.

"DCA Prez Schwartz Asks MPAA Board Take Own Focus of Camera After Nix By Shurlock." *Variety Daily,* 29 July 1955, 1ff.

de Lauretis, Teresa. *Alice Doesn't: Feminism, Semiotics, Cinema*. Bloomington and Indianapolis: Indiana University Press, 1984.

Dettmer, Roger. " 'Cabaret' Diluted 'Sweet Charity.' " *Chicago's American*, 28 November 1968.

"Distrib Fears 'I Am a Camera' May Be Too Candid to Win Production Code Seal." *Variety Daily*, 23 June 1955.

Doane, Mary Ann. "Film and the Masquerade: Theorising the Female Spectator." *Screen* 23 (1982): 74–87.

———. "Gilda: Epistemology as Striptease." *Camera Obscura* 11 (1983): 6–27.

———. "The Voice in the Cinema: The Articulation of Body and Voice." In Rosen, 335–48.

Durgnat, Raymond. *A Mirror for England: British Movies from Austerity to Affluence*. London: Faber, 1970.

Dyer, Richard. "Entertainment and Utopia." In Altman 1981, 175–89.

———, ed. *Gays and Film*. New York: Zoetrope, 1984.

Eagleton, Terry. *Criticism and Ideology*. New York: Schocken, 1978.

Ebb, Fred, and Alan Rich. "Aftermath: *Cabaret*." *World Journal Tribune* (15 Jan. 1967): 34.

Eisenstein, Sergei. "Dickens, Griffith, and the Film Today." *Film Form: Essays in Film Theory*. New York: Harcourt, 1949, 195–255.

Elsaesser, Thomas. "Lili Marleen: Fascism and the Film Industry." *October* 21 (1982): 115–40.

———. "Primary Identification and the Historical Subject." In Rosen, 535–49.

Ezrahi, de Koven Sidra. *By Words Alone: The Holocaust in Literature*. Chicago: University of Chicago Press, 1980.

Fell, John. *Film and the Narrative Tradition*. 1974. Berkeley, Los Angeles, and London: University of California Press, 1986.

Feuer, Jane. "The Self-Reflective Musical and the Myth of Entertainment." In Altman 1981, 159–74.

Finney, Brian. *Christopher Isherwood: A Critical Biography*. New York and Oxford: Oxford University Press, 1979.

Fischer, Lucy. "Sometimes I Feel Like a Motherless Child: Comedy and Matricide." *Comedy/Cinema/Theory*. Ed. Andrew Horton. Berkeley and Los Angeles: University of California Press, 1991, 60–78.

——— and Marcia Landy. " 'The Eyes of Laura Mars': A Binocular Critique." *Screen* 23 (1982): 4–19.

Foucault, Michel. *The History of Sexuality*. Trans. Robert Hurley. New York: Pantheon, 1978.

Fraser, G. S. *The Modern Writer and His World*. New York: Penguin, 1964.

Freedman, Barbara. "Frame-Up: Feminism, Psychoanalysis, Theatre." *Theatre Journal* 40 (1988): 375–97.

Freedman, Samuel G. "Bearing Witness: The Life and Work of Elie Wiesel." *New York Times Magazine*, 23 October 1983, 32–37ff.

Freud, Sigmund. *Jokes and Their Relation to the Unconscious*. Trans. James Strachey. New York: Norton, 1960.

Friedan, Betty. *The Feminine Mystique*. 1963. New York: Dell, 1970.

Fryer, Jonathan. *Isherwood: A Biography of Christopher Isherwood*. 1977. New York: Doubleday, 1978.

———. "Sexuality in Isherwood." *Twentieth Century Literature* 22 (1976): 343–53.

Garland, Robert. "Julie Harris Held Better Than Play." *Journal American*, 29 November 1951. *New York Theatre Critics' Reviews* 112 (1951): 158.

Gay, Peter. *Weimar Culture: The Outsider as Insider*. New York: Harper and Row, 1968.

Geherin, David J. "An Interview with Christopher Isherwood." *Journal of Narrative Technique* 2 (1972): 143–58.

Geraghty, Christine. "Diana Dors." *All Our Yesterdays: 90 Years of British Cinema*. Ed. Charles Barr. London: British Film Institute, 1986, 341–46.

Gibbs, Wollcott. Review of *I Am a Camera* by John Van Druten. *The New Yorker*, 8 December 1951, 64–66.

Gilligan, Carol. *In a Different Voice: Psychological Theory and Women's Development*. Cambridge, Mass., and London: Harvard University Press, 1982.

Gitlin, Todd. *The Sixties: Years of Hope, Days of Rage*. New York: Bantam, 1987.

Gottfried, Martin. Review of *Cabaret* by Joe Masteroff. *Women's Wear Daily*, 21 November 1966. *New York Theatre Critics Review* 27 (1966): 241.

———. *Opening Nights: Theater Criticism of the Sixties*. New York: Putnam, 1969.

Grossman, Atina. "The New Woman and the Rationalization of Sexuality in Weimar Germany." *The Powers of Desire: The Politics of Sexuality*. Eds. A. Snitow et al. New York: Virago, 1983, 153–71.

"Grosz Is a 'Camera.' " *New York Times Magazine*, 24 July 1955, 12.

Grubb, Kevin Boyd. *Razzle Dazzle: The Life and Work of Bob Fosse*. New York: St. Martin's, 1989.

Guernsey, Otis L., Jr., ed. *Broadway Song and Story*. New York: Dodd Mead, 1985.

Hamilton, Gerald. *Mr. Norris and I*. London: Allan Wingate, 1956.

Hart, Henry. "Economic Censorship." *Films in Review* 6 (1955): 507–10.

Hartung, Philip. Review of *I Am a Camera* by Henry Cornelius. *Commonweal*, 9 September 1955, 565.

Hasbany, Richard. "The Musical Goes Ironic: The Evolution of Genres." *Journal of American Culture* 1 (1978): 120–37.

Hausen, Karin. "Mother's Day in the Weimar Republic." In Bridenthal, 131–52.

Heilbrun, Carolyn. "Christopher Isherwood: An Interview." *Twentieth Century Literature* 22 (1976): 253–63.

Hewes, Henry. "Christopher Isherwood's Snapshots." *Saturday Review*, 12 April 1952, 38ff.

———. "Not Quite a Camera." *Saturday Review*, 10 December 1966, 64.

Hill, John. *Sex, Class, and Realism: British Cinema 1956–1963*. London: British Film Institute, 1986.

Hirsch, Foster. *Harold Prince and the American Musical Theatre*. Cambridge and New York: Cambridge University Press, 1989.

Hoffman, William M., ed. *Gay Plays: The First Collection*. New York: Avon, 1979.

Hofstader, Richard. *The Paranoid Style in American Politics, and Other Essays*. New York: Knopf, 1965.

Hope, Anthony. *The Dolly Dialogues*. London: Victoria House, 1899.

Horden, Anthony. *Legal Abortion: The English Experience*. Oxford: Pergamon, 1971.

Ilson, Carol. *Harold Prince: From "Pajama Game" to "Phantom of the Opera."* Ann Arbor: University Microfilms, Inc. Research Press, 1989.

Insdorf, Annette. *Indelible Shadows: Film and the Holocaust*. New York: Random House, 1983.

Isherwood, Christopher. *Berlin Stories: The Last of Mr. Norris and Goodbye to Berlin*. New York: New Directions, 1954.

———. *Christopher and His Kind*, 1929–1939. New York: Farrar, Straus & Giroux, 1976.

———. *Kathleen and Frank*. New York: Simon and Schuster, 1971.

———. *Lions and Shadows*. 1947. New York: Pegasus, 1969.

———. *Prater Violet*. New York: Random House, 1945.

———. *The World in the Evening*. London: Methuen, 1954.

"Is There Camp After Cruising ?" *Films and Filming* 345 (1983): 26–29.

Jacobs, Lea. "The Censorship of *Blonde Venus*: Textual Analysis and Historical Method." *Cinema Journal* 27 (1988): 21–31.

———. *The Wages of Sin: Censorship and the Fallen Woman Film, 1928–1942*. Madison: University of Wisconsin Press, 1991.

Johnstone, Iain. "The Real Sally Bowles." *Folio* (Autumn 1975): 32–38.

Johnstone, Iain, and Jenny Rees. "Bowles Players." *Radio Times*, 18 April 1974, 54ff.

Kaplan, Alice Yaeger. *The Reproduction of Banality: Fascism, Literature, and French Intellectual Life*. Minneapolis: University of Minnesota Press, 1986.

Kaplan, E. Ann. *Women and Film: Both Sides of the Camera*. New York and London: Methuen, 1983.

Kauffman, Stanley. Review of Fosse's *Cabaret*. *New Republic*, 4 March 1972, 22ff.

Kerr, Walter. "The Theater: 'Cabaret' Opens at the Broadhurst." *New York Times*, 21 November 1966. *New York Theatre Critics Review* 27 (1966): 242.

Klinger, Barbara Gail. *Cinema and Social Process: A Contextual Theory of the Cinema and Its Spectators*. Ph.D. dissertation, University of Iowa, 1986.

Komarovsky, Mirra. *Women in the Modern World: Their Education and Their Dilemmas*. Boston: Little Brown, 1953.

Koonz, Claudia. "The Competition for Women's Lebensraum, 1928–1934." In Bridenthal, 199–236.

———. *Mothers in the Fatherland: Women, the Family, and Nazi Politics*. New York: St. Martin's, 1987.

Kracauer, Siegfried. *From Caligari to Hitler: A Psychological History of the German Film*. Princeton, New Jersey: Princeton University Press, 1947.

Krutch, Joseph Wood. Review of *I Am a Camera* by John Van Druten. *Nation*, 22 December 1951, 554.

Kuhn, Annette. *Cinema, Censorship and Sexuality, 1909–1925*. London: Routledge, 1988.

———. *Power of the Image: Essays on Representation and Sexuality*. London: Routledge, 1985.

LaValley, Al. "The Great Escape." *American Film* 10 (1985): 28–34.

"Legion of Decency Nix on 'Camera' is Appealed to Cardinal Spellman." *Variety Daily*, 15 August 1955, 1ff.

Lehmann, John. *Christopher Isherwood: A Personal Memoir*. New York: Henry Holt, 1987.

———. *In My Own Time*. Boston: Little Brown, 1969.

Lenya, Lotte. Interview with George Voskovec, 1972. Videocassette, Lincoln Center Library for the Performing Arts, Theatre Collection.

Lewis, Peter. *The Fifties*. London: Heinemann, 1978.

"Liza Minnelli 'Cabaret' Role a Character Study." *Entertainment Today*, 31 March 1972, 2.

Lundberg, Ferdinand, and Marynia Farnham. *Modern Woman: The Lost Sex*. New York and London: Harper, 1947.

Macherey, Pierre. *A Theory of Literary Production*. Trans. Geoffrey Wall. New York: Routledge, 1978.

Marcus, Frank. "Ich Bin Ein Berliner." *Plays and Players* (May 1968): 14–17.

Mast, Gerald. *Can't Help Singin': The American Musical on Stage and Screen*. Woodstock, N.Y.: Overlook, 1987.

Masteroff, Joe. *Cabaret*. New York: Random House, 1967.

Mayne, Judith. "The Feminist Analogy." *Discourse* 7 (1985): 31–41.

———. "Marlene Dietrich, *The Blue Angel*, and Female Performance." *Seduction and Theory: Readings of Gender, Representation, and Rhetoric*. Ed. Dianne Hunter, 28–46. Urbana and Chicago: University of Chicago Press, 1989.

Mellen, Joan. "Fascism in the Contemporary Film." *Film Quarterly* 24 (1971), 2–19.

Meyer, Agnes E. *Out of These Roots: The Autobiography of an American Woman*. Boston: Little Brown, 1953.

Millett, Kate. *Sexual Politics*. New York: Avon, 1969.

Mizejewski, Linda. "Women, Monsters, and the Masochistic Aesthetic in *Cabaret*." *Journal of Film and Video* 39 (1987): 5–17.

Modleski, Tania. "A Father is Being Beaten: Male Feminism and Feminist Theory." *Discourse* 10.2 (1988): 62–73.

———. *The Women Who Knew Too Much: Hitchcock and Feminist Theory*. New York: Methuen, 1988.

Morehouse, Ward. "Sin, Sex and Mae West." *Sun*, 7 February 1949. *New York Theatre Critics' Reviews* 10 (1949): 372.

Morgan, Robin, ed. *Sisterhood is Powerful: An Anthology of Writings from the Women's Liberation Movement*. New York: Random House, 1970.

BIBLIOGRAPHY 249

Mosley, Leonard. "Does It Shock You to See a Girl Looking Like She's Sozzled?" *Daily Express*, 19 August 1955.

Mosse, George. *Masses and Man: Nationalist and Fascist Perceptions of Reality.* New York: Fertig, 1980.

———. *Nationalism and Sexuality: Respectability and Abnormal Sexuality in Modern Europe.* New York: Fertig, 1985.

"Mr. Isherwood's Berlin." *Times* (London), 17 October 1955, 3c.

Mulvey, Laura. "Afterthoughts on 'Visual Pleasure in Narrative Cinema' Inspired by *Duel in the Sun* (King Vidor, 1946)." *Framework* 15/16 (1981): 12–15.

———. "Visual Pleasure and Narrative Cinema." *Screen* 16 (1975): 6–18.

Nadel, Norman. " 'Cabaret' Fine New Musical." *World Journal Tribune*, 21 November 1966. *New York Theatre Critics Review* 27 (1966): 242.

Newton, Esther. *Mother Camp: Female Impersonators in America.* Chicago: University of Chicago Press, 1979.

Oberbeck, S. K. "Movies." A review of Fosse's *Cabaret. Newsweek*, 28 February 1972, 82.

Perry, George. *Forever Ealing: A Celebration of the Great British Film Studios.* London: Pavilion, 1981.

Petro, Patrice. *Joyless Streets: Women and Melodramatic Representation in Weimar Germany.* Princeton, New Jersey: Princeton University Press, 1989.

Piazza, Paul. *Christopher Isherwood: Myth and Anti-Myth.* New York: Columbia University Press, 1978.

Picard, Lil. "Interview With Bob Fosse." *Inter/View* (Mar. 1972): 8.

Plant, Richard. *The Pink Triangle: The Nazi War Against Homosexuals.* New York: Henry Holt, 1986.

Polan, Dana. "Above All Else to Make You See: Cinema and the Ideology of Spectacle." *Boundary 2* 11 (1982/83): 129–44.

———. "It Could Be Oedipus Rex: Denial and Difference in *The Bandwagon*, or The American Musical as American Gothic." *Ciné-Tracts* 14 (1981): 15–26.

Rector, Frank. *The Nazi Extermination of Homosexuals.* New York: Stein and Day, 1981.

Reich, Wilhelm. *The Mass Psychology of Fascism.* Trans. Theodore P. Wolfe. New York: Orgone Institute, 1946.

Renov, Michael. "From Fetish to Subject: The Containment of Sexual Difference in Hollywood's Wartime Cinema." *Wide Angle* 5 (1982): 16–27.

Review of *I Am a Camera* by Henry Cornelius. *English* 11 (1956): 20.

Review of *I Am a Camera* by Henry Cornelius. *Time*, 15 August 1955, 58ff.

Review of *I Am a Camera* by Henry Cornelius. *Times* (London), 17 October 1955, 3c.

Rich, Alan. "The Triumph of the Cliché." *World Journal Tribune*, 11 December 1966, 30.

Riviere, Joan. "Womanliness as Masquerade." *Psychoanalysis and Female Sexuality.* Ed. Henrik M. Ruitenbeek. New Haven: College and University Press, 1966, 209–20.

Robertson, James C. *The British Board of Film Censors: Film Censorship in Britain, 1896–1950*. London: Croom Helm, 1985.

Robinson, David. Review of *I Am a Camera*, by Henry Cornelius. *Sight and Sound* (Winter 1955/56): 150.

Rosen, Philip, ed. *Narrative, Apparatus, Ideology*. New York: Columbia University Press, 1986.

Rosenfeld, Alvin H. *Imagining Hitler*. Bloomington: Indiana University Press, 1985.

Ross, Andrew. *No Respect: Intellectuals and Popular Culture*. New York: Routledge, 1989.

Rove, John. "*The Berlin Stories, I am a Camera, Cabaret*: An Analysis and Comparison." M.A. dissertation, Memphis State University, 1976.

Russo, Mary. "Female Grotesques: Carnival and Theory." *Feminist Studies, Critical Studies*. Ed. Teresa de Lauretis, 213–29. Bloomington: Indiana University Press, 1986.

Ruth, Robin, et al. *Against Sadomasochism: A Radical Feminist Analysis*. E. Palo Alto: Frog in the Well, 1982.

Sarris, Andrew. *Politics and Cinema*. New York: Columbia University Press, 1978.

Sayre, Nora. *Sixties Going on Seventies*. New York: Arbor House, 1973.

Schultz, John. *No One Was Killed: Documentation and Meditation, Convention Week, Chicago, August 1968*. Chicago: Big Table, 1969.

Sedgwick, Eve Kosofsky. *Between Men: English Literature and Male Homosocial Desire*. New York: Columbia University Press, 1985.

Shurlock, Geoffrey. Letter to Fred J. Schwartz, 2 Feb. 1956. MPPDA Files, Herrick Library, Los Angeles.

———. MPPDA file memo, 7 Mar 1956. MPPDA Files, Herrick Library, Los Angeles.

Silverman, Kaja. "Masochism and Male Subjectivity." *Camera Obscura* 17 (1988): 31–66.

———. "Masochism and Subjectivity." *Framework* 12 (1983): 2–9.

Smith, Cecil, and Glenn Litton. *Musical Comedy in America*. New York: Theatre Arts, 1981.

Soloman, Stanley. *Beyond Formula: American Film Genres*. New York: Harcourt Brace, 1976.

Sontag, Susan. "Fascinating Fascism." *The Susan Sontag Reader*. New York: Farrar, Strauss, & Giroux, 1982. 305–25.

———. "Notes on Camp." In *The Susan Sontag Reader*, 105–19.

Spender, Stephen. *Journals 1939–1983*. New York: Random House, 1985.

———. *Letters to Christopher*. Santa Barbara: Black Sparrow, 1980.

———. "On Being a Ghost in Isherwood's Berlin." *Mademoiselle*, September 1974, 138–39ff.

———. *World Within World*. New York: Harcourt Brace, 1951.

Stoop, Norma McLain. "Christopher Isherwood: A Meeting by Another River." *After Dark* 7 (1975): 60–65.

Studlar, Gaylyn. *In the Realm of Pleasure: Von Sternberg, Dietrich, and the Masochistic Aesthetic.* Urbana and Chicago: University of Illinois Press: 1988.

Styron, William. "Chicago 1968." *The Quiet Dust and Other Writings.* New York: Random House, 1982.

Theweleit, Klaus. *Male Fantasies.* Vol. 1, *Women, Floods, Bodies, Histories.* Trans. Stephen Conway. Minneapolis: University of Minnesota Press, 1987.

———. *Male Fantasies.* Vol. 2, *Psychoanalyzing the White Terror.* Trans. Erica Carter and Chris Turner. Minneapolis: University of Minnesota Press, 1989.

Thomas, David P. "Goodby to Berlin: Refocusing Isherwood's Camera." *Contemporary Literature* 13 (1972): 44–52.

Thomas, Peter. " 'Camp' and Politics in Isherwood's Berlin Fiction." *Journal of Modern Literature* 5 (1976): 117–30.

Thompson, Mark. *Gay Spirit: Myth and Meaning.* New York: St. Martin's, 1987.

Troger, Annemarie. "The Creation of a Female Assembly-Line Proletariat." In Bridenthal, 237–70.

Turner, Chris, and Erica Carter. "Political Somatics: Notes on Klaus Theweleit's *Male Fantasies.*" *Formations of Fantasy.* Ed. Victor Burgin et al. New York: Methuen, 1986, 201–13.

Van Druten, John. *Bell, Book and Candle.* Final version, 1950. Billy Rose Theatre Collection. New York Public Library.

———. *I Am a Camera.* New York: Dramatists Play Service, 1955.

Waldorf, Wilella. "John van Druten's Latest: 'The Voice of the Turtle.' " *New York Post,* 9 December 1943. *New York Theatre Critics' Reviews* 4 (1943): 201.

Walker, Daniel. *Rights in Conflict: Convention Week in Chicago, August 25–29, 1968.* New York: Dutton, 1968.

Wallace, Robert. "Close Up: Julie Harris." *Life,* 7 April 1952, 154ff.

Watts, Stephen. "On Shooting a 'Camera.' " *New York Times,* 23 January 1955, sec. 2:5.

Weeks, Jeffrey. *Coming Out: Homosexual Politics in Britain from the Nineteenth Century to the Present.* New York: Quartet, 1977.

Weiler, A. H. "By Way of Report." *New York Times,* 20 June 1954, sec. 10:5.

Weinberg, Herman G. "Before the Putsch." *Film Culture* 1 (1955): 25.

Weininger, Otto. *Sex and Character.* 1906. New York: AMS, 1975.

Westerbeck, Colin L. Review of Fosse's *Cabaret. Commonweal,* 21 April 1972, 167.

White, Lynn, Jr. *Educating Our Daughters: A Challenge to the Colleges.* New York: Harper, 1950.

Whitebait, William. "Sally in Whose Alley?" *New Statesman,* 22 October 1955, 50.

Wilde, Alan. *Christopher Isherwood.* New York: Twayne, 1971.

———. "Language and Surface: Isherwood and the Thirties." *Contemporary Literature* 16 (1976): 478–91.

"Wildest Movie Binge." *Life* (8 August 1955): 35.

Williams, Dick. " 'I Am a Camera' Will Surely Jolt the Censors." *Mirror-News* (Los Angeles), 28 July 1955, 16.

Williams, Linda. "Film Body: An Implantation of Perversions." *Ciné-Tracts* 12 (1981): 19–35.

Wilson, Colin. "An Integrity Born of Hope: Notes on Christopher Isherwood." *Twentieth Century Literature* 22 (1976): 312–31.

Wood, Leslie. "The New Films." *Daily Film Renter*, 14 September 1955, 4.

Wood, Robin. "Art and Ideology: Notes on *Silk Stockings*." In Altman 1981, 57–69.

Wylie, Philip. *Generation of Vipers*. New York: Rinehart, 1942.

Zec, Donald. "Saucy Sal—the X Girl." *Daily Mirror*, 14 October 1955.

INDEX

abortion: in *Cabaret* (Fosse, 1972), 202, 210, 229, 232, 233, 234–35; in *Cabaret* (Masteroff, 1966), 185, 196–97; in *Goodbye to Berlin*, 43, 50–51, 52, 65–66, 67–68, 69, 80; in *I Am a Camera* (Cornelius, 1955), 122, 123, 125, 130, 151, 152, 154, 155; in *I Am a Camera* (Van Druten, 1951), 92, 93, 108, 111–13; and Nazi policy, 196, 196n

adaptation: and anti-Semitism, 5–6; as cultural history, 6–7, 9, 11–13; and feminist film theory, 7–10, 237; and generic conventions, 92–93, 98, 120–22, 159–60, 163, 172–73; and male hero, 10–11, 59, 134–35, 137–38, 150, 172–73, 224

Adorno, T. W., 20

After Auschwitz, 186

Allen, Jay Presson, 202–3

All the Conspirators, 45, 58

Altman, Rick, 214–15, 219, 220

antifascism: and camp, 168–69; as film genre, 19–20, 25–26; as male authorship, 93, 95, 96, 97, 98, 106, 147, 157, 185–86, 194; as masculinity, 96–97, 147, 151, 156–57, 219–20; and the musical, 168–69; and patriarchy, 193, 196, 198

anti-Semitism, 5–6, 67–68, 81–82, 93, 95–97, 116–17, 132, 168, 171, 176–79, 192, 202–3, 229, 239; and homophobia, 29, 30, 33; and misogyny, 28, 29, 30, 32–33, 67–68. *See also* Holocaust; Nazism

Arendt, Hannah, *The Origins of Totalitarianism*, 186

Auden, W. H., 45, 46

authorship, male, 68, 69, 70–74, 92, 93, 94–95, 107, 134–38, 147, 151, 155, 185–86, 194. *See also* antifascism: as male authorship

Babuscio, Jack, 63n

Bachardy, Don, 76

Bakhtin, Mikhail, 63, 69–70, 79. *See also* carnival (Bakhtinian)

Barefoot Contessa, The (1954), 129

Batman, 166

Bauer, Stephen, 7–8, 11, 12, 13, 221–22, 224

Baxter, Peter, 12n, 140n

Bell, Book, and Candle (Broadway), 86

Benjamin, Walter, 4, 13, 40, 83, 154

Bennett, Tony, and Janet Woollacott, *Bond and Beyond*, 23

Berenson, Marisa, 216

Berger, Helmut, 20, 201

Berger, John, 14

Bergman, Ingmar, 22

Bergmann, Martin S., and Milton E. Jucavy, *Generations of the Holocaust*, 186n

Bergonzi, Bernard, *Reading the Thirties*, 41n

Berkeley, Busby, 23, 63, 191–92, 220–21

"Berlin Diary (Autumn 1930), A" (*Goodbye to Berlin*), 43, 81–82

"Berlin Diary (Winter 1932–3), A" (*Goodbye to Berlin*), 43, 81–84

Berlin Stories, The, 43, 104. *See also Goodbye to Berlin*; Isherwood, Christopher; *Last of Mr. Norris, The*

Berman, Russell, 4, 13, 32n, 154–55

Bertolucci, Bernardo, 19

Blue Angel, The (1931), 3, 12, 14, 20–23, 139–41, 158, 201–2, 208, 216. *See also* Dietrich, Marlene; Lola Lola

Bogarde, Dirk, 20

Bond, James, 23

Booth, Mark, 62, 85, 110–11, 166n, 192n, 202

Bowlby, John, *Child Care and the Growth of Love*, 133–34

Bowles, Paul, 46, 64, 105

Bowles, Sally. *See also* abortion; *Blue Angel, The*; Dietrich, Marlene; Lola Lola; motherhood; Ross, Jean; satire; sexuality, female; spectacle: female; transvestism

—in *Cabaret* (Fosse, 1972): 206, 208–12; as dominatrix, 227–31; and gay male sexuality, 210–16, 218, 220, 224–26, 231–35; as musical star, 200–203, 215,